CARDINAL CAHAL B. DALY

THE BREAKING OF BREAD

Biblical Reflections on the Eucharist

VERITAS

First published 2008 by
Veritas Publications
7/8 Lower Abbey Street
Dublin 1
Ireland
Email publications@veritas.ie
Website www.veritas.ie

ISBN 978 1 84730 033 1

10 9 8 7 6 5 4 3

A catalogue record for this book is available from the British Library.

Scripture quotations taken from *The New Jerusalem Bible* © 1985 by
Darton, Longman & Todd Ltd and Doubleday & Company Inc. Psalm
quotations taken from *The Psalms: A New Translation* © 1963
by Fontana Books.

Lines from 'The Half-Way House', 'Nondum' and 'As Kingfishers Catch
Fire' by Gerard Manley Hopkins, taken from *Gerard Manley Hopkins – A
Selection of his Finest Poems*, courtesy of Oxford University Press, 1995.

Cover: Icon of Christ the Saviour, Russian, Moscow School, first quarter of
16th century. Rublyov Museum of Old Russian Art, Moscow.

Designed by Colette Dower
Printed in the Republic of Ireland by ColourBooks Ltd., Dublin

*Veritas books are printed on paper made from the wood pulp of managed
forests. For every tree felled, at least one tree is planted, thereby renewing
natural resources.*

· CONTENTS

I dedicate this book, as I dedicated
Steps on My Pilgrim Journey,
to the memory of my parents:

Charles Daly,
born Keadue, Co. Roscommon, 15 April 1879,
died Loughguile, Co. Antrim, 31 October 1939, aged 60

and

Susan Connolly,
born Glenbush, Co. Antrim, 8 December 1888,
died St Michael's (Bishop's residence), Longford,
28 January 1974, aged 86

They were the first to teach me to pray and to love
the Eucharist, in the Mass, in the Tabernacle
and in the Monstrance

NOTANDA

Quotations from the Bible, unless otherwise indicated, are from the *New Jerusalem Bible*.

Quotations from the Psalms, unless otherwise indicated, are from the Grail translation from the original Hebrew, as found in the Grail edition of the Psalms, published in 1963 as *The Psalms: A New Translation*, Fontana Books, Collins, St James Place, London.

There are two different ways of numbering the Psalms. The first is based on the translation into Greek made in Alexandria in the fourth century and known as the Septuagint. It was adopted by St Jerome in his Latin version and is the one used in Catholic versions generally up to the publication of the *Jerusalem Bible*. It is the version commonly used in the Catholic liturgy. The other numbering, based on the Hebrew Bible, is that used generally by scripture scholars; it is the numbering employed in the *Authorised Version* and in the *Jerusalem Bible*.

The differences are usefully summarised in a postscript to the Grail version. They begin with Psalm 9 and continue to the end, as follows:

Greek Septuagint	Hebrew
1–8	1–8
9	9–10
10–112	11–113
113	114–5
114–5	116
116–145	117–146
146–147	147
148–150	148–150

(*The Psalms, the Grail Version*, p. 255)

In the present book, the two numberings are given: the Septuagint/Vulgate numbering is given first and is followed (in brackets) by the Hebrew/*Jerusalem Bible* version.

FOREWORD

This book has been a long time in gestation. During a visit to Paris in 1970, I chanced to pick up a book by the distinguished French scripture scholar, Father André Feuillet, with the title *Retraite Eucharistique (Eucharistic Retreat)*. It was the outline text of a retreat which he had preached to a congregation of Sisters called Servants of the Blessed Sacrament. The book was not published commercially but privately, so I count myself fortunate in having obtained a copy in a second-hand bookshop. Personally, I feel that I derived great spiritual benefit to my prayer and to my eucharistic devotion from prayerful reading of this book. I was very struck by the richness of its biblical resources and by the way in which the Eucharist is shown to be at the heart of the Church's mystery – to be truly 'the mystery of faith' – and to be a focus for both the Old and the New Testament witness to Jesus. More than once in the gospels, Jesus explains to his disciples the passages from the Old Testament, which were about himself – and these passages relate also to the Eucharist.

From the time of my reading of Feuillet's book, I felt conscious of the fact that, so far as I knew, no book on the Eucharist in English provided such a rich biblical background to the mystery of the Eucharist, and that this represented a loss to English-speaking readers, anxious to deepen their eucharistic faith and devotion. The present book is by no means a translation of Feuillet's book or an attempt to re-write it. It is an attempt, rather, to do for English-language readers something along the lines of what Feuillet did for French readers in his admirable little book.

The proclamation by Pope John Paul II of the year from October 2004 to October 2005 as the Year of the Eucharist evoked in me, as it did in many, the desire to practice and to promote what the Pope called 'a more lively and fervent celebration of the Eucharist, leading to a Christian life transformed by love'. The Pope expressed the wish that each member of the faithful should 'assimilate through personal and communal meditation the values which the Eucharist expresses, the attitudes which it inspires, the resolutions to which it gives rise'. He asked: 'Can we not see here a spiritual charge which could emerge from the Year of the Eucharist?'

My own exploration of the scriptures relating to the Eucharist gave me a glimpse of how the Bible can deepen our prayer and revitalise our participation in the Mass and can renew our worship of the reserved Eucharist in the Tabernacle and in the Monstrance. This book is concerned primarily with the Mass; but obviously its reflections relate also to the reserved Eucharist.

This book takes whatever value it has from the Bible: hence the copious scriptural quotations throughout. As Father Feuillet advised in his book, this one should be read with the Bible in hand. My book is not a work of scriptural scholarship – I am not a scripture scholar. Nor is it an erudite theological study; it is something between a book of biblical theology and a prayer book. Karl Rahner once wrote that what the Church needs nowadays is 'theology on its knees'. This book is a humble attempt at such a theology. It is not intended to be read in one sitting, from cover to cover. Rather, each section, or even each part of a section, is meant to be a springboard for slow, meditative or contemplative prayer, whether by individuals or by groups. Pope John Paul II declared that 'the most holy Eucharist contains the Church's entire spiritual wealth'. May this book in some way help to a greater appreciation of that vast spiritual wealth. May it help the Church, which we are, to cast away our fears for the future and to be filled instead, as Pope John Paul II put it, with confident hope as we contemplate the Eucharist as the source and summit of the Church's entire life. For in each Eucharist we celebrate Christ is saying to us, as he so often said in his earthly life: 'Do not be afraid. I am with you. I am with you today and all days, till the end of time.'

PART I

OLD TESTAMENT: EUCHARIST VEILED

The Veil

St Paul returns several times to what is for him personally the great tragedy and the strange paradox: that so many who had listened to Christ's message and witnessed his miracles failed to see in him the fulfilment of the promises made to Abraham, and later to David and reiterated by the prophets, even though these promises are the central thread running through the whole of Israel's own sacred scriptures. Paul compares this lack of faith to the veil which Moses placed over his face when he turned towards the people, but removed when he turned towards the Lord. In contrast, Paul declared, the veil was never removed from the faces of some. When they listened to the scriptures, and even 'when Moses is read', 'the veil is over their minds' (2 Cor 3:15). The consequence is that they 'see' without seeing and hear but do not understand. The veil which prevents understanding will be removed only when they accept the grace which God is offering them through the Holy Spirit, namely when they accept Jesus as the Christ, the Son of God. 'This veil,' says St Paul, 'will not be removed until they turn to the Lord' in faith. Christ, for St Paul, is the true meaning of the Old Testament scriptures; he is the fulfilment of its promises and the realisation of its hopes. But Christ is veiled in the Old Testament, and only faith in Jesus Christ can remove the veil and enable those who hear and read the Hebrew scriptures to see the Christ who is present there but hidden, veiled.

I hope to show in Part I of this book that the same is true of the Eucharist. There are anticipations, foreshadowings, promises of the Eucharist in what Christians know as the Old Testament, but only Christ, revealed in the New Testament, can enable us to recognise them. Only Christ can remove the veil which conceals their full meaning. This is why I entitle Part I: 'The Old Testament: Eucharist Veiled'.

Jesus Christ is the Key

The religious language and the theological vocabulary of the Jews of the time of Our Lord were drawn entirely from what Christians know as the Old Testament. Devout Jews were closely familiar with Old Testament texts and habitually subjected Our Lord's teaching to questioning or to criticism by reference to the Old Testament scriptures. Our Lord frequently gave justification for his own teaching by quoting from texts in the Law or Torah, the Prophets or the Psalms – these being three titles under which the Jews grouped together the books of the Old Testament. After his resurrection, Jesus Christ explains to two disciples on the road to Emmaus passages from each category of the Hebrew scriptures, which, written long before his coming, were really about Jesus himself. In Luke's gospel we read of the Risen Lord, who, after walking, unrecognised, with these two disciples along the road to Emmaus, gently reproaches them as 'foolish men, so slow to believe the full message of the prophets'. He asks them: 'Was it not ordained that the Christ should suffer and so enter into his glory?' Then 'starting with Moses and going through all the prophets he explains to them all the passages throughout the scriptures that were about himself' (Lk 24:25-27). This was the experience which prepared them for the meal which he shared with them and in which the disciples' 'eyes were opened and they recognised him ... at the breaking of bread' (Lk 24:31, 35). I shall return to the Emmaus story on p. 146 where I explore further its eucharistic allusions.

Later on in the same chapter St Luke reports the Risen Lord as saying to all the Apostles: 'I said when I was still with you that everything written about me in the Law of Moses, in the Prophets and in the Psalms, has to be fulfilled. Then he opened their minds to understand the scriptures.' (Lk 24:44-47) Our Lord is here teaching his disciples, who were his first Church, that the full meaning of the Old Testament is found only in himself, the Christ, the Son of God. Faith in him and in his teaching is, therefore, for Christians, the key to the interpretation of the Old Testament scriptures. To know Christ fully we must know the Old Testament as well as the New; and to understand the full meaning of the Old Testament we must know Christ. Christ is the key to the full meaning of the Old Testament. As St Jerome puts it, ignorance of the scriptures is ignorance of Christ.

This is the message of a section of the Book of Revelation, the last book of the New Testament, namely the section on the Breaking of the Seven Seals. It opens with a passage recalling the great theophany of Isaiah and the song of the angels round the Throne of God:

> Holy, Holy, Holy
> is the Lord God, the Almighty. (Ez 1,10; Rev 4:1-8)

In this scene of the Book of Revelation, we see in the hand of the enthroned Lord a scroll with writing on back and front; but it is sealed with seven seals and cannot be read or understood because 'nobody is worthy to open the scroll and break the seals of it'. Then the seer catches sight of 'a lamb that seemed to have been sacrificed'; and, as he watched, the Lamb 'came forward to take the scroll from the right hand of the one seated on the Throne'. Then, in an atmosphere of sustained suspense, the Lamb breaks each of the seven seals, one after the other, and, at the end of a long wait, at last he breaks the seventh seal. Then, 'there was silence in heaven for the space of half an hour'.

In that dramatic scene, the true meaning of the Hebrew scriptures is at last revealed – in the Lamb who was sacrificed; and through him true worship is now given to God, through him the new covenant is ratified, and 'the one who sits on the throne will spread his tent over his people', 'and they will never hunger or thirst again; the Lamb will be their shepherd and will lead them to springs of living water'. Many refused to believe in Jesus, though he was the key to the meaning of their own scriptures. As Jesus himself said, 'they looked without seeing and listened without hearing or understanding' (Mt 13:14). In contrast, St Augustine writes that the Church, believing in Christ, 'has heard the promises and sees their fulfilment; she has heard in the prophecies and sees in the gospel'.[1]

All this is the scriptural basis for the teaching of the Second Vatican Council in its dogmatic constitution on Divine Revelation, *Dei Verbum*:

> God, the inspirer and author of both testaments, wisely arranged that the New Testament be hidden in the Old and the Old be made manifest in the New. For, though Christ established the new covenant in his blood, still, the books of the Old Testament, with all their parts, caught up with the proclamation of the Gospel, acquire and show forth their full meaning in the New Testament. (16)[2]

If I may be allowed to speak personally for a moment, I have vivid memories of visiting the Yad Vashem Museum in Jerusalem and the Holocaust Museum in Washington, D.C., in both of which there are many photographs of Jewish synagogues desecrated by the Nazis, with the sacred scrolls of the Hebrew scriptures lying torn or charred amid the rubble. Humankind must never be allowed to forget the unparalleled awfulness of the Shoah, or Holocaust; it reveals in a unique way the human capacity for evil. Because of all that links our faith with the faith of the Jews, we Christians should, more than any, remember the Holocaust. At a Jewish-Christian conference in Auschwitz in 1997, I found myself addressing an audience composed principally of Jews and I told them of the deep personal hurt and pain which I felt at the sight of the desecrated scrolls; 'These,' I said, 'are my scriptures too.'

The Church has treated the Old Testament scriptures as part of its own scriptural canon all through history, and made them familiar to the faithful long before books were printed or the masses of people were literate. An early Church heresy, named after Marcion, its chief exponent, wanted to exclude the Old Testament from the canon of Christian sacred scripture. Tertullian, at first a brilliant defender of Catholic faith, wrote a powerful refutation of this false doctrine;[3] sadly, he later espoused the puritanical doctrine of Montanism and left the Catholic fold.

The early and medieval Church used architecture, sculpture and stained glass as media for teaching the faith. A familiar thematic in these various media was the juxtaposition of Old Testament scenes with the New Testament scenes, which were their fulfilment. The stained-glass windows of medieval cathedrals – of which Chartres is one of the most famous – have many examples of this juxtaposition. These windows suggest an intimate familiarity on the part of the faithful of the late first and early second millennium with both the Old Testament and the New Testament and the relationships between both. The same is true of the sculptured scenes in many of our Irish High Crosses of the early medieval period. Our own knowledge of the Bible today can be tested by our ability to identify the scenes on the medieval stained-glass windows or the high crosses! In my own youth, a book called *Bible Stories*, containing selections of Old Testament texts with their New Testament correlatives, was used as a catechetical text, and served to familiarise people with both Testaments. Fortunately today, as a result of the Second Vatican Council, both school and adult catechetical programmes, as well as prayer groups and, above all, the revised liturgy, have given many people a much greater familiarity with the Bible, though there is much remaining to be done in this regard.

The continuity, and indeed the fundamental unity in Christ, of both Testaments means that familiarity with both is essential to a full catechesis in Christian and Catholic faith. The Catholic Church has provided for this in its Lectionary, revised after the Second Vatican Council, where the Sunday readings almost always include a reading from the Old Testament with its corresponding reading from the New Testament, the Old Testament reading in each case being selected because of its relation to the gospel of the day.

With the above by way of introduction, we can now turn to the Old Testament scenes that formed the backdrop to Christ's own teaching on the Eucharist.

I begin with the reference, found in our Eucharistic Prayer I (or the 'Roman Canon') to three sacrifices of the Old Law:

[Father] look with love on these offerings
and accept them, as once you accepted
the gifts of your servant Abel,
the sacrifice of Abraham, our father in faith,
and the bread and wine
offered by your priest, Melchisedek.

The Sacrifice of Abel

Abel's is the first sacrifice mentioned in the Book of Genesis.[4] Cain and Abel are the two sons of Adam and his wife Eve. They develop a bitter rivalry, all the more reprehensible because they are brothers. Cain, the elder, is a tiller of the soil; Abel is a shepherd who keeps flocks. They each offer a sacrifice to the Lord, Abel offering the first-born of his flock with some of its fat, Cain offering produce of the soil. The Lord is pleased with Abel and his offering, but is not pleased with the offering of Cain. Cain is very angry and downcast at this and his spite grows to such a point that eventually he murders Abel. The Lord then banishes Cain and he becomes a fugitive and a wanderer over the earth. The 'brand of Cain', originally intended by God for Cain's protection, passed into ordinary language as a mark of infamy.

After the story of Cain and Abel, the Book of Genesis passes to the story of the Flood and the choice by God of Noah, the 'good man' who 'walked with God' (Gen 6:9). The first covenant between God and mankind is made with Noah: it is a covenant 'between God and the earth, between God and every living creature of every kind ... every living thing that is on the face of the earth' (Gen 9:7-17). The sign of this covenant is the rainbow, the 'bow in the clouds'.

The survivors of the Flood, Noah and his family, offer sacrifice to God:

> Noah built an altar for the Lord and choosing from all the clean animals and all the clean birds he offered burnt offerings on the altar. (Gen 8:20-21)

In these, the Bible's first recorded sacrifices, we see distinctive features of the later Temple sacrifices. What is offered is something connected with life – either a living animal or some fruit of the soil which provides nourishment for human and animal life. Already at the very dawn of human history, human beings recognise that they owe their lives to God, their Creator, and they desire to offer their own life back to God. The worshipper's own life is symbolised by an animal that can be eaten or by something edible that nourishes life; hence the choice of animals from their flocks or of fruits or food that sustain life. In Hebrew sacrifice, from the beginning, there is present a longing to somehow share life with God; and in some forms of sacrifice this is acted out, as though in mime, by a meal 'shared' with God at the end of the sacrifice; where the food is the animal's flesh cooked and eaten by the worshippers, with part set aside to be consumed by fire and thus symbolically 'eaten' by God.

The story of Abel's sacrifice shows that God looks to the interior dispositions of the offerer as well as to the intrinsic worthiness of the offering. Cain, on the contrary, is 'ill-disposed' and 'sin is lurking at the door' of his conscience, and is not resisted; hence, his offering is rejected. The whole account is obviously reflective of a simple and primitive culture; nevertheless, these qualities continue to apply to subsequent sacrifices, as described throughout the Old Testament. We shall see that these attributes still have a place in the Christian understanding of Christ's sacrifice on the Cross, which is renewed sacramentally in the Eucharist.

The Sacrifice of Abraham

The Sacrifice of Abraham (recorded in Genesis 22:1-19) lends itself even more obviously to Christian linkage with the Eucharist. The roots of the Genesis account lie deep in the pre-Judaic culture of

Canaan. There are echoes of the human sacrifice practised in some of the Canaanite cults, particularly that of the god Molech or Moloch. Being asked by the Lord to offer his son Isaac in sacrifice, therefore, though it seems barbaric to us, was not unthinkable for Abraham. His awe before God was so great and his obedience so complete that without question he prepared the materials for the sacrifice of Isaac and started off for 'the place God had pointed out to him'. Abraham collected wood for the fire and placed it on the boy Isaac's back, while he carried the fire for the burnt offering and the knife for the immolation. The boy Isaac was already familiar with animal sacrifices and kept asking his father: 'Where is the lamb for the burnt offering?' Arrived at the place appointed for the sacrifice, Abraham built the altar of sacrifice and then arranged the wood for burning the holocaust on top of the altar. Next, he lifted the boy Isaac, stretched his body out and bound him tightly over the wood on top of the altar. Abraham raised the knife to kill his son. But God intervened; he wished only to put Abraham's obedience and faith to the test. Abraham passed the test without fault or hesitation. After the angel of God had witnessed this supreme proof of Abraham's awe before God, even to the point of not sparing his son, his only son, Abraham looked up and saw a ram caught in the bushes, and he offered the ram as his sacrifice in replacement of his son.

This test of Abraham's faith was a decisive moment in the history of Israel, the people of faith. It foreshadows the covenant between God and Israel which was to follow. In response to Abraham's faith the Lord spoke to him again, saying:

> Because you have done this, because you have not refused me your son, your only son, I will shower blessings on you, I will make your descendants as many as the stars of heaven and the grains of sand on the seashore. Your descendants shall gain possession of the gates of their enemies. All the nations of the earth shall bless themselves by your descendants, as a reward for their obedience. (Gen 22:16-18)

In the sacrifice of Abraham, we note again the distinctive features of all true sacrifices under the Old Law. The sacrifice is a sign of the worshipper's desire to give his own life to God in total obedience. The animal's life is a symbol of the offerer's life, and it is symbolically taken out of human ownership and given over to God by its killing. Some of the blood of the victim is dashed against the foot of the altar (representing God) as a sign of sharing human life with God. The sincerity of the worshipper's self-giving to God is more important than the value of the victim offered. The fire which consumes a portion of the victim symbolises the offerer's worship rising up towards God as smoke ascends towards heaven. The burning of incense often accompanies the offering of the sacrifice. The sacrifice is a sign of the worshipper's desire to enter into relationship with God or to repair that relationship when it has been broken by sin; the symbolism is of the sharing of life between God and mankind, represented by the killing of the victim and the conversion of part of its flesh into a burnt offering, the smoke ascending to the heavens, as the incense rises to the throne of God. The sacrifice is concluded by the worshippers' sitting down to a festive meal which has the remaining portions of the victim as its main course and which they feel they are sharing with God. Through all this ritual, human beings are seen somehow to share their lives with God and God is seen to share his life with them. We see these features reproduced in the sacrifice offered by Elijah at Carmel; there, we read:

> The fire of the Lord fell and consumed the holocaust, and the people fell on their faces and cried: 'The Lord is God, the Lord is God.' (1 Kings 18:38-39)

There are many parallels between the sacrifice of Abraham and the Passion and Death of Jesus. God accepts the sacrifice of his Son's own life offered freely by Christ in his love for mankind. Like Abraham, God the Father 'does not spare his Son, his only Son'. The son carried 'the wood for the sacrifice' (in the case of Christ, the wooden Cross) on his back to the place of sacrifice (in Christ's case, Calvary).

Christ is the Paschal Lamb, sacrificed at Passover time, at the hour when the lambs for the Passover sacrifice are offered, as the fourth gospel has it. On the way to the place of sacrifice, in response to Isaac's repeated question about the lamb for the burnt offering, Abraham had replied: 'God himself will provide the lamb for the burnt offering.' (Gen 22:7-8) During subsequent centuries, the Israelites – and often also the pagans in their religious search – continued to look for the perfect form of sacrificial worship and to ask, at least implicitly, Isaac's question: 'Where is the lamb for the sacrifice?' John the Baptist, whom Jesus in St John's gospel calls 'a witness to speak for the light' (Jn 1:7), was to be the one who would finally answer that question. Many centuries after Isaac, Jesus was walking one day along the river bank 'on the far side of the Jordan' when John the Baptist saw him, pointed to him and said to his disciples: 'Look, there is the Lamb of God that takes away the sins of the world' (Jn 1:29). Mankind's long search is ended. Isaac's question, 'Where is the lamb for the burnt offering?' at last is answered – in Jesus Christ and in the Eucharist. The Church came to repeat John the Baptist's words in every celebration of the Eucharist. This search for the perfect sacrifice, worthy of God and acceptable to him, is paralleled in the search for a 'sacrifice in spirit and in truth', which we find in St John's gospel, particularly in the encounter of Jesus with the Samaritan woman by the well at Sychar. I shall speak of this on pp. 26–7. Since the passion and resurrection of Christ, it was natural that the Church should see in the Eucharist the 'holy and perfect sacrifice', which resembles, but infinitely surpasses, the sacrifice of Abraham, the Church's 'father in faith' (Eucharistic Prayer I).

The Sacrifice of Melchisedek

In Genesis 14:17-24, we see that the sacrificial offering of Melchisedek, King of Salem and 'priest of God Most High', was bread and wine. It was natural that Christians should see this offering as a precursor of the Eucharist, the sacrament – sacrifice offered under the signs of bread and wine. The author of the Letter to the Hebrews sees in the mysterious figure of Melchisedek a prototype of Christ and a foreshadowing of the priesthood of Christ, surpassing and replacing the priesthood of the Old Law. I shall return to this theme in pages 204–11.

Sacrifice and the Exodus Event

The Exodus event was of central importance both in the history and in the faith of the Jewish people. It gave Israel their sense of identity as a people, and it determined their special relationship with God and their sense of having a unique mission from God, based upon the solemn covenant which God had made with them, first with Abraham, then with Noah, and finally with Moses.

The Book of Exodus tells us how the Jews were delivered by God's mighty hand out of slavery and suffering in Egypt. God's victorious power led them across the Red Sea, and guided them through the dangers and trials of the desert towards the Promised Land, where God himself would be their God and they would be his people.

The purpose of the Exodus was that God's people, Israel, might be set free to offer sacrifice to God. After God had revealed to Moses his sacred name, 'I Am', he instructed Moses to confront the King of Egypt, Pharaoh, and say to him:

> The Lord, the God of the Hebrews, has come to meet us. Give us leave, then, to make a three-days' journey into the wilderness to offer sacrifice to the Lord our God. (Ex 3:18)

When Moses does confront Pharaoh, he speaks to the Egyptian King as God's emissary and he says to Pharaoh on behalf of God: 'Let my people go that they may keep a feast in the wilderness in honour of me' (Ex 5:1). He receives a curt refusal: 'Who is the Lord that I should listen to him and let Israel go? I know nothing of him, I will not let Israel go.' (Ex 5:2)

Then there begins a series of plagues, bringing pressure on Pharaoh to listen to the pleas of Moses and let God's people go. The purpose is constantly reiterated: it is so that the Israelites may offer sacrifice to God, and indeed that they will learn what is the proper sacrifice to offer to God:

> The Lord, the God of the Hebrews, has sent me to say: 'Let my people go to offer worship to me in the wilderness.' (Ex 7:16)

The request is presented to Pharaoh over and over again, but meets each time with blunt refusal.[5] It is to be noted that the aim of the Exodus is not just the material liberation of God's people from slavery and oppression, but their being granted freedom to worship God.

Pharaoh eventually relents – to the point of being willing to let the people go to offer sacrifice, but to do so only within the territory of Egypt. Moses rejects this, on the grounds that the Jews sacrifice animals which Egyptians think it sacrilege to slaughter, and this would cause inter-religious conflict. Pharaoh relents again, but asks that the Jews do not go far; and, reflecting a degree of religious respect and tolerance, he adds: 'And intercede for me.' (Ex 8:20-29) Moses promises to pray for Pharaoh.

Dissatisfied with Pharaoh's response, Moses returns to the king and renews his plea. An argument ensues about who among the Israelites are to be allowed to go and about whether their flocks and herds are to accompany them. Moses insists that livestock must be included in their journey, because the Israelites do not yet know what animals will be required for sacrifice: 'Until we reach the place, we do not know ourselves what worship we shall offer to the Lord.' (Ex 10:26)

The plea of Moses is brought to Pharaoh before each of the ten plagues which fall on Egypt, but it meets each time with outright refusal. Pharaoh, sounding at times like a Marxist calling religion the 'opium of the people', or indeed like a Nazi crying *Arbeit macht frei*, or *Freiheit durch Arbeit*, says: 'They are lazy, and that is why their cry is, "Let us go and offer sacrifice to our God".'

His solution to the problem is to make the Israelites work harder than ever 'so that they do not have time to stop and listen to glib speeches' (Ex 5:8-9).

Then comes the climax, the tenth and most dreadful plague of all; it comes at Passover, when each first-born human being or animal in Egypt is to die, but the Israelites, their doorposts marked by the blood of a sacrificial lamb, will be spared. For the Israelites it is the first celebration of the great Feast of Passover, which is to be celebrated perpetually, year after year, in remembrance of the deliverance of the Jewish people from Egypt; for the Egyptians, it causes lamentation and doom, but brings about their final submission to God's demand through Moses. Pharaoh sends for Moses and Aaron and says to them:

> Go and offer worship to the Lord as you have asked, and as you have asked take your flocks and herds and go. And also ask a blessing on me. (Ex 12:31-2)

Sacrifice: What to Offer and Where?

The debate about what was the proper sacrifice to offer to God and where was the proper place to offer that sacrifice was to continue right through Jewish biblical history. In the Prophets and in the Psalms, a recurring question is that of whether true sacrifice consists in 'burnt offerings, wholly consumed' and 'young bulls offered on your altars', or in 'a contrite spirit, a humbled and contrite heart' (Ps 49(50):16-19). The prophets repeatedly contrast the mere offering of animals in sacrifice with the interior disposition and the moral rectitude of the worshipper, and stress that the latter is more important than the former. It should be remembered, however, that, in the Hebrew language of the Old Testament, contrast is often inclusive. When the psalmist prays in Psalm 39(40):

> You do not ask for sacrifice and offerings,
> but an open ear;
> you do not ask for holocaust and victim;
> instead, here am I

he is in fact proposing to offer sacrifice, but to accompany it with an offering of himself in a sincere determination to do God's will and to 'delight in [God's] law in the depth of [his] heart' (Ps 39(40):7-9). It is this which makes the external sacrifice genuine and authentic.

During their wanderings in the desert, Moses sets up the Tent of Meeting, with its altar and the Ark of the covenant and the Throne of Mercy, as the place of God's Presence among his people and, consequently, as the proper place to offer sacrifice to God. Later, David plans and Solomon builds the Temple as the place of God's Presence and the place of sacrifice. The question of where sacrifice is to be offered and what kind of sacrifice is required becomes acute when the Temple is destroyed. During the persecution of the Jews under Antiochus Epiphanes in the second century BC, the prophet Daniel laments:

> We have at this time no leader, no prophet ...
> no holocaust, no sacrifice, no oblation ...
> no place where we can offer you the first fruits
> and win your favour. (Dan 3:37-8)

We hear echoes of the debate in Our Lord's dialogue with the Samaritan woman. She, loyal to the traditions of her people, says to Jesus: 'Our fathers worshipped on this mountain, while you say that Jerusalem is the place where one ought to worship'. Jesus replies:

> The hour is coming when you will worship the Father
> neither on this mountain nor in Jerusalem ... The hour will
> come – in fact it is here already – when true worshippers will
> worship the Father in spirit and in truth. That is the kind of
> worshipper the Father wants. God is spirit and those who
> worship must worship in spirit and truth. (Jn 4:19-24)

Jesus then reveals to her his identity, saying: 'I who am speaking to you. I am he.' The latter words are in fact the same words that God had spoken to Moses when he revealed to him his Divine Name, 'I am' (Jn 4:20-26). The promise of worship in spirit and in truth is fulfilled in Jesus himself and in the Eucharist; and this is the final answer to the question posed by Moses to Pharaoh at the Exodus, as to what is true and acceptable worship and where it is to be offered.

Sacrifice and the Old Covenant

The linkage of the Exodus and Passover events with the Eucharist is still more explicit in the words of institution given to us by Jesus at the Last Supper. The Exodus reaches a climax in the solemn enactment by God of his covenant with the people of Israel, through the interceding of Moses. It is in fact the solemn and ritual ratification by God of the covenant first proclaimed amid the awesome signs of God's presence in the fire and smoke and thunder and deafening trumpet blast on Mount Sinai.[6] God had promised that, if his people obeyed his voice and held fast to his covenant, then Israel, 'of all the nations shall be [God's] very own' and God 'will make them a kingdom of priests, a consecrated nation' (Ex 19:5-8). The people responded by pledging full obedience and fidelity: 'We will observe all that the Lord has decreed; we will obey.' (Ex 24:3)

Moses had first given instructions for sacrifices to be prepared by the slaughter of animals. Moses cast on the altar half the blood of the slaughtered animals; the other half he put in basins, and, after reading the text of the Law of the covenant to the people, he sprinkled them with blood from the basins, with the words: 'This is the blood of the covenant that the Lord has made with you.' (Ex 24:5-8) In a clear recall of this covenant of God with his people, Jesus inaugurated a new covenant with the new People of God at the Passover meal on the eve of his Passion with the words: 'This cup is the new covenant in my blood, which will be poured out for you.' (Lk 22:19-20)

We shall examine more closely in Part II how Christ's blood shed in sacrifice on the Cross inaugurated a new and everlasting covenant with a people formerly excluded from the first covenant. We shall see also how the sharing of life between God and his people, symbolically represented by Moses' sprinkling of the people with sacrificial blood at Mount Sinai, is given an amazing new reality by Christ's sacrifice on the Cross, which is renewed sacramentally in the Eucharist.

Sacrifice according to Leviticus

Since the Eucharist is a sacrifice and a memorial of the Saving Sacrifice of Christ, it is relevant to look more closely at the Old Testament teaching of sacrifice. The Book of Leviticus lays down the ritual to be followed in a series of different kinds of sacrifice. A distinction is drawn between the sacrifice of an animal and an oblation. An oblation is an offering of wheat and flour on which the offerer is to pour wine and put incense, to be burnt by the priest on the altar 'as a memorial, a burnt offering whose fragrance will appease the Lord' (Lev 2:2). The flour may be baked and similarly offered, but it must be unleavened. The symbolism is that of one's life – represented by the flesh of an animal or by the bread which nourishes life – offered to God, and of life shared with God in memorial of his everlasting covenant of union with his people.

A holocaust is the offering of a male animal, 'without blemish', offered at the entrance of the Tent of Meeting 'so that it may be accepted before the Lord'. The worshipper is to lay his hand on the animal's head so that its immolation may be effectual for his atonement. The blood is offered by the priests; the flesh is burnt on the altar and 'the fragrance of it will appease the Lord' (Lev 1:1-17).

The communion sacrifice is the offering of an animal from the herd or from the flock, male or female, and without blemish. The ritual is similar to that of a holocaust, except that the fat is burnt on the altar 'as food, as a burnt offering for the Lord'.

The remaining edible parts of the animal are cooked and eaten by the worshipper and his family and friends, while the fat is burnt and thus 'eaten' by the Lord (Lev 3:1-17). Here the sharing of life between God and his covenant people becomes still more explicit, symbolised by the sharing of the sacrificial meal between God and the worshippers.

Sacrifices for sin are offered in atonement for grave violations of the law of God committed by priests or by the community or by individuals. The victim is an animal, or, if the sinner is a poor person, 'a pair of turtledoves or two young pigeons', or if even this is beyond the worshipper's resources, 'an ephah of wheaten flour'. As in the case of a communion sacrifice, the ritual combines elements of holocaust and of blood sprinkled around the altar (Lev 5:1-13).

The sacrifice of reparation introduces the further concept of 'restitution' of God's violated rights. It is required of anyone who sins inadvertently by not observing God's sacred rights. The victim here has to be 'an unblemished ram from [the sinner's] flock, subject to valuation', since the sinner 'must restore what his sin subtracted from the sacred rights, adding one fifth of the value' (Lev 5:15-19).

Covenant and Sacrifice

Covenant and sacrifice are closely linked with one another in the Old Testament and both of these are inseparable from the Eucharist in the New. The covenant with Noah had no sacrifice attached to it. There was, however, an external sign – the sign of the 'bow in the clouds', the rainbow; this was to be a perpetual recall of the covenant between God and the earth (Gen 9:14). God said to Noah:

> I will recall the covenant between myself and you and every living creature of every kind. ... This is the sign of the covenant I have established between myself and every living thing that is found on the earth. (Gen 9:15-16)

The covenant extended not just to humanity but also to: 'Every living creature to be found, birds and cattle and every wild beast with you.' (Gen 9:8-10) This covenant prohibited the eating of 'flesh with life, that is blood, in it'. It forbade the taking of human life: 'I will demand an account of your life-blood. I will demand an account of everyman's life from his fellow-men.' (Gen 9:4-6)

It is significant that the Noahic covenant was a covenant with 'the earth' and with all living creatures on the earth, including the animals. In anticipation of the great Flood, God made provision for all future propagation of animal species by including in the Ark two members, one male and one female, of every known species of animal. This earliest of covenants between God and his creatures is appropriately called 'The Cosmic covenant'.[7]

The covenant with Abraham, described in the Book of Genesis, was not marked by sacrifice but was given visual expression in the rite of circumcision. This was the external sign that Israel was a people apart, a people chosen by God as his very own people, while they had him alone as their God. This covenant was linked with the gift to them by God of 'the whole land of Canaan, to own in perpetuity' (Gen 17:9-13). Later, however, came the testing of Abraham's faith and obedience by the divine command to sacrifice his son, his only son, Isaac.

Abraham is the great Patriarch of Jewish faith; he is also the Patriarch of Christian faith. In the Latin original of our present Eucharistic Prayer he is called 'our Patriarch Abraham'. It is Abraham's faith which wins for him that dignity: 'Abraham put his faith in the Lord, who counted this as making him justified.' (Gen 15:6) In the earliest accounts of Abraham in the Book of Genesis, we find a different name for Abraham, the great Patriarch of Jewish faith: he is called Abram. The names are interchangeable. 'Abram' is what the *New Jerome Bible Commentary* terms a 'dialectal variant' of the name 'Abraham'. The Genesis account of Abraham begins with God's call to him to leave 'his country, his family and his father's house for the land which God will show him', with a promise that '[God] will make you a great nation. ... All the tribes of the earth shall bless themselves by you' (Gen 12:3).

Abraham was accompanied on his journey to the 'Promised Land' by his wife Sarai, his nephew Lot and his household. They settled in the Negeb and here Abraham built an altar to the Lord and invoked the name of the Lord. Famine struck the land and Abraham took refuge in Egypt. From here, when the famine ended, Abraham returned to the Negeb. At this point, Abraham and Lot agreed to separate and live apart. Lot settled in the Jordan plain and Abraham settled in the land of Canaan, which the Lord promised to 'give to [him]' and to '[his] descendants forever' (Gen 13:15).

After the separation of Abraham and Lot the Genesis narrative inserts the story of Melchisedek. Since the theological significance of Melchisedek is developed principally by the author of the Letter to the Hebrews, I shall explore this story, along with other New Testament themes, in Part II (see pp. 204–11).

Sometime later, Genesis continues, 'a word of the Lord was spoken to Abraham in a vision: "Have no fear Abram, I am your shield, your reward will be very great."' (Gen 15:1-2) Abraham asked God for an heir, since Sarai was childless. Sarai gave her Egyptian slave-girl, Hagar, to Abraham as his wife; and of her was born Abraham's son, Ishmael. Then God renewed the covenant with Abraham and his descendants forever:

> I will establish my covenant between myself and you and your descendants after you, generation after generation, a covenant in perpetuity, to be your God and the God of your descendants after you. I will give to you and to your descendants after you the land you are living in, the whole land of Canaan, to own in perpetuity, and I will be your God. (Gen 17:7-8)

The covenant will be marked by a visible sign: every Jewish male is to be circumcised; and 'this shall be the sign of the covenant between myself and you' (Gen 17:9-14). Abraham's wife, Sarai, is to be called Sarah and she is to give birth to another son, Isaac, a son of Abraham's old age; whose birth is promised for a time when Sarah was herself well past child-bearing age; then the covenant will be renewed between God and Isaac and all Isaac's posterity.

The narrative continues with the divine apparition at Mamre. Three men arrive at Abraham's tent during the hottest part of the day. Abraham and Sarah quickly prepare a meal for them. The 'guest' promises to return within the year, and Isaac will be born at this time. It is noteworthy that the guests are described alternatively as three and as one. This apparition is to become in Christian times the theme of the *icon* of the Trinity, so greatly venerated in the Orthodox Churches, and, particularly in recent decades, so lovingly and so devotedly honoured by Catholics as well. Catholics have stressed the eucharistic aspects of this *icon* of the Trinity. The three Persons are seen as the three Members of the most Holy Trinity. They are seated at an altar, on which stands the cup and food for a meal. The person representing Christ has his hand extended towards the cup. The figure of the cup is found also in the shape of the altar itself, and can indeed be further discerned in the disposition of the figures and their attire. The *icon* reflects the Church's teaching that in the Eucharist we receive the Father and the Holy Spirit together with the Divine Son. We are reminded of the words of the Lord in St John's gospel: 'If anyone loves me he will keep my word and my Father will love him, and we shall come to him and make our home with him.' (Jn 14:23)

Returning to the Genesis narrative, we find two visible signs of God's covenant with Abraham, firstly: the three guests at Mamre – surely an indication that the people of the Eucharist are a people made one in the unity of the Father, the Son and the Holy Spirit (this is the phrase applied to the Church by St Cyprian: it is quoted by the Second Vatican Council in its Constitution on the Church, *Lumen Gentium*); and secondly: the birth of a son, Isaac, to the old and childless Abraham –

surely an indication that the mystery of the Church is one with the mystery of Christ, and that the sacrifice of Christ, foretold in the sacrifice of Isaac, is the saving sacrifice which makes the Church saved, redeemed and holy.

The covenant is then renewed between God and Abraham and 'his descendants after him, a covenant in perpetuity', whereby God will give to them the whole land of Canaan to own in perpetuity, 'and [he, the Lord], will be their God' (Gen 17:1-7).

Finally, a strange rite was performed by Abraham in compliance with a message from God. At a time when Abraham was still childless, he had a vision in which God spoke to him, saying: 'Have no fear; I am your shield.' But Abraham did have fear for the future: how could God's promises of a multitude of descendants be fulfilled while Abraham was childless? He was told by God: 'Look up to heaven and count the stars if you can. Such will be your descendants.' (Gen 15:2-5) God gave Abraham a sign to strengthen his faith in God's promise. The sign took the form of a strange and ancient rite, in accordance with which Abraham was to get together three animals, each of them a three-year-old, namely a heifer, a goat and a ram, and together with them, two birds, a turtledove and a young pigeon. He was to cut the animals in half and lay the pieces out in rows with a space between each row. Abraham fell into a deep sleep and then was seized with the awe and 'terror' associated with one overcome by the sense of the presence of God. God then spoke to Abraham, renewing his promise. Later, in the darkness of the night 'there appeared a smoking furnace and a firebrand that went between the halves'. This was a sign of God's covenant with Abraham, a covenant carrying God's guarantee of the promised land: 'To your descendents I give this land from the wadi of Egypt to the great river.' (Gen 15:12-18)

This strange ritual is described again in a totally different context in the Book of Jeremiah. In this case, the covenant is solemnised by the killing and the cutting into two halves of a calf. The people are warned through the prophet that, since they had violated the covenant that God had made with them – a covenant attested by the ritual of 'the halves' of the calf – they would deserve to suffer the fate signified by the slain calf.[8] It would seem that this ritual was a solemn way of sacralising important covenants between individuals or tribes. If one of the parties broke the contract, then that party was seen as implicitly calling down upon himself the fate of the dismembered animals. Although this ritual is not sacrificial, there are similarities between it and the ritual of sacrifice; its symbolism overlaps with that of sacrifice. In the case of Abraham, the ritual symbolises an interweaving of two lives, the life of God and the life of the chosen people. God, represented by the firebrand, walks between 'the halves' of the people, symbolised by the slain animals.

In the Eucharist, which perpetuates the new and everlasting covenant won for us by the death and resurrection of Christ, one could perhaps think of the worshipping community as being enveloped between the 'two halves' of the Body of Christ at the *fractio panis* or breaking of bread before the communion. This can be seen as a sign of the union with the 'broken Christ' of the crucifixion into which we enter at our eucharistic communion, and our entering thereby into union with the resurrected Christ – an anticipation of our being finally and forever clasped in the eternal embrace of God, the one and undivided Trinity, who is our first beginning and will be at one and the same time our last end and our new beginning. This image is nowhere suggested in the liturgy, but I suggest it is a permissible thought as a matter of personal devotion.

These thoughts re-echo the teaching of Jesus in St John's gospel, to which we have just referred: 'We shall come to him and make our home with him.' (Jn 14:23. See p. 32).

This 'being at home with Jesus' in our own holy communions, and the consequent uninterrupted 'having Jesus at home with us' in our daily lives, is the greatest consolation we enjoy in our faith in Jesus Christ. Our prayer in this sceptical modern age can often be taken up with questions: are the gospels historically reliable? Is

Jesus a man-made myth or is there solid evidence for his life and his teaching? Is it reasonable and rational to believe in Jesus Christ? It is consoling to recall the words ascribed to Jesus by St John in his Farewell Discourses after the Last Supper:

> You are sad now but I shall see you again and your hearts will be full of joy and that joy no-one shall take from you. When that day comes you will not ask me any questions. (Jn 16:22-23)

The account in Genesis of the birth of Isaac is enough to indicate the importance of Isaac in God's plan of salvation; it is by God's direct intervention that Isaac is born. Isaac is a prototype of Jesus Christ:

> The Lord dealt kindly with Sarah as he had said, and did what he promised. So Sarah conceived and bore a son to Abraham in his old age, at the time God had promised. Abraham was one hundred years old when his son Isaac was born to him. (Gen 21:1-6)

The Manna in the Desert

A most important Old Testament link with the Eucharist is the Exodus story of the manna.[9] Our Lord refers to the manna with which God fed his people in their forty years of wandering in the desert before entering the promised land. He does so particularly in the great eucharistic discourse in the sixth chapter of St John's gospel. We shall reflect on this gospel in Part II. The mysterious food on which the people of Israel survived the hardships of the desert is described in Exodus as a 'fine flake-like thing', falling like dew each morning 'on the face of the wilderness, as fine as hoarfrost on the ground'. It was 'like coriander seed, white ... like bdellium'. It could be boiled like porridge or ground and baked like cakes; it tasted like wafers sweetened with honey.[10] The manna, as we are told in Exodus, was miraculously provided by God after the people complained about the lack of food on their desert journey and grumbled that it would have been better for them to die in Egypt than starve to death in the desert. God, the account in Exodus continues, 'heard the complaints of the sons of Israel', and gave them also meat to eat, in the shape of quails whose flight darkened the sky each evening, while in the morning he gave them 'bread to [their] heart's content'. The word 'manna', according to the Exodus account, is taken from the question which the Israelites asked when they first saw this mysterious substance. 'What is that?' they asked one another. In Hebrew, the question was: '*Man hu?*' Moses answered their question in the words: 'That is the bread the Lord gives you to eat.'

There are several special features about this 'bread from heaven'. Each person was able to gather each day exactly enough of this food for his needs for that day; and, no matter how much he gathered over and above this amount, only his allowance for that day remained. For tomorrow's bread they had to have faith that God would provide – and he never failed. There are echoes of this in the 'Our Father', the prayer that Jesus taught us: 'Give us this day our daily bread' is a petition for the Eucharist and also for material bread 'just for today', leaving all our tomorrows trustingly in God's hands.

The Book of Deuteronomy tells us that manna was sent by God to the people of Israel as their daily food for forty years in the desert; not simply, however, as their material nourishment, but also as a sign of their total dependence on God and to test their faith in God's Word, their observance of his Law and their fidelity towards him. The text of Deuteronomy states:

> Remember how the Lord your God led you for forty years in the wilderness, to humble you, to test you and to know your inmost heart – whether you would obey his commandments or not. He humbled you, he made you feel hungry, he fed you with manna ... to make you understand that man does not live on bread alone but that man lives on everything that comes

from the mouth of the Lord ... Take care you do not forget the
Lord your God. ... Do not then forget the Lord your God.
(Deut 8:2-3, 11, 14)

Deuteronomy goes on to teach that the manna is a sign of the
covenant which God made with his people; it showed that God was
faithful to his covenant and it was a reminder to the people that
they must be faithful to their covenant with God. Above all, the
manna was a reminder to the people that they should hunger more
for the words of the Lord than for material food. These words are
quoted by Jesus on the occasion of his temptation in the desert. The
devil, knowing that Jesus was hungry after his fast of forty days,
invited him to use his power to turn a stone into a loaf. Jesus
replied: 'Scripture says: "Man does not live on bread alone, but on
every word that comes from the mouth of God".' (Mt 4:4)

The manna and the desert experience of Israel are closely
linked to the covenant between God and his people. God warns
the people through Moses in the desert that they are never to
forget the Lord and his commandments:

When the Lord has brought you into [the promised land] ...
with vineyards and olives you did not plant, when you have
eaten these and had your fill, then take care you do not forget
the Lord who brought you out of the land of Egypt. (Deut
6:10-13).

Take care you do not forget the Lord your God, neglecting his
commandments and customs and laws which I lay on you
today. When you have eaten and had all you want, when you
have built fine houses to live in, when you have seen your
flocks and herds increase, your silver and gold abound and all
your possessions grow great, do not become proud of heart.
Do not then forget the Lord your God. ... Remember the Lord
your God. It is he who gave you this strength and won you this
power, thus keeping the covenant then, as today, that he swore
to your fathers. (Deut 8:11-18)

The manna narrative is re-echoed in the accounts of the multiplication of the loaves in the three synoptic gospels. In the gospel accounts, the place where the loaves are miraculously multiplied is another desert place. As the Israelites of old are miraculously fed by God with manna, so the loaves are miraculously multiplied in the desert place by Jesus Christ. The manna was in part a testing of the faith of the Israelites in God and in his words and his promises; the miracle becomes in the gospel the prelude to a session of teaching by Jesus of the assembled crowd: 'Jesus set himself to teach them at some length.' (Mk 6:34) This teaching in turn becomes the occasion for Peter's confession of faith. As God manifested his supreme being and power to the Israelites in the desert by the miracle of the manna, so, after another desert experience, Jesus reveals his divine Name, 'I Am', to his disciples as he walked on the waters in the storm at sea. Afterwards, by a series of miraculous cures, he reveals his power and compassion.[11] We examine these passages in greater detail in Part II.

The association of the gospel miracle of the loaves with the Eucharist is clear already from the language used in the gospels to introduce the actual miracle: Jesus, we read in St Mark's gospel, 'took the loaves, raised his eyes to heaven and said the blessing, then he broke the loaves and handed them to the disciples to distribute among the people'. The words are substantially the same as those used by Mark in his account of the institution of the Eucharist; and the same is true for Luke and Matthew. Since the earliest days of the Church and following the first eucharistic kerygma, as we find this in St Paul and in the synoptic gospels, the Church has interpreted the miracle of the loaves in a eucharistic sense.

Indeed, in all biblical texts relating to the Eucharist, the same theme as in the manna narrative recurs, namely the theme of listening to the words of the Lord and believing them.

'Eating' God's Word

We have seen that the manna in its deeper meaning included God's teaching and faith in his word. The concept of 'eating' the words of God recurs repeatedly across the whole of the Old Testament. The psalms speak frequently of 'eating' or 'thirsting for' the words of God. The lovely psalm 'The Lord is my Shepherd' has the verse: 'You have prepared a banquet for me in the sight of my foes. My head you have anointed with oil, my cup is overflowing.' (Ps 22(23):5) In Psalm 33(34) we have the well-known words: 'Taste and see that the Lord is good.' (Ps 34(35):8)

Psalm 41(42) compares yearning for God to the thirsting of a parched deer for running streams and goes on: 'My soul is thirsting for God, the God of my life.' (Ps 41(42):2) In Psalm 106 we learn of how God's people suffered sickness because of their sins and had:

> A loathing for every food
> and came close to the gates of death;
> then they cried to the Lord in their need
> and he rescued them from their distress.
> He sent forth his word to heal them
> and saved their life from the grave. (Ps 106(107):17-20)

Psalm 118(119) is an extended commentary on the theme of the Word of God, using a variety of terms for that Word, such as will, precepts, commands, statutes, decrees, law, wonders, love, promise, truth, justice, mercies, saving help. One of its verses says: 'Your promise is sweeter to my taste than honey in the mouth.' (Ps 118(119):103)

Through the prophet Amos, God warns the Israelites of a famine which is to strike the country: 'a famine, not of bread, a drought, not of water, but of hearing the word of the Lord.' (Am 8:11) The prophet Jeremiah 'devours' the words of God: 'When your words came I devoured them; your word was my delight and the joy of my heart.' (Jer 15:16)

The prophet Ezekiel is commanded by God to take the scroll which is handed to him and to eat it. When he has done so, God says to him: 'Son of man, feed and be satisfied by the scroll I am giving you.' Ezekiel goes on to say: 'I ate it, and it tasted as sweet as honey.' (Ez 2:8-3:3)

We find similar language in the Book of Wisdom. There we read: '[It is not] the various crops that nourish human beings, but your Word which sustains those who trust in you.' (Wis 16:26) In the Book of Ecclesiasticus or The Wisdom of Ben Sirach we read: '[Wisdom] will give him the bread of understanding to eat and the water of wisdom to drink.' (Ecclus 15:3) Later, Wisdom addresses her own people:

> Approach me, you who desire me,
> and take your fill of my fruits,
> for memories of me are sweeter than honey
> inheriting me is sweeter than the honeycomb.
> They who eat me will hunger for more,
> they who drink me will thirst for more. (Ecclus 24:19-29)

This language passed over to the New Testament. In the Book of Revelation, a voice from heaven bids the seer: 'Take [the scroll] and eat it. It will turn your stomach sour, but in your mouth it will taste as sweet as honey.' (Rev 10:9-10)

The Old Testament language, of which I have given examples, is a key to the fuller understanding of the manna in the desert. It is also important for the reading of the first part of the eucharistic discourse in St John's gospel, as we shall see later.

It may be remarked that, somewhat similarly, ordinary English usage speaks of someone's having a 'voracious appetite' for books, or 'devouring' newspapers, or having a 'hunger for learning', or of an audience's 'eating' an orator's words, or 'drinking in' his message. We speak of 'ruminating' on a piece of scripture.

The above is the scriptural source for the teaching of the Second Vatican Council about the 'two tables' at the Eucharist, first the 'table of God's Word' and second the 'table of the Lord's body'.[12] This, as we shall see, is reflected in the two phases, distinct but inseparable, of the eucharistic liturgy, first the liturgy of the Word, and second the liturgy of the Eucharist.

Yom Kippur, the Day of Atonement

Special solemnity attaches to the sacrifice for sin offered on the Great Day of Atonement (Yom Kippur), which is prescribed for 'the tenth day of the seventh month ... as a perpetual law' (Lev 16). This day was set aside as a day of atonement or reconciliation between God and his people. It was a day when the priests, for themselves and also on behalf of their people, and the people through their priests, offered contrition and reparation to God for their own sins and for their inadvertent offences and ritual uncleannesses. Leviticus describes in detail the 'rite of atonement over the sanctuary for the uncleanness of the sons of Israel, for their transgressions and for all their sins' (Lev 16:16). A series of sacrifices of atonement is prescribed for this day. In particular, Aaron is to offer the sacrifice of a bull for his own sins, taking the blood behind the veil of the Tent of the Divine Presence and sprinkling its blood on and before the Throne of Mercy and at the same time burning incense.

Then, for the sins of the people, Aaron is to select two goats and cast lots for one to be set aside for God and one for Azazel (a demon of the desert). The goat allotted for God is immolated and its blood is carried inside the veil in the Tent of Meeting and is sprinkled on and before the Throne of Mercy. Then Aaron is to 'lay his hands on [the other goat's] head and confess all the faults of the sons of Israel, all their transgressions and all their sins and lay them to the charge [of the goat]'. An attendant then takes the goat and leads it off to be set free to wander across the desert. The word 'scapegoat' derives from this ancient ritual, and there is a special poignancy for us in reflecting that Jesus freely makes himself the scapegoat for our sins. The ritual is a kind of sacred mime, symbolising the people's desire to banish sin from their midst. There are parallels in other religions, such as Islam.[13]

There are echoes of the Day of Atonement in the gospel accounts of the Passion and death of Jesus Christ. There are echoes also in the second part of the Book of Isaiah. This is a collection of prophecies, Isaiah 40–55, by an unnamed prophet who, after the Babylonian conquest, preached to the Israelite exiles 'by the rivers of Babylon'. The unnamed author is usually called the 'Deutero-Isaiah'. This collection was added on to the prophecies of the historical Isaiah who preached before the Babylonian exile. The collection is otherwise known as the 'Book of the Consolation of Israel'. It offers comfort from God to the people of Israel at one of the lowest points in their tragic history. It offers them the hope of the covenant renewed, the return of the exiles to the promised land and salvation achieved, through the sufferings of a Servant of the Lord who chooses to suffer for his people. This is the theme in particular of the Four Songs of the Servant of the Lord.[14]

The whole book of Isaiah, and the Book of the Consolation of Israel in particular, had an important place in Hebrew spirituality and messianism in the time of Our Lord. Indeed, Jesus undoubtedly identified himself with the suffering Servant. The disciples came to interpret and explain the mission of Jesus Christ, his Passion and his death in terms of these passages from Isaiah. The first song of the Servant has indeed been termed the fifth gospel of the Passion. The Isaian image of the substitutory and expiatory sacrifice offered to God by the Servant through his sufferings and his death corresponds closely with Jesus Christ's own understanding of his 'laying down his life for his friends' (Jn 15:13) and of his words of institution of the Eucharist: 'This is my body, given up for you and for all.' (Lk 22:19) 'This is my blood, which is to be poured out for many for the forgiveness of sins.' (Mt 26:23) The Passion and death of Jesus Christ cannot be fully understood without reference to these Isaian passages. We examine them later in greater detail.

The Prophets and Sacrifice

After his resurrection, Jesus appeared to two disciples on the road to Emmaus, and later he spoke to them and to their fellow disciples in Jerusalem, explaining to them 'all the passages in the Law of Moses, in the Prophets and in the Psalms which were about himself' (Lk 24:27, 44). I wish now to look at these same books in the Bible, particularly at some passages which relate to the sacrifices which were an important part of Jewish worship. Since the crucifixion and death of Jesus Christ were regarded, from the earliest days of the Church, as the sacrifice offered by Christ to his Eternal Father in atonement for the sins of mankind, it is obviously relevant to our purpose to examine the teaching of the Prophets and the Psalms about sacrifice. We have already mentioned the Servant Songs of Deutero-Isaiah, which correspond so exactly with the mind of Jesus before and during his passion and which express so clearly the sacrificial and expiatory nature of Christ's suffering and death.

Contrary to what one might expect, however, the prophets, at first sight, speak negatively about sacrifice in general. Already Samuel, condemning Saul for disobedience to God following the defeat of the Amalakites, pronounced God's rejection of Saul with the words: 'Is the pleasure of the Lord in holocausts and sacrifices or in obedience to the voice of the Lord? Yes, obedience is better than sacrifice, submissiveness better than the fat of rams.' (1 Sam 15:22)

One of the severest critics of Jewish sacrifices is Isaiah. He presents God as asking: 'What are your endless sacrifices to me?'; 'away with your worthless offerings.' (1:11-20) Amos has God saying:

> Offer sacrifices each morning, burn your thanksgiving offerings, boast of your free-will offerings – if that is what makes you happy! (Am 4:4-5)

Later Amos, still more vehemently, has God saying: 'I hate and scorn your festivals. I do not accept your burnt offerings, oblations and communion-sacrifices.' (Am 5:21-4) Micah speaks in similar terms (6:6-8).

Each of these apparent condemnations of sacrifice is, however, accompanied by statements of what God does desire and does expect from worshippers. Samuel asks for obedience and submissiveness to the voice of the Lord. Isaiah, in the passage quoted, continues as follows: 'Search for justice, help the oppressed, be just to the orphan, plead for the widow.' (1:17) Jeremiah puts it thus: 'Sincerity is no more; it has vanished from their mouths.' (7:28) Similarly, Amos continues: 'Let justice flow like water and uprightness like a never-failing stream.' (5:24) Micah adds: 'You have already been told what the Lord wants of you, only this: To act justly, to love tenderly, and to walk humbly with your God.' (6:8)

The genius of the Hebrew language itself suggests, however, that what the prophets are saying is that sacrifices are genuine when certain dispositions are present; when these are absent, sacrifice is useless. Sacrifices offered by people who are lacking in love, justice, sincerity, forgiveness, mercy and kindness are worthless before God.

These dispositions, however, are precisely those lived and taught by Jesus Christ and exemplified in his sacrificial death on the Cross. In his life and in his death, Jesus Christ manifested what Hosea calls the 'faithful love which pleases [God]'.

There are in fact many favourable references to sacrifice throughout the prophets.[15] The prophets speak also of the perfect sacrifice which will be offered and accepted by God after the great return of the exiles and in the Messianic Age.[16]

These warnings of the prophets should be applied by us to our eucharistic worship. The infinite value of Christ's sacrifice remains, even if our dispositions are unworthy; but the fruitfulness in our own lives of that sacrifice is reduced by our unworthiness; to the point, indeed, of our incurring further sin, even sacrilege, through our unworthy reception of the Eucharist. Conversely, our way of living should reflect the qualities required by the prophets for every true sacrifice. Since all true sacrifice is an offering of our own lives to God and a desire to have God present in our lives, there must be consistency between our lives and our offering; there must be sincerity in our prayer and our lives. We must be honest with God; we must mean what we say when we speak to God and when we offer the eucharistic sacrifice to God. Let the prophet Daniel be our guide in prayer and in life:

> May the contrite soul, the humbled spirit,
> be as acceptable to you as burnt offerings.
> Such let our sacrifice be to you today.
> May it please you that we follow you whole-heartedly.
> May we put our whole heart into following you,
> fearing you and seeking your face.
> Treat us gently as you yourself are gentle and very merciful.
> (3:38-42)

But, when we do our best to bring to the eucharist our 'contrite soul' and 'humbled spirit', and try to follow the Lord 'whole-heartedly', putting our whole heart into following God, 'fearing him and seeking his face', then we have from the prophet Zephaniah the assurance that God has delirious joy in coming to us in holy communion: 'The Lord will rejoice over you with happy song. He will dance with shouts of joy for you as on a day of festival.' (3:17)

The Servant Songs and the Eucharistic Sacrifice

More strikingly still, the Servant Songs of Deutero-Isaiah form the unspoken background to many of the actions and words of Jesus. In the Fourth Song, we find the Servant freely embracing suffering and death in atonement for the sins of humanity:

> ... for our faults struck down in death ...
> If he offers his life in atonement
> he shall see his heirs, he shall have a long life
> and through him what the Lord wishes will be done. ...

By his sufferings shall my servant justify many,
taking their faults on himself. (Isa 53)

Already at his baptism by John in the Jordan, Jesus takes upon
himself the guilt of sinners, accepting a Messiahship which is
expiatory and self-sacrificing. He sees his baptism by John as an
anticipation of his Passion, and later speaks of his Passion as a
baptism still to be undergone.[17] In the temptations in the desert, he
is tempted by the devil to choose a messiahship of worldly power
and pomp, but he firmly rejects this and chooses instead a
messiahship of unworldly weakness and of suffering for others.[18]
In the Agony in the Garden Jesus rejects power and violence ('put
your sword into its scabbard ...') and chooses vicarious suffering,
symbolised by the cup of God's anger against sin, which he agrees
to drink.[19] His predictions of the Passion contain repeated implicit
references to the Suffering Servant and especially to the Fourth
Song.[20] The eucharistic implications of all this are obvious.[21]

Jesus' understanding of his messiahship and his mission
correspond closely with what is written in chapters 40 to 45 in the
Book of Isaiah, as I have already said on p. 42. This 'book' has some
of the most moving and tender declarations of love given by God to
his people to be found in the entire Bible. In reading these professions
of God's love, we remember that they are fulfilled in that greater love
than any man has, the love which led Jesus to 'lay down his life for
his friends' (Jn 15:13) on the Cross; and this is the love which is
made present for us in the Eucharist. I quote here a few examples of
the Deutero-Isaian words of love:

Do not be afraid, for I am with you;
stop being anxious and watchful, for I am your God.
I give you strength, I bring you help,
I uphold you with my victorious right hand. ...

For I, the Lord your God,
I am holding you by the right hand;

I tell you, 'Do not be afraid,
I will help you'.
Do not be afraid, Jacob, poor little worm,
Israel, tiny little mite.
I will help you – it is the Lord who speaks –
the Holy One of Israel is your redeemer. (Isa 41:10-14).

Listen to me, House of Jacob,
all you who remain of the House of Israel,
you who have been carried since birth,
whom I have carried since the time you were born.

In your old age I shall be still the same,
when your hair is grey I shall still support you.
I have already done so, I have carried you,
I shall still support you and deliver you. (Isa 46:3-4)

He who pities them will lead them
and guide them to springs of water. ...
Shout for joy, you heavens; exult, you earth!
You mountains, break into happy cries!
For the Lord consoles his people
and takes pity on them who are afflicted. (Isa 49:10-13)

Does a woman forget her baby at the breast
or fail to cherish the child of her womb?
Yet, even if these forget,
I shall not forget you. (Isa 49:15)

Do not be afraid, you will not be put to shame,
do not be dismayed, you will not be disgraced;
for you will forget the shame of your youth
and no longer remember the curse of your widowhood.
For now your creator will be your husband,
his name, the Lord Sabaoth;
your redeemer will be Holy One of Israel,
he is called the God of the whole earth. ...

I did forsake you for a brief moment,
but with great love I will take you back.
In excessive anger, for a moment
I hid my face from you.
But with everlasting love I have taken pity on you,
says the Lord your redeemer. ...
For the mountains may depart,
the hills be shaken,
but my love for you will never leave you
and my covenant of peace with you will never be shaken,
says the Lord who takes pity on you. (Isa 54:4-10)

The Church draws upon this Book of Consolation as it awaits the coming of the Saviour during the liturgical season of Advent. The haunting antiphon, '*Rorate Coeli Desuper*', sung during Advent, is composed of extracts from this book. The opening line is indeed the opening line of the Book of Consolation: '*Consolamini, consolamini.*' The association of this book with preparation for the birth of Christ is found already in the Infancy gospel of Luke, in the account of the Presentation of the child Jesus in the Temple. Here we find the old man, Simeon, referred to as one who 'looked forward to Israel's comforting'. This term seems to be a reference to the 'Book of the Consolation of Israel'. The book contains the outlines for a theology of salvation which, in many of its aspects, anticipates the theology of redemption which we find in the gospels and in St Paul, and which is found specifically in the words of institution of the Eucharist. What is still more important is that Jesus Christ identified himself with the 'Servant of the Lord', to whom the four 'Songs of the Servant' in this book are addressed. It is also clear from the gospels and the writings of St Paul that the earliest Christian preaching often spoke of Jesus in terms of the 'Servant of the Lord' of Second Isaiah.

Jesus constantly presented himself to his disciples as a servant, indeed a servant who would be despised and rejected and who would suffer for the redemption of all. Jesus said: 'The Son of Man himself did not come to be served but to serve and to give his life as a ransom for many.' (Mk 10:45)[22] Matthew applies to Jesus the words of the first of the Deutero-Isaian Servant Songs:

> Jesus withdrew from the district ... but warned them not to make him known. This was to fulfil the prophecy of Isaiah:
>
> 'Here is my servant whom I have chosen,
> my beloved, the favourite of my soul. ...
> He will not break the crushed reed,
> nor put out the smouldering wick ...'
> (Mt 12:15-21 quoting Isa 42:1-4)

The emphasis here is on the gentleness and the patience of the Servant Jesus. When he finds a splintered rod, he will not throw it away as useless but will splice it and make it usable again; when he finds a lighted wick spluttering for lack of oil, he will not extinguish the flame but will find a new supply of oil and keep the flame alight.

St Luke reports Jesus as saying to the disciples at the Last Supper, after the institution of the Eucharist and before the departure from the Upper Room for the Garden of Gethsemane: 'These words of Scripture have to be fulfilled in me: "He let himself be taken for a criminal." Yes, what scripture says about me is even now reaching its fulfilment.' (Lk 22:37)

The reference is to the Fourth Song of the Servant.[23] St Paul, in his first Letter to Timothy, says that Jesus is the only one mediator between God and mankind, 'himself a man, Christ Jesus, who sacrificed himself as a ransom for them all' (1 Tim 2:6).

I deal on pages pp. 130 – 40 with the words of the institution of the Eucharist, where we find a similar theology of redemption to that adumbrated in the 'Servant Songs'.

As is well known, St John is the only gospel writer who does not report the words of institution. Instead, he describes the washing of the feet of the disciples by Jesus at the Last Supper. This scene of the washing of the feet is a particularly vivid portrayal of Jesus as the Servant – one who, in full knowledge of his divine nature and mission, 'got up from table, removed his outer garment and, taking a towel, wrapped it round his waist; then poured water into a basin and began to wash the disciples' feet and to wipe them with the towel he was wearing'. The dress he chose to wear for the occasion and the menial task he insisted on performing were a visible statement by Jesus that he is indeed the Servant of the Lord. Indeed, his action contains already an allusion to the humiliations and indignities, the mockeries and the spittings, he was soon to endure in his Passion. I look more closely at this theme on pp. 159–60, when I examine the washing of the feet scene in St John's gospel.

Jesus, the Suffering Servant

What strikes one above all in the 'Songs of the Servant' is the closeness of the resemblance of the Deutero-Isian 'Servant of the Lord' to the person, the message and the mission of Jesus Christ, as well as to his Passion and his death. Deutero-Isaiah depicted a person, present or future, who would suffer and by his sufferings would bring victory over sin and death and would lead mankind to everlasting life and glory. It was a messianism of self-sacrificing love, not a messianism of earthly power, much less of military victory. The first song (Isa 42) introduces the servant as God's 'chosen one', in whom God's 'soul delights'. He is gentle, quiet, patient. God has appointed him as 'covenant of the people and light of the nations'. Reference to the covenant is re-echoed in the words of institution of the Eucharist. The words 'the light of the nations' are recalled in Simeon's canticle at the Presentation of the child Jesus in the Temple. Simeon was the one who 'looked forward to Israel's comforting'.

In the second song, the servant is at times identified with the chosen people of Israel and at times he is depicted as the one chosen by God to bring his people back to God and to their own land. He will be despised and loathed by the pagans; yet he is the one who will bring about the great Return from Exile, and the kings of the earth will honour him. God's people had been in deep despondency and near despair; it seemed that God had forgotten them; but God replied in the unforgettable words which we have quoted already: 'Does a woman forget her baby at the breast ...? Yet, even if she should forget, I will never forget you.'

In the third song, we again have a servant of the Lord who suffers. But first he listens to his Lord and relays to the people the message given him by the Lord. He submits to the suffering without complaint, knowing that the Lord will vindicate his innocence and that he shall not be shamed:

> I offered my back to those who struck me, my cheeks to those who tore at my beard. I did not cover my face against insult and spittle. The Lord comes to my help so that I am untouched by the insults. ... My vindicator is near at hand. (Isa 50:4-9)

The prophet might have been an eyewitness of the trial of Jesus before Annas and Caiaphas and of the scourging, so accurately does he describe, centuries in advance, the events of the Passion.

It is the Fourth Song of the Servant which has been called 'the fifth Passion gospel'. Yet, as in reality, so also in prophecy, the Passion is not separated from the resurrection, or the degradation of Jesus from his exultation: 'See, my servant will prosper, he shall be lifted up, exalted, raised to great heights.'

No words can replace or even summarise the original language of the Fourth Song of the Servant: I reproduce it here in full:

> As the crowds were appalled on seeing him, so disfigured did he look that he seemed no longer human – so will the crowds be astonished at him, and kings stand speechless before him; for they shall see something never told and witness something never heard before: 'Who could believe what we

have heard, and to whom has the power of the Lord been revealed?' Like a sapling he grew up in front of us, like a root in arid ground. Without beauty, without majesty [we saw him], no looks to attract our eyes; a thing despised and rejected by men, a man of sorrows and familiar with suffering, a man to make people screen their faces; he was despised and we took no account of him.

And yet ours were the sufferings he bore, ours the sorrow he carried. But we, we thought of him as someone punished, struck by God, and brought low. Yet he was pierced through for our faults, crushed for our sins. On him lies a punishment that brings us peace, and through his wounds we are healed.

We had all gone astray like sheep, each taking his own way, and the Lord burdened him with the sins of all of us. Harshly dealt with, he bore it humbly, he never opened his mouth, like a lamb that is led to the slaughter-house, like a sheep that is dumb before its shearers never opening its mouth.

By force and by law he was taken; would anyone plead his cause? Yes, he was torn away from the land of the living; for our faults struck down in death. They gave him a grave with the wicked ... though he had done no wrong and there had been no perjury in his mouth. The Lord has been pleased to crush him with suffering. If he offers his life in atonement, he shall see his heirs, he shall have a long life and through him what the Lord wishes will be done.

His soul's anguish over he shall see the light and be content. By his sufferings shall my servant justify many, taking their faults on himself. Hence I will grant whole hordes for his tribute; he shall divide the spoil with the mighty for surrendering himself to death and letting himself be taken for a sinner, while he was bearing the faults of many and praying all the time for sinners. (Isa 52:13-15, 53:1-12)

One can never read this passage without being awed at the way in which the prophet, five centuries before Christ, foresaw the nature of the sufferings of Christ, and foresaw also the spirit in which Jesus accepted them and the purpose for which he endured them. The theology of the Fourth Song of the Servant is very close to that of Christ's own words of institution, and close furthermore to the theology of St Paul. We shall explore these in a later section. There is abundant reason to see in the songs of the Servant a prevision of the One who, as St Paul was to put it, in words remarkably similar to those of Deutero-Isaiah:

> did not cling to his equality with God but emptied himself to assume the condition of a slave ... even to accepting death, death on a Cross. But God raised him high. ... [so that] every tongue should acclaim Jesus Christ as Lord to the glory of God the Father. (Phil 2:6-11)

The Passover

All four gospels link the Last Supper of Jesus and his institution of the Eucharist with the Passover. Some familiarity with the ritual of Passover is therefore helpful to fuller understanding of the Eucharist. Mark and Matthew make a point of telling us that the twelve Apostles shared the Passover with Jesus. Mark writes: '[Jesus] arrived [at the large upper room prepared for Passover] with the Twelve.' (14:17) Matthew says: 'When evening came, he was at table with the twelve disciples.' (26:20) Luke has it that 'Jesus took his place at table and the apostles with him.' (22:14) John speaks of 'the disciples', naming Simon Peter, Judas Iscariot and Thomas and Philip (13:14).

Being a celebration of Passover, the Last Supper of Jesus was not an ordinary meal; it was also a religious Service with a set programme of scripture readings, psalms and prayers, with an ordered sequence of words and gestures and actions. Special vessels were kept for use at the meal. Misunderstanding of the nature of the Passover Meal has led some, particularly in the immediate aftermath of the Second Vatican Council, to celebrate the Eucharist in a manner as like as possible to an ordinary meal, with ordinary bread and everyday vessels, celebrated on a kitchen table. This is gross misunderstanding. The Passover was primarily a sacred meal, and it required a sacred setting. St Paul, in fact, may have had situations like what I have described in mind, as well as other abuses, when he reprimanded the Corinthians for some objectionable practices concerning the Eucharist.[24]

The Passover was one of the most important feasts in the Jewish sacred calendar and is still celebrated as such across the Jewish world. It is at once a memorial of God's salvation of his people from slavery and oppression in Egypt, and an anticipation of the great blessings which God still has in waiting for his people in the future. First let us summarise the directions laid down in the Book of Exodus for the Feast of Passover and then turn to a description of the typical Passover of modern times.

Chapter 12 of the Book of Exodus conflates instruction for the proper celebration of the Feast with events of the Exodus. The Feast is to be a memorial of the most important events of Israel's history, most of which are celebrated in the first month of the Jewish year: on the tenth day of this month each man is to take an animal, usually a lamb, from his flock and keep it until the fourteenth day of the month; then, together with 'the whole assembly of Israel', he shall slaughter it 'between the two evenings'. A sprig of hyssop shall then be dipped into the blood of the lamb and the two doorposts and the lintel of the house shall be marked with the blood. That night, the flesh of the lamb is to be roasted over the fire and eaten, together with unleavened bread and bitter herbs. Nothing is to be left over; if any portion remains till morning it is to be burned. Not a single bone of the lamb is to be broken. The flesh is to be eaten with a girdle around the waist, sandals on the feet and a staff in the hand. It is to be eaten hastily: 'it is a Passover in honour of the Lord.' On that same night the Lord shall 'go through the land of Egypt and strike down all the first-born of men and beast alike and deal out punishment to all the gods of Egypt'. But when God sees the blood on the houses of the Israelites he will pass over these houses and spare the inhabitants:

> This is to be a day of remembrance [for all Israelites] and [they] must celebrate it in the Lord's honour. For all generations you are to declare it a day of festival, for ever. (Ex 12)

For the seven days following Passover, the Feast of Azymes or of Unleavened Bread is observed: no bread with leaven shall be eaten, only unleavened bread shall be baked or eaten.

In later times, as the feasts of Azymes and Passover are celebrated, a child is to ask: 'What does the ritual mean?' and the head of the house is to answer: 'It is the sacrifice of the Passover in honour of the Lord who passed over the houses of the sons of Israel and struck Egypt but spared our houses.' It was a commemoration of the actual event whereby Pharaoh, devastated by the deaths of the first-born all over Egypt and 'seeing not a house without its dead', told Moses and Aaron to 'get away from the [Egyptian] people'. 'Go, and worship God as you have asked, take your flock and herds and go, and also ask a blessing on me.' The Egyptians told the Israelites to hurry and to leave their land. 'So the people carried off their dough still unleavened on their shoulders and their kneading bowls wrapped in their cloaks.' Before leaving, however, they asked the Egyptians for gold and silver ornaments and fine clothing.

The signs of haste (girdle around the waist, staff in hand, sandals on feet, bread unleavened because there is not time to bake proper bread) are a reproduction in mime-like form of the conditions of departure from Egypt. This will be for the Jews of all time a reminder, 'like a sign on the hand or a memento on the forehead, of how the Lord brought them out of Egypt with a mighty hand' (Ex 12). On Passover night the head of the household will explain to the youngest son: 'This is because of what the Lord did for me when I came out of Egypt.' (Ex 13)

The Passover ritual is fundamentally a recall of Israel's history and an affirmation of the truth that Israel's birth as a nation comes from the covenant God made with his chosen people; its whole identity is its covenant relationship with God. Israel's very identity as a nation is a sacred identity and it is spelled out in Israel's sacred texts. For biblical Israel, the sacred and the secular are fused together. Passover has been celebrated throughout the whole history of Judaism as one of Israel's chief festivals. There have been minor variations across the centuries, but the essential elements remain as outlined in the Book of Exodus. I now turn to the typical modern Passover.[25]

Terms for the Passover festival varied over the centuries. The name 'Passover' itself derives from the Hebrew word, 'Pesach', which means simply 'Pass over'. The word may refer to God's 'passing over' the houses of the Jews while the houses of the Egyptians are stricken with the deaths of their first-born. The word may also refer to the Israelites' passing safely over the Red Sea while the Egyptian forces and their chariots are submerged. The term can refer also to the 'passing over' of the Jews from slavery in Egypt to freedom in the Promised Land and thereby, it is hoped, from oppression and fear to freely chosen obedience to God and to his commandments. For Christians the name 'Pesach' itself mutated into the Christian term, 'pasch'. In Jewish circles, two names for Passover emerge later – *Haggadah* and *Seder*. 'Haggadah' is the name usually given to what we may call the 'script' or programme of the feast, setting down the 'rubrics' for the various readings and prayers and psalms which are to be recited as the different courses are served and cups of wine poured out. The 'Seder' is the term usually applied to the ordering of those gathered to celebrate Passover. Either term can also describe the Passover feast itself.

The meal is both a religious service and an enjoyable family party. In both of these aspects, the Passover is a strictly lay occasion and primarily a family occasion. In this it reflects some of the great strengths of the Jewish faith: namely that this faith is strongly embedded in the family and is transmitted across the generations primarily by lay persons in and through their families. Like Passover, many of the religious observances of Judaism are conducted by lay people within the family.

The meal is characterised by the eating of bitter herbs (*maror*) and of unleavened bread (*matzah*). The bitter herbs recall the drudgery and slavery of Egypt. The unleavened bread recalls the haste with which the exodus from Egypt had to be completed; it also marks the notes of cleansing and purification which accompany Passover. Houses had to be cleansed of all impurities, such as those associated with accumulated stocks of leaven. This meant a kind of 'spring cleaning' of houses as Passover time came round each year. There was also a call to spiritual 'spring cleaning' in preparation for the feast. Those who are familiar with the tradition of 'station Masses', still surviving in some parts of Ireland, will notice here some parallels with the Passover celebration.

We read in the gospels of how Jesus asked his disciples to make 'the preparations for him to eat the Passover with his disciples' (Mt 26:17-19). The preparations included the obtaining of a suitable room, with dining table and couches, suitable for reclining during the meal – for family and guests reclined, rather than sat, for this very special meal; together with the procuring of the paschal lamb, which was killed in sacrifice and then roasted so as to be served as the main course at the meal itself. The lamb was roasted whole and no bone of it was to be broken. The gospel writers relate the fact that the legs of Jesus as he hung on the Cross were not broken and they see this fact among others as identifying Jesus with the Paschal Lamb. Only unleavened bread (*matzah*) was allowed at Passover and this was prepared in advance. A bone was placed on the table – the shank bone of the lamb; this, in times when sacrifice was no longer possible for Jews as a form of worship, was a symbol and a reminder of the once-sacrificed Passover lamb.

After the initial blessing and prayers, four questions are asked by the youngest child present. In one form or another, all four questions ask the same thing: 'Why is this night different from all other nights?' For the child, the differences are the use of unleavened bread, the use of bitter herbs, these being dipped twice instead of once, and the family and guests reclining as they eat, rather than sitting for the meal, as on all other nights. The answer is given by the head of the house. It begins:

> Our ancestors were slaves to Pharaoh in Egypt, but God brought us out from there with a strong hand and an outstretched arm.

But, as the answer develops, the unique character of Passover becomes clear: 'we' becomes 'I' and the memory becomes individual and personal. The head of the house goes on to say: 'It is because of what God did for me when I came out of Egypt.' In every generation each and every Jew must be brought to feel as if he himself or she herself was personally set free by the power and mercy of God.

First served at the meal are bitter herbs (*maror*). A sweet paste called *haroset* is served; it is a concoction of apples, nuts and cinnamon, with a little wine. Lettuce or celery is served; this is eaten dipped in a dish of salt water – another symbol of the bitter past from which the Passover people were delivered by God.

Four cups of ceremonial wine are provided for each person to drink at four specified points of the celebration. Four 'toasts' are called in the course of the meal, two before the main course and two after it. In the order in which they are announced, these toasts are 'To Life', 'To Freedom', 'To Peace', and 'To Jerusalem'. Each phase of the meal is introduced by blessings or prayers, biblical readings and rabbinical interpretations of these from the Talmud, and psalms or songs. It is an unusual melange of solemn religious service and of festive relaxation.

A special place is given at the Passover meal to the Hallel Psalms, a group of psalms of praise of God. Using the Vulgate or Latin numbering of the psalms, these comprise Psalms 112(113)–117(118) and Psalm 135(136), the latter being called the 'Great Hallel'. Psalms 112(113) and 113(114-115) are recited or sung after the 'Four Questions' are answered, and at this point the first 'toast' is called.

This is followed by the second 'toast', after which the main course or the Passover 'meal' proper, is served and eaten. After this course is eaten, Psalm 126(127) is sung and this is followed by a prayer of thanksgiving after the meal.

After the psalm and the prayer, the third 'toast' is called. The third cup is called 'Elijah's Cup'. Elijah, the mightiest of prophets, was expected to reappear to prepare for the great coming of the Messiah; so, at this point of the Passover celebration, a chair is produced for Elijah and a knock on the door would, at some future time, at a fortunate Passover meal, announce his coming to a chosen family. Children were in readiness to open the door for Elijah if he should knock. Jewish writers have later recalled their childish excitement at that point of the Passover: it was a blend of eager anticipation and of unspoken anxiety. The 'coming of Elijah' spoke of victory and security, but also of the judgment of nation and individual.

The 'coming of Elijah' has its place also in the gospels. In St Luke's infancy narrative, John the Baptist is spoken of as coming 'in the spirit and power of Elijah' (Lk 1:17). Jesus is cited in St Matthew's gospel as saying that John the Baptist is in fact the 'Elijah who was to return' (Mt 11:14). Others thought that Jesus, the Son of Man, was himself Elijah (Mt 16:14). Elijah appears with Moses at the transfiguration: he represents the prophets, while Moses represents the law (Mt 17:3-4). Jesus' cry to God on the Cross, 'Eloi, Eloi', was interpreted by some bystanders as a cry to Elijah (Mk 15:35).

The Elijah interlude in the Passover meal is followed by psalms of thanksgiving and praise: these also are taken from the Hallel sequence, Psalms 113(114-115), 114(116) and 117(118) being sung. Psalm 117(118) has the words: 'Blessed is he who comes in the name of the Lord'; these words are associated in the gospels with Jesus Christ himself.

Then the 'Great Hallel' psalm (135(136)) is sung, preceded by a prayer. The verses of this psalm enumerate the reasons for praising and thanking God: his wonderful deeds in creation, in the exodus and in the desert, in the Canaanite wars and in God's constant care for his people, giving 'food to all living things'. The mention of each of God's mighty deeds of mercy evokes the sung refrain: 'Great is his love, love without end.'

The Passover celebration ends with prayers of praise and blessing and thanks:

> Blessed art thou –
> great in praise –
> God of thanksgiving –
> Lord of wonders –
> King, God, eternal.

Then the fourth cup of wine is quaffed to the toast of 'To Jerusalem'. The Passover ends with an expression of Israel's ancient longing:

> End thy people's endless cry,
> joyful and in Zion free,
> next year in Jerusalem.

As for the precise moment of the Passover celebration at which Jesus took and blessed the bread and the cup and thereby instituted the Eucharist, the gospels do not give sufficient information for us to be certain. Mark merely tells us that 'as they were eating' Jesus took bread and said the blessing (Mk 14:22 cf. Mt 26:26). Luke tells us that Jesus 'took some bread, blessed it, broke it and gave it to the apostles'; and then he goes on to say: 'he did the same with the cup after supper.' (Lk 21:19-20) The word 'supper' here could refer either to the entire Passover feast, including the hors d'oeuvre and the four cups of wine, or it could refer to the main course. The cup which Jesus took could therefore be the third or the fourth Passover cup. However, it seems more likely that the Passover ritual was completed before Jesus took the bread and wine which were to become the new Passover or Pasch for his followers to the end of time.

The lamb for this new sacrifice was Jesus himself. John, particularly anxious to stress the paschal aspect of the Passion and

Death of Jesus, points to the fact that the soldiers did not break the legs of Jesus on the Cross; he says that this fulfils the scriptural words about the paschal lamb (Ps 33(34):20).[26]

The Passover ritual is in great part a memorial service of praise and thanksgiving for the covenant which God made with his people on Mount Sinai. The Eucharist is a memorial of the new and eternal covenant which God made with his people on Calvary. The 'memorial' aspect of the Passover has the effect that each participant feels that he or she has been personally delivered from slavery in Egypt and led safely through the desert to the Promised Land. In some sense the past event becomes a personal experience. We could call the Jewish Passover a quasi-sacramental act of remembering. In the Eucharist, the memorial, enacted 'in memory of me', is fully sacramental: the past event is made present reality under the sacramental signs; the crucified and risen Christ is a real presence before the gathered community and for each of its members. Each one can say: 'I was there when they crucified my Lord. ... I was there when he rose up from the tomb.' The power and the amazing grace of these great saving events are made really and truly present as if we each had stood with Mary at the foot of the Cross or as if, with the other Mary, we had clasped his feet after he had risen from the tomb. Pope John Paul speaks of the 'mysterious contemporaneity' of the Eucharist with Golgotha, with Emmaus and the Resurrection.[27]

In Matthew's account of the Last Supper, we read that 'after Psalms had been sung' Jesus and the Twelve left for the Mount of Olives and the Garden of Gethsemane.[28] We know what these psalms were: they were the Hallel Psalms and we recall them here. Psalms 112(113) and 113(114-115) were sung between the first and second cups of wine. After the main course Psalm 126(127) is sung: this is a pilgrim's song, expressing the joy of the returned exiles as they rediscover the Jerusalem of their dreams. After the third cup of wine comes the Elijah interlude; and after this Psalms 113(114-115), 114(116), 115(116) and 117(118), and finally 135(136), are sung. These psalms give us a precious insight into the mind of Our Lord in these last hours just after the institution of the Eucharist and before the Agony in the Garden. It is deeply moving to think prayerfully of these psalms as being prayed aloud by Our Lord in the Upper Room after the Last Supper. Jesus's human dread of the thought of the cruel Passion and degrading death which awaited him is expressed in Psalm 114(116):

> They surrounded me, the snares of death
> with the anguish of the tomb;
> they caught me, sorrow and distress.
> I called on the Lord's name:
> O Lord my God deliver me.

The consolation which he drew from the foreknowledge of what the Eucharist would mean for his followers in the new future made possible by his Passion is clear from Psalms 115(116) and 116(117):

> How can I repay the Lord
> For all his goodness to me?
> The cup of salvation I will raise,
> I will call on the Lord's name.
>
> My vows to the Lord I will fulfil
> before all his people.
> O precious in the eyes of the Lord
> is the death of his faithful. ...
> a thanksgiving sacrifice I make;
> I will call on the Lord's name. (Ps 115(116))
>
> O praise the Lord all you nations,
> acclaim him all you peoples!
> Strong is his love for us,
> He is faithful for ever. (Ps 116(117))

Psalm 117(118) as prayed by Jesus, shows his trust in the Lord and his confidence that, in spite of everything, God would have the victory and that life would prevail over death and love over hate:

The Lord is at my side; I do not fear.
What can man do against me? ...
It is better to take refuge in the Lord
than to trust in princes.

The Lord's right hand has triumphed;
I shall not die, I shall live,
and recount his deeds. ...

The stone which the builders rejected
has become the corner stone. ...[29]

Blessed in the name of the Lord
Is he who comes. (Ps 117(118))[30]

Finally, the great Hallel is sung in praise of the mighty deeds of
God during the Exodus; with each line followed by the refrain:
'Great is his love, love without end.' For Christians, the last verses
have a eucharistic reference:

He gives food to all living things,
great is his love, love without end;
to the God of heaven give thanks,
great is his love, love without end. (Ps 136)

Passover, as we have seen, is a memorial feast. The remembering
is not just a recall of past history; it is intended to dispose each
one present to identify with the remembered events and to realise
that he or she was, in God's eyes, involved in those dramatic
events. Each one round the table of the Seder was, through
remembering, to be brought to realise that this present individual,
this present family and this present people of Israel was personally
and communally redeemed and spared and saved by God on the
first Passover night. From the earliest history of the Jews up to the
present day, as a Jewish family sits down to its Passover meal

anywhere across the world, the father answers his child's question with the words of the Book of Exodus describing the actual event of the historical Passover out of Egypt: 'This is because of what the Lord did for me when I came out of Egypt.' (Ex 13:8)

This kind of remembering (*anamnesis*) is given a new and deeper meaning in the Eucharist, offered in memory of Christ. The linkage of Passover and the Eucharist is made clear in all the gospel accounts of the institution of the Eucharist. This is clear also from the title of 'Lamb of God' or 'Lamb' given by John the Baptist to Christ and repeated throughout the New Testament.[31]

Food for Elijah's Journey

Hints of the coming Eucharist can be found also in the life of Elijah. Elijah was ranked as one of the greatest prophets of Israel and his story was very familiar in the time of Jesus. In an appendix to the words of the prophet Malachi it had been foretold that Elijah would return to the earth before the coming of the Messiah. Through Malachi the Lord said:

> Know that I am going to send you Elijah the prophet before my day comes, that great and terrible day. He shall turn the hearts of the fathers towards their children and the hearts of children towards their fathers. ... (Mal 3:23-24)

This passage is quoted in St Luke's narrative of the birth of John the Baptist, where the new-born child is predicted to be one who will go before the Lord 'in the spirit and power of Elijah ... preparing for the Lord a people fit for him' (Lk 1:17).

There are several links between events in the life of Elijah and events in the life of Jesus Christ: and there are specific links between Elijah's story and the Eucharist. In the 'Elijah Cycle' in the first book of Kings[32] we read of Elijah's confrontations with the sinful and idolatrous King Ahab, and of how the Lord sent a severe drought upon the land, meanwhile telling Elijah to go eastwards to the Brook Cherith, where ravens would bring 'bread in the morning and meat in the evening' and where he could 'quench his thirst at the stream'. But, as the drought continued, even the stream dried up. Elijah is now ordered to go to Zarephath, a Sidonian town. Here a Sidonian widow was gathering sticks when Elijah came up and pleaded with her for a little water to drink and a scrap of bread to eat. She had no baked bread in the house, only 'a handful of meal in a jar and a little oil in a jug'. She explained that she was just about to gather sticks to kindle a fire, in order to prepare a meal for 'herself and her son to eat, and then we shall die'. Elijah renewed his plea for just a 'little scone' for himself, promising her in the Lord's name that the jar of meal would not be left empty nor the jug of oil spent before the rains would come. The woman complied and all three ate. From then on, there was meal in the jar and oil in the jug until the drought ended. The sign for the ending of the drought was 'the cloud no bigger than a man's hand, rising from the sea'. Then 'rain came in torrents'. Christians have seen the daily refilled jar and replenished jug as symbols of the Eucharist.

Later we read of Elijah's confrontation with the priests of Baal, the god of the Canaanites. Elijah challenged them to offer sacrifice to their god, while he would offer sacrifice to the true God: the one who was truly God would 'answer by fire'. God accepted Elijah's sacrifice, by the sign of fire which came down from heaven and consumed the sacrificial victim. No fire came in response to the repeated invocations of Baal by the pagan priests. Baal and his priests were completely discredited in the eyes of the crowd. Elijah ordered the priests to be arrested and brought down to the Wadi Kishon, and, we read, 'he slaughtered them there'.

Jezebel, the wife of Ahab, was enraged at what Elijah had done and sent him a messenger with an immediate death threat. Elijah 'was afraid and fled for his life'(1 Kings 19). Elijah set out on a long journey across the desert to Mount Horeb. After a day's journey, Elijah threw himself down on the ground, completely exhausted and in deep depression. He had had enough; he wanted to die. Sleep came, but an angel touched him as he slept, saying: 'Get up and eat.'

He got up and saw a scone and a jar of water nearby. He ate and drank and fell asleep again. The angel came a second time, awoke him, and said: 'Get up and eat or the journey will be too long for you.' The story continues: 'So [Elijah] got up and ate and drank, and strengthened by that food he walked for forty days and forty nights until he reached Horeb, the mountain of God.' (1 Kings 19)

Horeb is another name for Mount Sinai, the place of the great Theophany granted to Moses and the scene of the covenant God made with Moses and the people of Israel. The Elijah story is a repetition in the life of one great prophet of the journey of Moses and the Israelites through the desert for forty years. For the Mosaic journey, God provided the daily manna; for Elijah's he provided 'food for the journey'. Both are seen by Christians as forerunners of the Eucharist, the food given us by God for our life journey. Elijah's 'food for the journey' is recalled in the term 'Viaticum', which is the term often used for the Eucharist when it is administered to the dying. In the Christian context, it is food for life's last journey to the final Mountain of God.

Elijah's completion of his journey to Horeb is followed by the granting to him of a beautiful experience of God, recalling, but contrasting with, Moses's experience of God on the top of that mountain (otherwise called Mount Sinai). God manifested himself to Moses and the people amid peals of thunder and lightning flashes, trumpet blast and violent shaking of the mountain, making the people tremble with fear and dread. Elijah's experience is different: God reveals himself in gentleness and stillness and quiet, recalling the words of Psalm 45: 'Be still and know that I am God.' Elijah has spent the night in a cave. In the morning, God spoke to him, asking him: 'What are you doing here, Elijah?' The prophet replied: 'I am filled with jealous love for the Lord of Hosts, because the sons of Israel have deserted you. ... I am the only one left and they want to kill me.'

Then Elijah was told, as Moses had been told, to stand on the mountain before the Lord. Then:

The Lord himself went by. There came a mighty wind, so strong that it tore the mountains and scattered the rocks. But the Lord was not in the wind. After the wind came an earthquake. But the Lord was not in the earthquake. After the earthquake came a fire. But the Lord was not in the fire. And after the fire came a gentle breeze. (1 Kings 19:9-14)

Elijah covered his face with his cloak and went out of the cave. He is asked by God to go back to where he had come from and anoint a new king of Aram and a new king of Israel and to prepare for his own departure from earth by anointing Elisha as his successor. Meanwhile, God promises that seven thousand in Israel will be spared because they had not bent the knee before the pagan god Baal. Cardinal John Henry Newman likened the gentle breeze to the still small voice of conscience, the echo of the voice of God. We are reminded of the voice of Christ spoken over the stormy sea: 'Peace. Be still.' (Mk 4:39)

Elijah himself appeared with Moses in conversation with Jesus at the Transfiguration; this occurrence was, as we shall see, the conclusion of the 'section on the loaves' in the synoptic gospels. Elijah's spiritual son and successor, Elisha, is reported as working a miracle closely resembling Jesus Christ's miracle of the loaves. A man brought twenty barley loaves and fresh grain to the 'man of God', Elisha. The latter said: 'Give it to the people to eat.' The man protested: 'How can I serve this to a hundred people?' Elisha insisted; the Lord, he said, 'would see that all would eat and have some left over'. The narrator concludes that 'it happened so as the Lord had said' (2 Kings 4:42-44).

The Wisdom Books and the Eucharist

The Sapiential or Wisdom Books of the Old Testament have a specially important place in the backdrop to the eucharistic teaching of the New Testament. These books are fully in line with Jewish religious tradition but also reveal influence from the Greek culture in which many Jews lived in the century before Christ. The

Book of Wisdom itself was written in Greek and was never accepted into the canon of Hebrew Scripture. It was, however, well known to the writers of the New Testament.

Wisdom, Sophia, is given divine attributes in the Book of Wisdom, though its precise relationship with God is not entirely clear. There are, nevertheless, some analogies with the Logos of St John's Prologue and with the eucharistic discourse in Chapter 6 of St John's gospel. This is particularly true of the theme of the Banquet of Wisdom. Wisdom is spoken of as indwelling in souls that are just and honourable:

> Wisdom will never make its way into a crafty soul nor stay in a body that is in debt to sin. Wisdom is a spirit, a friend to man. (Wis 1:4, 6)

These words are re-echoed in St John's gospel, where Wisdom is identified as the Holy Spirit:

> If you love me you will keep my commandments. I shall ask the Father and he will give you another Advocate to be with you for ever,
> that Spirit of truth whom the world can never receive since it neither sees him nor knows him; but you know him because he is with you, he is in you. (Jn 14:15-17)

We shall call attention later to the role of the Holy Spirit in the eucharistic mystery. There are hints in these passages from the Book of Wisdom of the mutual indwelling of Jesus in us and of us in him which is a recurring theme in the eucharistic teaching of St John and St Paul.

In other passages, Wisdom is presented as offering itself as food and drink to be enjoyed by people of faith and good will:

> Whoever fears the Lord will act like this
> and whoever grasps the Law will obtain wisdom. ...
> She will give him the bread of understanding to eat
> and the water of wisdom to drink. (Ecclus 15:1-3)

Wisdom implores people to accept her invitation:

> Approach me, you who desire me,
>   and take my fill of your fruits,
> for memories of me are sweeter than honey,
>   inheriting me is sweeter than the honeycomb.
> They who eat me will hunger for more,
>   They who drink me will thirst for more. (Ecclus 24:19-21)

In these writings, often called the Sapiential writings of the Old Testament, Wisdom is sometimes described in similar terms to those used for the promised Messiah, 'the One who is to come'. There are distinctive echoes of these Wisdom passages in the Prologue to St John's gospel and in other parts of the fourth gospel. Wisdom is shown as participating in God's creation of the world:

> The Lord created me when his purpose first unfolded,
>   before the oldest of his works.
> From everlasting I was firmly set,
>   from the beginning, before earth came into being. ...
> Before the mountains were settled
>   before the hills, I came to birth. ...
> When he fixed the heavens firm, I was there,
>   when he drew a ring on the surface of the deep,
> when he thickened the clouds above
>   when he fixed fast the springs of the deep
> when he assigned the sea its boundaries
>   when he laid down the foundations of the earth,
> I was by his side, a master craftsman,
>   delighting him day after day
> ever at play in his presence,
>   at play everywhere in his world,
> delighting to be with the children of men. (Prov 8:22-31)

Then Wisdom again issues an invitation to the banquet she has prepared:

> Wisdom has built herself a house,
>   she has erected her seven pillars,
> she has slaughtered her beasts, prepared her wine,
>   she has laid her table.
> She has dispatched her maid servants
>   and proclaimed from the city's heights:
> 'Who is ignorant? Let him step this way.'
> To the fool she says,
>   'Come and eat my bread,
>   drink the wine I have prepared.
> Leave your folly and you will live,
>   walk in the ways of perception'. (Prov 9:1-6)

The Book of Wisdom has a beautiful prayer, imploring God to grant the gift of Wisdom to his servant. The prayer is placed on the lips of Solomon, who, having been chosen by God as king over God's people, Israel, feels overcome by the responsibilities entrusted to him by God, and confesses his utter unworthiness, and even his inability, to carry these responsibilities unless Wisdom from God is granted to him. I quote some parts of this prayer:

> God of our ancestors, Lord of mercy, ...
> grant me Wisdom ...
> and do not reject me from the number of your children.
>
> For I am your servant, son of your serving maid,
> a feeble man, with little time to live,
> with small understanding of justice and the laws.
> With you is Wisdom, she who knows your works,
> she who was present when you made the world;
> she understands what is pleasing in your eyes and what agrees
> with your commandments.
> Despatch her from the holy heavens,
> send her forth from your throne of glory
> to help me and to toil with me

and teach me what is pleasing to you,
for she knows and understands everything.
She will guide me prudently in my undertakings
and protect me by her glory. ...
What man indeed can know the intentions of God?
who can divine the will of the Lord?
The reasonings of mortals are unsure
and our intentions unstable;
for a perishable body presses down the soul,
and this tent of clay weighs down the teeming mind.
It is hard enough for us to work out what is on earth,
laborious to know what lies within our reach;
who, then, can discover what is in the heavens?
As for your intention, who could have learnt it,
had you not granted Wisdom
and sent your Holy Spirit from above?
Thus have the paths of those on earth been straightened
and men been taught what pleases you,
and saved by Wisdom. (Wis 9:1-18)

In such passages as these there are surely intimations of the incarnation of God's Son and Word. There are intimations also of Jesus Christ's rejection by many of his contemporaries and of his condemnation to death.

The account given in the Book of Wisdom of 'the virtuous man who is poor' and who 'annoys us and opposes our way of life', reproaching us 'for our breaches of the law and accusing us of playing false to our upbringing', has remarkable similarities to the descriptions in the gospels of how the scribes and the Pharisees reacted to Jesus Christ when he came.[33] Another page of the Book of Wisdom has strange resemblances to the excuses that might have been given by the scribes and Pharisees for their part in planning the condemnation of Christ and his death:

If the virtuous man is God's son, God will take his part
and rescue him from the clutches of his enemies.

Let us test him with cruelty and with torture,
and thus explore this gentleness of his
and put his endurance to the proof.
Let us condemn him to shameful death
since he will be looked after – we have his word for it.
(Wis 2:18-20)

The third section of the Book of Wisdom is devoted to the
theme of 'Wisdom and God in History'. It speaks of how God
chose the people of Israel as the privileged people among whom
his Wisdom should dwell. Wisdom dwells and acts in a
particular manner through the Law. God, through his Wisdom
and his law, ensured that 'for [God's] holy ones all was great
light'; and, through Israel, 'the imperishable light of the Law
was to be given to the world' (Wis 18:1-4). The coming of
God's Wisdom and Word into the midst of Israel at the time of
Passover in Egypt at the Exodus required no alterations in order
to be applied to the birth of Jesus, the incarnate Word of God,
in Bethlehem:

When peaceful silence lay over all,
and night had run the half of her swift course,
down from the heavens, from the royal throne, leapt your all-
powerful Word;
into the heart of a doomed land [Egypt] the stern warrior leapt.
(Wis 18:14-15)

Reference is made in the Book of Wisdom to the manna, and
Christians cannot fail to find eucharistic overtones in this passage:

How differently with your people! You give them the
food of angels,
from heaven untiringly sending them bread already prepared,
containing every delight, satisfying every taste.
(Wis 16:20)

Many passages are in fact echoed in the gospel of St John. John too speaks of the Word as being with God 'in the beginning', proclaiming that:

> All that came to be had life in him that life was the light of men, a light that shines in the dark, a light that darkness could not overpower. (Jn 1:3-5)

The account of the wedding at Cana in Galilee has echoes of the Messianic Wedding Feast and of the Feast which is to mark the eschatological Kingdom of God.

Ben Sirach (or Ecclesiasticus) has a passage in which Wisdom invites to a banquet all those who desire to possess and to learn from Wisdom:

> Approach me, you who desire me,
> and take your fill of my fruits,
> for memories of me are sweeter than honey,
> inheriting me is sweeter than the honeycomb.
> They who eat me will hunger for more,
> they who drink me will thirst for more. (Eccl 24:19-21)

These words are echoed in the eucharistic discourse in St John's gospel: 'I am the bread of life; he who comes to me will never hunger and he who believes in me will never thirst.' (Jn 6:35)

The conflict between the words of Jesus and the words of Ben Sirach is only apparent. Jesus is teaching that the one who comes to him to receive the bread of life will never hunger for bread that does not satisfy, for his or her hunger will be satisfied only by 'every word that comes from the mouth of God'; and every tasting of that word, every drinking of that water, will make one hunger and thirst for more. This is substantially the same teaching as that of Ben Sirach: each receiving of Wisdom will make the receiver hunger and thirst for more of the Wisdom which God alone can give.

The foreshadowings of the Eucharist in the Wisdom Books find a parallel in the writings of the prophets of Israel. I cite two passages from Isaiah as typical of such passages:

On this mountain,
the Lord of Hosts will prepare for all peoples
a banquet of rich food, a banquet of fine wines,
of food rich and juicy, of fine strained wines.
On this mountain he will remove
the mourning veil covering all peoples,
and the shroud enwrapping all nations,
he will destroy Death forever.
The Lord will wipe away
the tears from every cheek;
he will take away his people's shame,
everywhere on earth,
for the Lord has said so.
That day, it will be said: See, this is our God
in whom we hoped for salvation;
the Lord is the one in whom we hoped.
We exalt and we rejoice
that he has saved us;
for the hand of the Lord rests on this mountain. (Isa 25:6-10)

Thus says the Lord, your redeemer, the holy One of Israel:
I, the Lord, your God, teach you what is good for you,
I lead you in a way you must go
if only you had been alert to my commandments,
your happiness would have been like a river,
your integrity like the waves of the sea. ...

I will say to the prisoners, 'Come out',
to those in darkness, 'Show yourselves'. ...

They will never hunger or thirst,
scorching wind and sun shall never plague them,
for he who pities them will lead them

and guide them to streams of water …
Some are on their way from afar,
others from the land of Sinim,
shout for joy you heavens;
exult you earth!
you mountains break into happy cries!
For the Lord consoles his people
and takes pity on those who are afflicted. (Isa 49:7-13)

Then follows in Deutero-Isaiah one of those unforgettable declarations of love made by God to his people:

For Zion was saying, 'the Lord has abandoned me,
the Lord has forgotten me'.
Does a woman forget her baby at the breast,
or fail to cherish the son of her womb?
Yet, even if these forget, I will never forget you.
See, I have branded you on the palms of my hands.
(Isa 49:14-15)

We note the eschatological fulfilment described in these passages: all our needs, all our longings, all our hopes, are unfailingly fulfilled when God admits us to his presence and seats us at his heavenly table. We express that eschatological desire and affirm our hope of its fulfilment in every Eucharist we celebrate. Features of this future in God are described in the Wisdom Books, in the prophets and in the New Testament: they include the 'destruction of death' and its replacement by our life in God or God's life in us, namely eternal life; they include joy and celebration, surprise and wonder at God's greatness and glory, his mercy and love, thanksgiving and praise of God for just *being* and for being Who He is, namely *He Who Is*.

These passages point to the Messianic Age which is to come, and which begins with the coming of Our Lord, Jesus Christ. André Feuillet stresses the parallel between these Wisdom passages and the Messianic Banquet foretold by the prophets. He pronounces these Wisdom passages the most significant Old Testament foreshadowings of the Eucharist.[34]

The Canticle of Canticles

Closely linked with the Sapiential Books in the Bible is the Canticle of Canticles. This is a great love poem in the form of a dialogue between Bride and Bridegroom, in which each expresses passionate love for the other. There is grief and desolation when they are apart, there is longing to be together again, there is search for the absent one and lavish praise by each of the other's beauty; there is the bride's desire to surrender totally to the bridegroom. There is throughout the poem an alternation of presence and absence, loss and search and presence again; but in the end there is only presence and possession and peace.

The Canticle may be based on secular prototypes in the form of love songs of Hebrew or even pagan culture. The theme of human love and marriage would not of itself be enough to gain for the Canticle its place in the Canon of Hebrew and then Christian scripture, or make it an important text for Christian mysticism. The love in question in the Canticle is the love between God and his people, where God is the bridegroom and Israel the bride, or where the Church is the bride and God the bridegroom. What is certain is that the Canticle has provided rich spiritual nourishment for Christian saints and mystics over the centuries and has profoundly influenced Christian mystical theology. St Teresa of Avila and St John of the Cross were each deeply influenced by it and each wrote explanations of it. St Thomas Aquinas was engaged in dictating a commentary on the Canticle in his last illness as he awaited death.

Christians interpret the loss and rediscovery, the absence and the search and the finding again, in terms of the loving relationship between God and his Church or between God and the individual soul. As in the Canticle, this relationship is marked on the human side by alternations between light and peace in God's presence and distress and 'dark nights' at his apparent absence. Both of these are manifestations of God's unchanging love; at times he seems to be all light, and at other times all darkness; sometimes hidden, though more present than one is to one's own self. God is always a mystery to be acknowledged with loving reverence rather than a problem to be explained or explained away by human science or reason.

We have hints of this pattern of alternation already in the Old Testament; God is referred to as 'a hidden God', who 'hides himself' from his people because of their sins, or from whose presence his people hide themselves by their sins. The Prophets and the Psalms plead with the people to desist from sin and to 'seek the Lord' again with contrite hearts.[35] We recall also the cloud or *shekinah* which was the sign of God's presence with his people on Sinai, or the 'pillar of cloud' by day and the 'pillar of fire' at night during the desert journeys of the exodus. The cloud filled the tabernacle of God's presence among his nomad people in the desert, and later filled the Temple in Jerusalem. The cloud reappears at decisive moments in Jesus Christ's life, as at the Annunciation to Mary of his conception through the overshadowing of the Holy Spirit, and again at the Transfiguration and yet again at the Ascension. Always it is a sign of the incomprehensible mystery of God – not so much a darkness as a brightness blinding human eyes by excess of light. We recall the title of Walter Hilton's fourteenth-century mystical writing, *The Cloud of Unknowing*.

John of the Cross – commenting on the gospel account of the appearance of the Risen Lord in the garden when Mary Magdalene clasped his feet – compares Mary with the Bride of the Canticle, who sought for traces of her lover through the City in the night, seeking him whom her heart loved in the streets and the squares. When at last she found him, she says: 'I held him fast, I would not let him go.' (Canticle 3:4)

Mary's clasping is certainly similar to that of the bride in the Canticle and the words of the Canticle can surely be applied to Mary, whose gesture eloquently expresses her feelings at being reunited with her Lord. The heart of this Canticle is love, love that nothing can break. The bridegroom says:

Set me like a seal on your heart …
for love is as strong as death. …
Love no flood can quench
no torrents drown.

And the last word of the Bride is peace:

Under his eyes I have found true peace. (Canticle 8:6-7, 10)

The Eucharist being the supreme gift of love left by Christ to his Church, it would be surprising if there were not a deep affinity between God's own love song for his Bride, the Church, and the Eucharist, in which, as St John tells us, Jesus Christ, '[having always] loved those who were his own in the world, now showed how perfect his love was' (Jn 13:1). To this declaration of Christ's love for his Bride the appropriate response of the Church is in the first verse of the Canticle: 'How right it is to love you.' (Canticle 1:4)

St Thérèse of Lisieux had a special predilection for the Canticle and quotes it often in her *Story of a Soul*, her letters and her poems. She once remarked that, if she had the time, she would love to write a commentary on the Canticle because she found in it such profound thoughts on the union of the soul with its Beloved:

The service of love – the words keep sounding gently in the ear of my soul. That is the only science I long for. Having given away all my riches for that science, I feel, like the Spouse in the Canticle, that I have given nothing.[36]

God's Vine

Linked with the Wisdom Books are the passages in both Old and New Testaments about God's 'Vine'. In St John's gospel, Jesus speaks of himself as 'the true Vine' and, as we shall see in Part II, he does so in a eucharistic context. In doing so Jesus seems to depart from some Old Testament texts; indeed when Israel is called

God's Vine in the Old Testament, it is often being spoken of as an unfaithful and disloyal people, who have betrayed their vocation and have been undeserving of God's unending generosity and patience towards them. Thus, we read in Isaiah 5:1-7 of God's love for the House of Israel, who are his vineyard. After all his care for the vineyard, God had expected a fine vintage of rich grapes, but instead he finds only sour grapes: 'What could I have done for my vineyard that I have not done?' There remains no outcome for the vineyard except that it should sink further and further into wasteland, 'unpruned, undug and overgrown by briar and thorn' (Isa 5:6).

In another passage of Isaiah, however, God speaks of 'the delightful vineyard' and says:

> I, the Lord, am its keeper;
> every moment I water it
> for fear its leaves should fall;
> night and day I watch over it. …
> if thorns and briars come
> I will declare war on them,
> I will burn them every one. (Isa 27:2-4)

Ezekiel speaks of how the wood of the vine is 'thrown on the fire for fuel' because it was fit for nothing else (15:1-8). This passage is alluded to in the chapter on the vine in St John's gospel, where Jesus speaks of disciples who do not 'remain in him'; they are like 'branches that have been thrown away', they wither and are 'collected and thrown on the fire and they are burnt' (Jn 15:6). But the Johannine text completely changes the meaning of Ezekiel's allegory. In St John's chapter, Jesus identifies himself as the Vine and speaks of the disciples as branches of the vine, called to 'make their home' in him as he makes his home in them. This relationship or 'reciprocal indwelling' between Jesus and his followers is a new and unprecedented revelation by Jesus of his relationship with his disciples. I explore it more fully on pp. 160 – 3, showing that the

Eucharist is the most complete indwelling of Jesus in his followers and of them in him.

A sign given in the prophets, especially in Isaiah, of the coming of the Kingdom of God is the sign of the Banquet to which the Lord God will invite the exiled and scattered children of Israel at the time of the great Return. It is the triumphant consummation of the covenant of God with his people. As God fed his people in the desert and gave them water from the rock to drink, so will he serve his liberated and reunited people with 'a banquet of rich food, a banquet of fine wines', as Isaiah described it in a passage (25:6-10) quoted on pp. 74 – 5.

The biblical descriptions of the Messianic Banquet were echoed by Jesus when he delivered his great eucharistic discourse in the gospel of St John. The Isaian text promised that God 'will destroy death forever' and that when a people listen to God's word their 'soul will live'. Jesus in the eucharistic discourse promises 'food that endures to eternal life' (Jn 6:27); he speaks of 'bread that comes down from heaven so that a man may eat of it and not die', in contrast with the manna in the desert which their fathers ate but died (Jn 6:49-51). Jesus declares that 'it is [his] Father who gives bread from heaven and gives life to the world (Jn 6:32-3). He declares that he is himself 'the bread of life' (Jn 6:35).

The Messianic Banquet texts form the backdrop to the account in the fourth gospel of the Wedding Feast at Cana. The Johannine account calls attention to the worthlessness at a wedding feast of the Jewish ablutions.[37] The Christian commentator will point to the incommensurable value of the wine of the Eucharist, the 'best wine kept for the last', the 'last' being the time of Jesus. The crucial intervention of Mary, Mother of Jesus, is also stressed. We return to the Cana scene in Part II of this book.

Glory to God in the Highest

The primary purpose of the Eucharist is to give glory and praise, honour and thanks to God. There are many great prayers in the

Bible expressing these sentiments, and these prayers obviously influenced the public worship of the early Christian Church. I quote a selection of them, from the Law, the Historical Books, the Prophets, the Wisdom Books and, on pp. 98 – 125, Psalms.

The prayers of Moses are particularly marked by these notes of praise and wonder at God's greatness and glory, his faithfulness and his mercy, and his nearness to his people. In what is known as the First Discourse, Moses said: 'What great nation has its gods as near as the Lord our God is to us whenever we call to him?' (Deut 4:7) St Thomas Aquinas cites this passage in his theological study of the Eucharist.

Later, after recalling the covenant and the Ten Commandments, Moses says:

> The Lord set his heart on you and chose you, not because you were the most numerous of all peoples – for indeed you were the smallest of all – but because he loved you and meant to keep the oath that he swore to your ancestors. ... The Lord your God is the true God, the faithful God, who is true to his covenant and his faithful love for a thousand generations. You will be the most blessed of all peoples. (Deut 7:7-9, 14)

Moses asks his people to put a question to past ages 'from the time God created the human race on earth':

> Was there ever a word so majestic from one end of heaven to the other? ... Did ever a people hear the voice of the living God speaking from the heart of the fire as you have heard it? ... This he showed you so that you might know that the Lord is the true God and that there is no other. (Deut 4:32-5)

This passage refers directly to God's words spoken amid the thunder, the fire and the dense smoke and the earthquake that marked God's awesome self-revelation on Mount Sinai; but it refers also to the Word of God wherever spoken or by whom-so-ever read: whoever the reader of that Word may be, the One who speaks is the

Lord and he speaks that Word out of 'the heart of the fire' which is his intense love for us.

After the installation of the Ark of the covenant in Jerusalem, King David leads the people in prayers of thanksgiving and praise:

> Give thanks to God, call his name aloud,
> proclaim his deeds to the peoples.
> Chant to him, play to him,
> sing about all his wonders.
>
> Take pride in his holy name,
> let your heart rejoice, you seekers of the Lord.
> Seek out the Lord, seek his strength,
> continually seek out his presence.
>
> The Lord it was who made the heavens,
> in his presence are splendour and majesty ...
> Give the Lord his due of glory and power,
> give the Lord the glory due to his name.
> (1 Chron 16:8-11, 27-9)

'To which', we read, all the people said, 'Amen Alleluia' (1 Chron 16:36).

When David had accumulated all the gold and silver and all the precious materials needed to build the Temple in Jerusalem, and had left all in readiness for Solomon his son to erect the building, he composed a song of praise of the Lord, based mainly on the above psalm, and asked Asaph and his kinsmen to chant it. Then David poured out his own soul before God in prayer and praise:

> May you be blessed, Lord, for ever and ever. Yours Lord is the greatness, the power, the splendour, length of days and glory, everything in heaven and on earth is yours. Yours is the sovereignty, Lord; you are exalted, supreme over all. ... We give thanks to you, our God, and praise your majestic name, for who am I and what is my people ... since everything comes from you

and we have given you only what you bestowed in the first place. ... With integrity of motive I willingly give all this and have been overjoyed to see your people, now present here, willingly offering their gifts to you. Lord, God of Abraham, Isaac and Israel our ancestors, watch over this for ever, shape the purpose of your people's heart and direct their hearts to you. (1 Chron 29:10-18)

Firm has he made the world and unshakeable.
Let the heavens be glad, let earth rejoice ...
Let the sea thunder and all it holds,
let the fields exult and all that is in them,
let all the woodland trees cry out for joy
at the presence of the Lord,
for he comes to judge the earth ...
Say, 'God of salvation, save us,
gather us, rescue us from among the heathen
to give thanks to your holy name
and to find our happiness
in praising you. (1 Chron 16:30-33, 35)

Then, we read, David addressed the whole assembly: 'Now bless the Lord your God', and the whole assembly blessed the Lord (1 Chron 29:10-14, 20). These words are particularly appropriate for the dedication of a new Church, but they form a fitting prayer before any celebration of Mass when people are gathered to bless and to praise the Lord our God.

Later, when David's son Solomon had completed the Temple building and was conducting the rite of dedication he prayed kneeling, with his 'hands stretched out to heaven'.

Lord, God of Israel, there is no God like you in heaven or on earth, you who are loyal to the covenant and show faithful love to your servants as long as they walk whole-heartedly in your way. ... Yet, will God really live with people on earth? Why, the heavens and the heavens of heavens cannot contain you! How much less this house which I have built! Even so, listen favourably to the prayer and entreaty of your servant. ... Day and night may your eyes watch over this temple, over this place, in which you have promised to put your name ...

When (your people) sin against you ... and (then) turn back to you with all their heart and soul ... and pray ... then listen from heaven where you reside, hear their prayers and entreaties, uphold their cause and forgive your people for having sinned against you. (2 Chron 6:13-20, 36-39)

Solomon concluded his prayer with the words:

Lord God, go up to your resting place. ...
Let your priests be robed in salvation,
Let your faithful rejoice in what is good. (2 Chron 6:41)

Finally, Solomon, to the accompaniment of musical instruments, offered praise to God, while the people alternated his calls for praise with the words: 'Great is his love, love without end.' (cf. 2 Chron 7:6)

These words coincide with the refrain of Psalm 135, the Great Hallel. The repetition of praise and thanks in these great Hebrew prayers reminds us of the relative absence of those themes in the personal prayers of most of us. We excel in prayers of petition and these tend to arouse our greatest fervour. We should learn from the Hebrew tradition and from the Church's liturgy, influenced in this sense by Jewish prayer, the importance of also giving praise and thanks and glory to God in our prayer.

Solomon knew and all the people knew that God is shrouded in mystery: he 'dwells in thick cloud' (2 Chron 6:1-2); yet, in his desire to be near to us and to allow us to feel his nearness, God 'came down from heaven for us and for our salvation'; he became man and dwelt amongst us. When, with our salvation accomplished, he ascended into heaven, he left us himself in the holy Eucharist and he dwells amongst us still in buildings and tabernacles made by human hands – so that he might dwell amongst us in human hearts. Thus he fulfils his own wish and his own promise that he would not 'leave us orphans' here on earth. No people has its god so near as our God is to us.

The Book of Wisdom has Solomon praying to God for the gift of wisdom, without which no ruler can hope to lead his people wisely and judge them justly. The Christian Church recognised in Wisdom the Holy Spirit 'who proceeds from the Father and the Son' and who is given to the Church through Christ's redemptive death and resurrection. Solomon's prayer is one of the great biblical prayers on which the prayers of the Church's liturgy, and especially her Eucharistic Prayers are modelled.

Solomon is represented in the Book of Wisdom as praying for God's gift of wisdom:

> God of our ancestors, Lord of mercy,
> who by your word have made all things,
> and in your wisdom have fitted man
> to rule the creatures that have come from you,
> to govern the world in holiness and justice,
> and in honesty of soul to wield authority,
> grant me Wisdom, consort of your throne,
> and do not reject me from the number of your children. ...
> For I am your servant, son of your serving maid,
> a feeble man
> with little time to live
> with small understanding
> of justice and law ...
>
> Dispatch Wisdom from the holy heavens,
> send her forth from your throne of glory
> to help me and to toil with me
> and teach me what is pleasing to you,
> since she knows and understands everything.
> She will guide me prudently in my undertakings
> and protect me by her glory. (Wis 9:1-5, 10-11)

The same Book of Wisdom gives praise and thanks to God for his power and his mercy:

> Your great strength is always at your call;
> who can withstand the strength of your arm?
> In your sight the whole world
> is like a grain of dust
> that tips the scales,
> like a drop of morning dew
> falling on the ground.
> Yet you are merciful to all,
> because you can do all things
> and overlook men's sins
> so that they can repent
> yes, you love all that exists,
> you hold nothing of what you made in abhorrence,
> for if you had hated anything
> you would not have formed it,
> and how, if you had not willed it,
> could a thing persist,
> how could it be conserved
> if not called forth by you?
> You spare all things
> because all things are yours, Lord,
> lover of life,
> you whose imperishable spirit is in all. (Wis 11:21-12: 1)

The prophet Isaiah has a lovely prayer of thanksgiving and praise:

> O Lord, you are my God.
> I exult you, I praise your name,
> for you have carried out your wonderful design,
> long planned, trustworthy and true. ...
> For you are a refuge for the poor,
> a refuge for the needy in times of distress,
> a shelter from the storm,
> a shade from the heat. ... (Isa 25:1-5)

This prayer in Isaiah is immediately followed by his description of the Messianic Banquet, which I have quoted in full on p. 74. For Christians, the implied reference to the Eucharist is unmistakeable.

Jeremiah hears the following word from the Lord, addressed to 'all the clans of Israel'; Christians read in it the story of divine love which leads God to give us the amazing gift of the Eucharist:

> I have loved you with an everlasting love,
> so I am constant in my affection for you. ...
> Is Ephraim, then, so dear a son to me,
> a child so favoured,
> that after each threat of mine
> I must still remember him,
> and still be deeply moved for him,
> and let my tenderness yearn over him?
> It is the Lord, who speaks. (Jer 31:3, 20)

In the Book of Lamentations, we find a prayer expressing the deep depression which has overcome Israel:

> Happiness has gone out of our lives;
> grief has taken place of our dances.
>
> Nothing is left of all that we were proud of.
> We sinned, and now we are doomed.
>
> We are sick at our very hearts
> and can hardly see through our tears.
>
> Because Mount Zion lies lonely and deserted,
> and wild jackals prowl through its ruins.
>
> As you, O Lord, are King forever
> and will rule to the end of time,

Why have you abandoned us so long?
    will you ever remember us again?

Bring us back to you, Lord! Bring us back!
    restore our ancient glory.

Or have you rejected us forever?[38] (Lam 5:15-22)

The Books of Judith and Esther were later additions to the
Canon of Scripture and are sometimes called 'Deuterocanonical'.
They are stories rather than history, and were designed to bring
hope to Israel in face of its danger of extinction as a race, at the
hands respectively of the Assyrians and the Persians. Judith and
Esther are symbols of the Jewish people, both in their military
weakness and in their spiritual strength. Esther is trembling
with fear as she prepares to confront Ahasuerus or Xerxes, King
of the Persians, and she prays fervently:

You, Lord, have chosen Israel out of all the nations and our
ancestors out of all before them to be your heritage forever.
(Esth 4:17n)

Come to my help for I am alone and have no one but you, Lord
... Nor has your servant found pleasure from the day of her
promotion until now except in you, Lord, God of Abraham.
(Esth 4:17t, 17y)

It is significant that the reason given in the Books of Judith and
Esther for the survival of Israel is that it may continue to give
praise to God. This is the purpose also of what St Paul calls 'the
new Israel', namely, that the Christian Church may continue to
give worship and praise, glory and honour and thanks, to God.

From Berakah to Eucharistic Prayer

I turn now to examine a recurring form of Hebrew prayer, the Berakah, which was developed by the Christian Church and adapted so as to help to form the present Eucharistic Prayer. Four versions of this are found in the present Roman Missal and are authorised for public worship. The Latin version of the eucharistic liturgy, commonly called the Pius V or Tridentine Mass, is now more freely authorised, following the Motu Proprio of Pope Benedict XVI, *Summorum Pontificum*. It is close in many respects to the present Eucharistic Prayer I.

The Eucharistic Prayer, which is the heart of the eucharistic liturgy, was in its beginnings a Christian development of the Jewish prayer-form known as *Berakah*.[39] The gospel accounts of the Last Supper and of the institution of the Eucharist tell us that Jesus 'took the bread' and 'said the blessing', and then 'took a cup' (of wine) and 'returned thanks' (Mt 26:26-28). The Berakah was not just a prayer before meals as we understand it. It was not a formula asking God to bless the food. It was rather an act of thanks and praise to God for providing this food for us, leading to a prayer of praise and thanks to God for all his mighty deeds of power and mercy throughout the long history of his people, Israel, and especially for the everlasting covenant, sealed in the blood of sacrifice, by which God linked his own life with the life of Israel. It is significant that the word 'Berakah' is translated in early Christian times by the word *Eucharistia*. The prayer with which the first Christians celebrated the sacred meal bequeathed to them by Christ at the Last Supper took the form of a Berakah. This prayer in the Jewish usage could take the form of a very short prayer or of a long compendium of Israel's history, recalled in love and praise and thanks to God. An example of the 'short' Berakah is Eliezer's prayer on meeting Rebecca, the destined wife of Isaac. Eliezer, the servant of Abraham, on seeing Rebecca, prayed:

> Blessed be the Lord, God of my master Abraham, who has never ceased showing goodness and kindness to my master. He has guided my steps to the house of my master's brother.[40]

Jethro, 'father-in-law of Moses', when he came to visit Moses in the camp near Mount Sinai, prayed:

> Blessed be the Lord who has rescued you from the Egyptians and from Pharaoh and has rescued the people from the grasp of the Egyptians. Now I know that the Lord is greater than all the gods. (Ex 17:10-11)

Then, we read, Jethro 'offered a holocaust and sacrifices to God and Aaron came with all the elders of Israel to share the meal with the father-in-law of Moses in the presence of God' (Ex 17:12). Here we have the Berakah associated with sacrifice and sacred meal, as it later familiarly became in Jewish usage.

The greatest of the 'long' Berakoth reported in the Bible is that of Nehemiah, who proclaimed it on the occasion of the return of the exiles and the rebuilding of ruined Jerusalem. Throughout this particular Berakah there is a strong note of repentance for the repeated sins of Israel, penitently contrasted with the unfailing mercy of God and his unflinching fidelity to the covenant he had made with his people. This Berakah begins:

> Blessed are you, Lord our God,
> from everlasting to everlasting,
> and blessed be your name of glory
> that surpasses all blessing and praise. ...
> For [your people's] hunger you gave them bread from heaven,
> for their thirst you brought them water spurting from the rock.

In spite of the people's obstinate relapses into sin,

> Greatly loving,
> you did not make an end of them,
> you did not forsake them,
> for you are a gracious and a loving God. (Neh 9:5-17)

There are many examples in the psalms and elsewhere of the more developed Berakah, taking the form of the recital of God's mighty deeds in favour of his beloved people, Israel, remembered in gratitude and praise to God by a grateful people. Psalms 77(78), 104(105), 105(106), 106(107) and 113(114-115) are psalms of this kind. Emphasis is placed on the need for God's people constantly to recall God's mighty deeds and his fidelity to an often sinful people. Interestingly, these psalms have many references to God's providing food and drink, manna and water, for his starving and thirsty people during their long wandering in the desert. There are also recurring references to the covenant God made with his people and frequently renewed:

> The things our fathers have told us
> we will not hide from their children
> but will tell them to the next generation:
> the glories of the Lord and his might
> and the marvellous deeds he has done. ...
> He gave a command to our fathers
> to make it known to their children
> that the next generation might know it,
> the children yet to be born.
> They too should arise and tell their sons
> that they too should set their hope in God
> and never forget God's deeds
> but keep every one of his commands ...
> He commanded the clouds above
> and opened the gates of heaven.
> He rained down manna for their food
> and gave them bread from heaven.
> Mere men ate the bread of angels ...
> He rained food on them like dust
> Winged fowl like the sands of the sea. ... (Ps 77(78):3-7, 23-27)

He remembers his covenant forever
his promise for a thousand generations. ...
When they asked for food he sent quails,
he filled them with bread from heaven.
He pierced the rock to give them water
it gushed forth in the desert like a river. (Ps 104(105):8,40-41)

God's fidelity is regularly met with forgetfulness and infidelity on the part of Israel, who are prone to lapse into the idolatrous practices and the sinful lifestyle of the pagan nations surrounding them:

... exchanging the God who was their glory
for the image of a bull that eats grass.
They mingled with the nations
and learned to act like them. ...
they broke their marriage bond with the Lord... (Ps 105(106):20)

Nevertheless, God remained ever faithful to his covenant with them: 'For their sake he remembered his covenant.' In sorrow and remorse, his people pray:

O Lord, our God, save us!
gather us from among the nations
that we may thank your holy name
and make it our glory to praise you.

Blessed be the Lord, God of Israel
forever, from age to age.
Let all the people cry out:
Amen! Amen! Alleluia! (Ps 105(106):44-45, 47-48)

Another psalm of this series extols God's mastery of nature, which he exerts in favour of his people on land or on sea:

> For he satisfies the thirsty soul,
> he fills the hungry with good things. ...
> he sent forth his word to heal them
> and saved their life from the grave.

The people are invited to praise:

> 'O give thanks to the Lord for he is good,
> for His great love is without end.'
> They staggered, reeled like drunken men
> for all their skill was gone.
> Then they cried to the Lord in their need
> and he rescued them from their distress
> He stilled the storm to a whisper
> all the waves of the sea were hushed. (Ps 106(107):1, 27-29)

Psalm 115(116) is one of the Hallel group of psalms of which I treat on pp. 60–3. This is another recital of the wonders of the Exodus, and a call to Israel to give thanks and glory to God:

> Not to us, Lord, not to us,
> but to your name give the glory;
> for the sake of your love and your truth,
> lest the heathens say:
> 'Where is their God?' ...
> We who live bless the Lord, now and forever. (Ps 115(116):1-2)

The Berakah therefore is 'essentially a proclamation, a confession, of the wonderful works of God'.[41] It is our response in faith to God's self-revelation of himself to us in his Word and in his Law.[42] God reveals himself to us and we respond by receiving God into our lives and into our very selves in faith, through prayer and the sacraments, and especially through the Eucharist. Let us now survey the Eucharistic Prayer in the Roman Missal and see how far it resembles the Jewish Berakah.

First of all, we note that the offertory prayers for the preparation of the gifts are themselves short Berakoth, one said over the bread and one over the wine:

> Blessed are you, Lord, God of all creation.
> Through your goodness we have this bread to offer,
> which earth has given, and human hands have made.
> It will become for us the bread of life.
>
> Blessed are you, Lord, God of all creation.
> Through your goodness we have this wine to offer,
> which earth has given, and human hands have made.
> It will become our spiritual drink.

Next, it is important to note that each Eucharistic Prayer begins with the Preface and this sets the tone for the whole Eucharistic Prayer. The Preface is an integral part of the Eucharistic Prayer. The Preface begins, and therefore the entire Eucharistic Prayer begins, with the dialogue between priest and people in which the people are invited to 'lift up their hearts' in joy and wonder and praise. The priest invites the people to 'give thanks to the Lord our God', and the people reply: 'It is right always and everywhere to give him thanks and praise.' The priest follows by saying: 'It is indeed right always and everywhere to give you thanks ... through Jesus Christ, our Lord.' Then follows the *Sanctus*, which is itself based on the great description of the Theophany or self-revelation of God in the sixth chapter of Isaiah, when the Lord God is seen 'seated on a high throne', while seraphs cry out to one another:

> Holy, holy, holy is the Lord God of hosts.
> His glory fills the whole earth.

Meanwhile, Isaiah tells us, the foundations of the threshold shake at the sound of the voices and the Temple is filled with smoke. Isaiah is overcome with awe and with a sense of his own unworthiness in the presence of the all-holy God; but he is seized also with the urge to proclaim the holiness of God so that people may 'be converted and healed' (Isa 6).

The *Sanctus* is said or sung by choir and people in union with the angels and the saints in heaven. It is preceded by the following or similar words: 'Now we join the angels and the saints as they sing their unending hymn of praise.'

The Eucharistic Prayer continues: 'We come to you, Father, in praise and thanksgiving, through Jesus Christ, your Son.' The Eucharistic Prayer then proceeds in the manner of all Berakoth to praise and thank God and give glory to him for his wonderful deeds. In Eucharistic Prayer I these great deeds are enumerated: above all, Christ's passion and death and his resurrection and ascension into glory – the great marvels of the New Testament – while the sacrifices of the Old Testament are also remembered – those of Abraham, Abel and Melchisedek.

Our thanks and praise to God are united with those of the Blessed Virgin Mary and the apostles and martyrs and saints. Our glory and praise to God are finally expressed in the concluding words:

> Through Christ, with him and in him,
> in the unity of the Holy Spirit,
> all glory and honour is yours,
> almighty Father,
> for ever and ever. Amen.

Just as the Jewish Berakah had place also for prayer of petition – the Hebrew *Tefillah* – so too has the Eucharistic Prayer. We pray for the Church, for the Pope, the bishops and the clergy; we pray for the living, we pray for the dead. Central to the Eucharistic Prayer is the prayer of Epiclesis, prayed with the priest's hands extended over the bread and wine, inviting the Holy Spirit to:

make [these gifts] holy
so that they may become for us
the body and blood of our Lord, Jesus Christ.

The Holy Spirit is invoked also to help us, the congregation, to 'become one body, one spirit in Christ' (Eucharistic Prayer III).

Another petition found in each Eucharistic Prayer is a prayer for the coming (of Christ) in glory when,

in your kingdom,
freed from the corruption of sin and death,
we shall sing your glory with every creature,
through Christ, Our Lord,
through whom you give us
everything that is good.

This prayer is the echo within us of the High Priestly prayer of Christ himself on the night of the Last Supper, before he crossed the brook at Kedron to the Garden of Gethsemane:

Father, I want those whom you have given to me to be with me where I am, so that they may always see the glory you have given me because you loved me before the foundation of the world. (Jn 17:24)

The paramount themes of the Eucharistic Prayer – praise and thanks and glory to God – are perhaps best expressed in Eucharistic Prayer IV:

Countless hosts of angels
stand before you to do your will;
They look upon your splendour
and praise you, night and day.
United with them
and in the name of every creature under heaven,
we too praise your glory as we say:
'Holy, holy, holy, Lord ...'

Then God's great deeds are enumerated, beginning with the creation of the world and of mankind and proceeding with the covenant formed with God's people and culminating in God's sending of his own Son,

> conceived through the power of the Holy Spirit
> and born of the Virgin Mary,
> a man like us in all things but sin.
> To the poor he proclaimed
> the good news of salvation,
> to prisoners, freedom,
> to those in sorrow, joy.
> In fulfilment of your will
> he gave himself up to death,
> but by rising from the dead,
> he destroyed death and restored life.
> And that we might live
> No longer for ourselves but for him,
> He sent the Holy Spirit from you Father,
> as his first gift to those who believe,
> to complete his work on earth
> and to bring us the fullness of grace.

In and through the Eucharistic Prayer, we pass from faith, received through God's self-revealing Word, to faith lived in our sharing of God's life, through Jesus Christ, in the power of the Holy Spirit. The result is that we are gathered 'into the one body of Christ, a living sacrifice of praise'. We are prepared already in this present life for an eternal life of praise, when 'we shall sing [God's] glory with every creature through Christ, our Lord'. Let us note, contrary to what is suggested by some critics of our faith, that this is not because our God is some solipsistic being absorbed in his own greatness, who needs and demands incessant flattery. Instead, the need is entirely on our part – the need to ensure that the One whom we praise and glorify is indeed the One God, and there is no other. This praise of God is God's destiny for us human beings; it is also the realisation of our full human potential. St Irenaeus wrote:

> The glory of God is in living men and women; and full life for men and women is the vision of God.[43]

The Psalms and the Eucharist

The psalms have from the beginning provided the framework of prayer in which the Church has celebrated the Eucharist. As we have just seen in the section on the Berakah, the Eucharistic Prayers of the Church come from the same tradition of prayer as the psalms; and many of the psalms are themselves examples of Berakah. Indeed, the whole Psalter has been called an extended Berakah.[44] The entrance hymn in the eucharistic liturgy has traditionally been a psalm or part of a psalm, chanted as the presiding priest and 'servers' made their processional way to the altar. For many decades before the Second Vatican Council, the entrance hymn was Psalm 42(43), proclaimed in alternate verses by priests and servers. Altar servers of those times will still remember the opening lines spoken by the priest in Latin:

> *Introibo ad altare Dei,*
> *Ad Deum qui laetificat iuventutem meam.*
>
> I shall go in to the altar of God
> the God who gives joy to my youth.

The priest continued:

> *Judica me Deus et discerne causam meam*
> *a gente non sancta,*
> *ab homine iniquo et doloso*
> *erue me.*

> Defend me, O God, and plead my cause
> against a godless nation.
> From deceitful and cunning men
> rescue me, O God.

The psalm goes on:

> O send forth your light and your truth,
> let these be my guide.
> Let them bring me to your holy mountain
> to the place where you dwell.
> (Ps 42(43))

The words of this psalm still form an excellent prayer of preparation for the celebration of the Eucharist.

In pre-Vatican II days the priest, as he left the altar, was encouraged to pray the Canticle of the Three Young Men from the Book of Daniel, together with Psalm 150(151), the last of the psalms, a great prayer of praise of God – a prayer that resonates with our *Gloria in excelsis*:

> Praise God in his holy place
> praise him in his mighty heavens ...
> Oh praise him with resounding cymbals,
> praise him with clashing of cymbals.
> Let everything that lives and that breathes,
> give praise to the Lord.

This psalm can serve as a wonderful prayer of thanks and praise to God for the surpassing gift of the Eucharist – a reminder that the word 'Eucharist' itself means 'Thank you'.

The psalms were usually associated with the processional movements in the Liturgy: the solemn entrance to the sanctuary, the carrying of the Book of the Gospels to the Lectern for the reading of the gospel, the offertory procession or the procession with the gifts, the movement of the faithful towards the sanctuary for the reception of Holy Communion, the departure of priest and servers from the sanctuary. Originally, an entire psalm was read or chanted at these points in the liturgy, but over time this had been reduced to one or two verses. Before the great liturgical renewal of Vatican II, the processions were scarcely recognisable. The gospel procession, for example, had become reduced to the server's moving the missal from one side of the altar to the other. Here as elsewhere, the reforms of Vatican II were often a matter of return to an earlier and more authentic tradition.

The scripture readings were also traditionally accompanied by psalms. The first reading was followed by a psalm called the 'gradual'. This was followed by a further psalm reading, called the 'tract'. The post-Vatican II Liturgy restores the psalms to their full place in eucharistic worship. It also ensures that the laity, through the ministry of readers or through the choir, can lead the people in proclaiming or singing the psalms. The responsorial psalm, following the first reading, is selected in view of its harmony with the first reading and with the gospel reading of the day; it is a prayerful reflection on the first reading and a preparation for the attentive reading and hearing of the gospel. The gospel reading is the climax of the Liturgy of the Word, and this is itself, with the homily, a precious opportunity for reawakening and deepening our faith in the Lord, in preparation for the coming of him who enters into such close and intimate union with us individually and as a community in the Liturgy of the Eucharist.

For the communion procession and our prayers after communion the Church regularly returns once more to the psalms as her favoured way of expressing thanks to God for the inexpressible gift which he makes of himself to us in Holy Communion. The psalms, therefore, have a very important place in the liturgy of the Eucharist, as they had in the whole Jewish tradition of prayer and had in the prayer of Jesus himself and of his holy Mother and his Apostles and in the prayer of the Church across the ages. It is fitting, therefore, that we explore the psalms more fully in the course of our biblical reflections.

I begin with the psalms which Christ himself may have been praying as he hung upon the Cross. The gospel accounts of the Passion preserve for us words spoken by the dying Lord: some of these are quotations from the psalms. Jews normally prayed aloud. As Jesus' strength ebbed away on the Cross, his voice became more faint: we recall that bystanders thought he was calling upon Elijah when he was calling upon God, 'Eloi'. Only occasional words or short sentences from the lips of the dying Jesus could be heard. We can confidently assume that Jesus on the Cross was praying entire psalms, as he had done throughout his life.

The Passion narratives of Mark and Matthew record that Jesus cried out on the Cross: 'My God, my God, why have you forsaken me?' The words are taken from Psalm 21(22). We can reasonably conclude that Jesus prayed the entire psalm, or at least that the verses of the psalm passed through his mind and expressed his feelings, as he hung on the Cross. Other verses of the psalm are referred to in Matthew's gospel.[45] We can confidently turn to this psalm, therefore, as giving us insight into the thoughts and feelings of Jesus in the hours of his slow and dreadfully painful dying. We speak of ex*cruc*iating pain precisely because '*crux*' is the Latin word for 'cross'.

The verse quoted above is itself very revealing in this regard. Jesus addresses his Father as 'my God', 'Eloi', 'Elohim'. It is the only time in all the gospels in which Jesus prays to God his Father without calling him 'Abba', 'Dear Father'.[46] This gives us a glimpse of the loneliness and desolation of Jesus as death approached. God seems to be no longer his 'Abba', his dear Father; he feels rejected, abandoned, forsaken, at the time when he most needs acceptance, affirmation and support. His disciples had run away. Peter had denied him. Even God seems not to care:

> You are far from my plea and the cry of my distress,
> I call by day and you give no reply,
> I call by night and I find no peace.

Through the psalm, Jesus contrasts his plight with the goodness God had shown to his people across the ages:

> But I am a worm and no man,
> the butt of men, the laughing-stock of the people.

Still following Psalm 21(22), we can learn how Jesus contrasts this state of abandonment in which he is left to die with the love which God had lavished upon him when he was so secure in his mother's arms:

> You entrusted me to my mother's breast.
> To you was I committed from my birth.

Jesus pleads:

> Do not leave me alone in my distress.
> Come close, there is no-one else to help.

With the psalmist, Jesus seems to cry out in sheer terror, admitting that he feels as if 'fierce bulls of Bashan' were closing in on every side around him, with jaws wide open to rip his body apart, 'like lions rending and roaring', or like dogs that 'tear holes in my hands and my feet'. He no longer has the physical energy to protect himself, his bones seem disconnected, his throat is parched 'like burnt clay'. In something like desperation, Jesus may have prayed the verses of the psalm:

> Save my life from the jaws of these lions,
> my poor soul from the horns of these oxen.

The despair and the fear and sheer human terror which seem to hold Jesus in their remorseless grip are very real; but they cannot prevail over his 'hope against hope' in God, his Father. The last verses of the psalm express Jesus' trust in God, his Abba. He remembers God's mercy towards the poor and his faithfulness to the covenant which he made with his people, and particularly with the poor. The psalm ends, and Jesus on the Cross, praying the psalm, would have ended, with the words:

> My soul shall live for him,
> my children serve him.
> They shall tell of the Lord to generations yet to come,
> declare his faithfulness to peoples yet unborn:
> 'These things the Lord has done.'

Psalm 21(22) speaks to us directly from Calvary, as we gather before the altar of the Eucharist. They tell us of the dreadful cost to Jesus of his words instituting the Eucharist:

> This is my body, given up for you ...
> This is my blood which shall be shed for you.

They tell us of the love 'greater than man has ever seen' (Jn 15:13), with which Jesus laid down his life for us. Listening to these words at Mass, we cannot but see the Eucharist as among the greatest 'things the Lord has ever done' (Ps 21(22):31) to show his love for us, imparting his love unto death to each of us individually and to all of us who form the Church, the body of Christ, as we celebrate the Eucharist in memory of Jesus.

St Luke, in his account of the Passion, quotes another verse spoken by Jesus on the Cross: 'Into your hands I commend my spirit.' (23: 46) They are the last recorded words of the Lord; they are taken from Psalm 30(31). As in the case of Psalm 21(22), we can be confident that this psalm too was prayed by the dying Christ, though his voice was so faint that only some of his words were heard by those standing near the Cross. Jesus is now again at peace. He now *feels* what he always *knew*, that God is his 'rock', his 'stronghold', his 'refuge', and in deep trust he places his soul in the loving hands of his dearest Abba. The distress, the tears and the sighs, the bodily exhaustion and the spiritual affliction which he had felt, the hurtful rejections by his friends, the taunts and jeers of the bystanders, all are turned by Jesus into total trust in God:

> I trust in you Lord,
> I say 'You are my God',
> my life is in your hands, deliver me
> from the hands of those who hate me.
> ...
> Let your face shine on your servant
> Save me in your love. ...
> Blessed be the Lord
> who has shown me the wonders of his love.

St Thérèse, whose name in religion included the Holy Face of Jesus, loved the phrase, 'Let your face shine on your servant'; she refers to it often in her poems.[47]

Jesus' praying of this psalm would have ended with words addressed to us, the people 'who trust God' as Jesus did:

> Be strong, let your heart take courage,
> all you who hope in the Lord.

Jesus himself used very similar words to address his disciples in the context of his future Passion. He said to them, as recorded in St John's gospel:

> Listen; the time will come – in fact it has come – when you will be scattered, each going his own way and leaving me alone. And yet I am not alone, because the Father is with me. I have told you all this so that you may find peace in me. In the world you will have distress, but be brave. I have overcome the world. (Jn 16:32-33)

The gospel writers link other psalms with the passion narrative, but without any suggestion that Jesus was praying these psalms on the Cross. Psalms 34(35) and 68(69) are referred to in connection with the false accusations made against Jesus at his trial.[48] John's Passion gospel quotes Psalm 68(69) in proof that Jesus was fulfilling the scriptures when he cried, 'I am thirsty', and was given vinegar to drink.[49] One verse of Psalm 68(69) is quoted as describing Jesus' sense of aloneness on the Cross:

> I looked in vain for compassion
> for consolers, not one could I find. (Ps 68(69):20)[50]

Psalm 88 is not associated with the Passion of Christ in the gospels. As pilgrims to the Holy Land will know, however, it is associated by tradition with a place described as the 'prison cell' of Jesus where, it is claimed, Jesus was detained while awaiting his trial. The 'cell' is a hole in the ground, with just enough room for a person to stand, but not to recline. There is no means of escape.

There is no evidence to support this story. Nevertheless the psalm could be read as a possible expression of the feelings of Jesus at certain moments of the passion:

> Lord my God, I call for help day by day:
> I cry at night before you …
>
> For my soul is filled with evils;
> My life is on the brink of the grave
> Your fury has swept down upon me
> Your terrors have utterly destroyed me.
>
> They surround me all the day like a flood,
> They assail me all together.
> Friend and neighbour you have taken away,
> My one companion is darkness. (Ps 87(88))

Jesus, however, was vouchsafed joy on the Cross – and that joy surely came in great part from his foreknowledge that his people, 'those who love [his] cause', will celebrate the Eucharist in memory of his passion and death and his resurrection victory, in which the whole Church will share. Psalm 68(69) has these words of joy:

> I will praise God's name with a song,
> I will glorify him with thanksgiving,
> a gift pleasing God more than oxen,
> more than beasts prepared for sacrifice ...
> the poor when they see it will be glad
> and God-seeking hearts will revive;
> for the Lord listens to the needy
> and does not spare his servants in their chains.
> Let the heavens and the earth give him praise
> the sea and all its living creatures.
> For God will bring help to Zion
> and rebuild the cities of Judah
> and men shall dwell there in possession.
> The sons of his servants shall inherit it
> those who love his name shall dwell there. (Ps 68(69):30-36)

The opening verses of this extract enunciate a common teaching of the psalms, namely that the good dispositions of the worshipper offering sacrifice are more pleasing to God than the number or quality of the beasts offered in sacrifice. This is super-eminently true of the sacrifice of the Eucharist, where Christ is both sacrificing priest and sacrificial victim. It is touching to think that Jesus took comfort and joy on the Cross from his foreknowledge of the faith and love with which we in time to come would celebrate the Eucharist in memory of him.

Another theme of Psalm 68(69) is the return of the exiles to Judah and the restoration of God's holy city of Jerusalem and of the Temple to their former glory. We have seen already that the primary effect of the Eucharist is the growth in holiness and in extent of Christ's body, the Church, and the repair of the damage done to it by human sin and especially by the sins of its members. A group of psalms[51] share this theme and can be used by us as our prayer, united with the Eucharist, for the Church, beset by so many difficulties and humiliated by clerical child abuse scandals in our time. Many of the psalms were composed in times of great distress for God's people, Israel. Some are lamentations for the destruction of the Temple of Jerusalem. Others express the desolation felt by Israel at the exile of its people to Babylon, and implore the Lord to bring about the return of the exiles and the restoration of Israel's former glory. But there are also many recalls of God's great deeds of might and mercy throughout Israel's history, accompanied by urgent pleas to God to act now on behalf of his people in their present distress. The psalmist is quite bold in reminding God that Israel has not 'forgotten him', though he seemed to have forgotten them! Pleading for Israel, the psalmist cries:

> Awake, Lord, why do you sleep?
> Arise, do not reject us forever.
> Why do you hide your face
> and forget our oppression and misery?
> For we are brought down low to the dust,
> our body lies prostrate on the earth.
> Stand up and come to our help.
> Redeem us because of your love. (Ps 43(44):23-26)

In Psalm 73, the psalmist begs God to renew his ruined Temple:

> Turn your steps to these places that are utterly ruined!
> The enemy has laid waste the whole of the sanctuary.
> Your foes have made uproar in your house of prayer:
> they have set up their emblems, their foreign emblems,
> high above the entrance to the sanctuary.
>
> Their axes have battered the wood of its doors.
> They have struck together with hatchet and pickaxe.
> O God, they have set your sanctuary on fire:
> they have raised and profaned the place where you dwell. ...

> How long, O God, is the enemy to scoff?
> Is the foe to insult your name forever?
> Why, O Lord, do you hold back your hand?
> Why do you keep your right hand hidden? (Ps 73(74):3-7, 10-11)

Psalm 76(77) is the prayer of a perplexed man who simply cannot understand how God's love seems to have 'vanished forever' and his promise to have 'come to an end'. 'The way of the Most High has changed.' Yet this is the same God who manifested his almighty power over nature at the creation and who again showed himself as Lord of nature and of history on behalf of his people at the Exodus and on Mount Sinai (Ps 76(77):9-11, 16-20).

Psalm 78(79) and 79(80) are moving laments over the destruction of Jerusalem and God's Temple.

> The nations have invaded your land,
> they have profaned your Holy Temple.
> They have made Jerusalem a heap of ruins ...
> they have poured out blood like water in Jerusalem,
> leaving no-one to bury the dead.

Enemies have taunted God's people in their defeat, pouring 'mockery and scorn' on their beliefs. Unbelievers are taunting them: 'where is [your] God?' (Ps 78(79):1-5, 10)

Psalm 79(80) expressed the grief of a divided people, contrasting the decline of King Solomon's great united Israel with the pitiable state of divided Israel in the psalmist's day. The psalmist cried to God:

> You brought a vine out of Egypt ...
> before it you cleared the ground,
> it took root and spread through the land. ...
> It stretched out its branches to the sea
> to the great river [Euphrates] it stretched out its shoots.
> (Ps 79(80): 8-11)

Now it can be ravaged by any passerby. The psalmist prays for a new king who will 'visit this vine and protect it, the vine your right hand has planted' (Ps 79(80):14-15). The 'new king' was seen as the Messiah, who would bring deliverance to God's people and install the Kingdom of God on earth. We can make this psalm our prayer for the spiritual welfare of the Church and for the Pope, seeing in him 'the man [God] has chosen, the man [God] has given [his] strength' (Ps 79(80):17).

Indeed, these psalms are re-echoed in our Eucharistic Prayers. In these, we pray:

> We offer [these gifts] for your holy Catholic Church,
> watch over it, Lord, and guide it.
> Grant it peace and unity throughout the world.
> We offer them for N., our Pope,
> For N., our Bishop,
> and for all who hold and teach the Catholic faith
> that comes to us from the Apostles.
> (Eucharistic Prayer I)

> May all of us who share in the body and blood of Christ
> be brought together in unity by the Holy Spirit.
> Lord, remember your Church throughout the world,
> makes us grow in love
> together with N., our Pope,
> N., our Bishop, and all the clergy.
> (Eucharistic Prayer II)

> Grant that we, who are nourished by his body and blood
> may be filled with his Holy Spirit
> and become one body, one spirit in Christ.
> May he make us an everlasting gift to you. ...
> Strengthen in faith and love your pilgrim Church on earth,
> Your servant Pope N., our Bishop N.,
> and all the bishops

with the clergy and the entire people
your Son has gained for you.
(Eucharistic Prayer III)
Look upon this sacrifice which you have given to your Church
and by your Holy Spirit gather all who share this one bread
and one cup into the one body of Christ, a living sacrifice of
praise. Lord, remember those for whom we offer this sacrifice,
especially N. our Pope, N. our Bishop and bishops and clergy
everywhere.
(Eucharistic Prayer IV)

In the communion rite of every Eucharist we pray:

Deliver us Lord from every evil
and grant us peace in our day.
In your mercy keep us free from sin
and protect us from all anxiety,
as we wait in joyful hope
for the coming of our Saviour Jesus Christ.

We must never forget that the Church depends on the Eucharist as
her greatest source of life and strength, her inexhaustible fountain of
hope, her certainty of ever new beginnings. In all her trials and
seeming defeats, Israel was confident that God would intervene, that
he would be faithful to his new and eternal covenant and would
ensure his people's victory. For, in him, as the psalmist prayed:

Mercy and faithfulness have met,
justice and peace have embraced.
Faithfulness shall spring from the earth
and justice look down from heaven. (Ps 84(85):10-11)

This is spoken by the psalmist even as he described the defeats and
humiliations of God's people, when God's mercies 'sworn in your
faithfulness to David' seemed to have ended. But no! God is
faithful; he has solemnly declared:

I will never violate my covenant
nor go back on the word I have spoken. (Ps 88(89):34)

This psalm can well express our 'joyful hope' of God's intervention in all the trials of the Church. It is filled with the joyful hope in the coming of the Messiah. This is why St Thérèse of Lisieux loved Psalm 88(89), which so powerfully expressed her total trust in God's mercy, even at times when God seemed no longer 'there' for her. In her translation the psalm began with the verse: 'I shall sing forever of the mercies of the Lord.' In her *Story of a Soul*, Thérèse wrote:

> I'm only going to do one thing: I'm going to begin here below to sing what I want to be saying over and over for ever in eternity: 'the mercies of the Lord.'

She repeats the phrase, 'the mercies of the Lord', no less than nine times in the *Story of a Soul*.[52]

In the translation I have been using, the opening verse of Psalm 88(89) reads:

> I will sing forever of your love, O Lord,
> through all ages I will proclaim your truth.
> Of this I am sure, that your love lasts forever. (Ps 88(89):1-2)

Thérèse used to repeat: 'Even if he should slay me, I shall still trust in him.' Whatever the darkness engulfing her soul, she still prayed, in the words of Psalm 88(89):

> Of this I am sure
> that your love lasts forever,
> that your truth is firmly established in the heavens.
> (Ps 88(89):3)

The group of psalms known as the 'Seven Penitential Psalms'[53] feature in the liturgy particularly in the penitential seasons of Advent and Lent and also on Fridays, as we recall Good Friday, cause of such atrocious pain to Jesus, source of all goodness to us. In our time, when receiving Holy Communion seems to be seen as the natural thing to do when we are at Mass – good in itself though this may be – there is a danger of our forgetting that, if we are conscious of grave sin, we must seek God's forgiveness in the sacrament of reconciliation before receiving him in Holy Communion. This is part of what St Paul meant when he wrote of 'recognising the Body' and warned of the danger of our 'eating and drinking our own condemnation' through unworthy reception of holy communion (1 Cor 11:29). The penitential psalms have, therefore, a special relevance for the Eucharist in our times.

The best known of these is Psalm 50(51), the *Miserere*. This psalm expresses sorrow for sin in almost physical terms, speaking of 'the bones [God] has crushed'. Something of this survives in the term 'contrition', a word whose Latin source conveys the sense of our being 'crushed' both by sin and by sorrow for sin. The psalm longs for and prays for 'truth in the heart' to replace the lies of sin. The phrase is recalled by St Paul's description of Christians as 'doing the truth'.[54]

Psalm 50(51), like many of the psalms and like many passages in the Prophets, seems to condemn the offering of sacrifice to God. The psalmist says to God:

> In sacrifice you take no delight,
> burnt offering from me you would refuse.

Instead, the psalm seems to suggest what true sacrifice is – namely,

> A contrite spirit,
> a humbled, contrite heart.

As we have seen, however, this is Hebrew idiom for saying that sacrifice in itself does not please God, unless it is accompanied by interior dispositions like humility and repentance.

The same teaching is found in Psalm 49(50), where God is presented as pronouncing judgement on his people:

> I find no fault with your sacrifices,
> your offerings are always before me.
> I do not ask more bullocks from your farms,
> nor goats from among your herds.

Instead, God invites his people:

> Pay your sacrifice of thanksgiving to God
> and render him your votive offerings. (Ps 49(50):8-9, 14)

God asks them to remember his commandments, not as a list to be recited, but as a solemn agreement to be honoured. He asks them to remember his covenant, not as a story to be repeated but as a reality to be lived.

Psalm 31(32), another plea for forgiveness, was the favourite psalm of St Augustine. It speaks of the heavy-heartedness of a man whose sin is unconfessed, and of the joy of confessing one's sin to the Lord and being forgiven by him.

> Happy the man whose offence is forgiven,
> whose sin is remitted.
> O happy the man to whom the Lord
> imputes no guilt,
> in whose spirit is no guile. (Ps 31(32):1-2)

Psalm 25(26) is the prayer of one who strives to live in full awareness of God's love and to 'walk according to God's truth'. The psalmist declares:

> O Lord, I love the house where you dwell,
> the place where your glory abides ...
> I will bless the Lord in the assembly. (Ps 25(26):8, 12)

It is a psalm which expresses longing to be in God's house, in his presence, praising him along with God's people gathered there.

Psalm 15(16), an affirmation of trust in God and of delight at being called to God's service, is often invoked as a prayer of priestly or religious vocation:

> O Lord, it is you who are my portion and my cup,
> it is you yourself who are my prize. ...
> You will not leave my soul among the dead
> nor let your beloved know decay.

The words are quoted by St Peter in the Acts of the Apostles, in reference to the resurrection of Christ (2:25-32, 13:36-37). They are also sometimes quoted in reference to the Assumption of the Blessed Virgin Mary into heaven. They are re-echoed in Psalm 16(17):

> As for me, in my justice I shall see your face,
> and be filled when I awake
> with the sight of your glory. (Ps 16(17):15)

Frank O'Connor, in *An Only Child,* quoted these words in reference to the death of his mother, and called them the most beautiful words in the Bible.

Psalm 8(9) is a wonderful hymn of praise of God, Creator of the universe and Creator of human beings, whom he appointed stewards of the cosmos. It is striking that, when the Apollo spacecraft carried its crew to the moon to take the 'great step for mankind' which was the landing on the moon, the astronauts brought with them messages from the world leaders of the time, including Pope Paul VI. The Pope chose Psalm 8(9) as his message; and a disc of indestructible metal, inscribed with the words of the psalm, is embedded on the moon's surface: 'O

Lord, our God, how wonderful is your name over all the earth.'
(Ps 8(9):9)

Similar in theme is Psalm 18(19), which begins:

> The heavens proclaim the glory of God
> and the firmament shows forth
> the work of his hand.

Archbishop Robinson, Anglican Archbishop of Armagh, chose
these words as the inscription carved on his telescope at the
Observatory which he founded in Armagh. Both of these psalms
can be linked with the theme of the cosmic Eucharist, of which I
treat on pp. 211–15.

Psalm 33(34) has a special link with Ireland. It was the psalm
which St Colm Cille was copying when death overtook him in his
monastery on the island of Iona. He had reached verse 11 of the
psalm when he had to hand over his pen to another monk, saying:
'Here at the end of the page I must stop. Let Baithene write what
follows.' The last lines Colm Cille himself copied were: 'Those
who seek the Lord lack no blessing' (Ps 33(34):10) Some verses
earlier, Colm Cille had copied the lines:

> Look towards [God] and be radiant ...
> this poor man called, the Lord heard him
> and rescued him from all his distress ...
> Taste and see that the Lord is good ... (Ps 33(34):5-6)

The manuscript Colm Cille was writing is called the *Cathac*: it is the
oldest Irish illuminated manuscript. It was kept in a special shrine,
consisting of a metal box with a gilt silver panel in the centre of its
side. The manuscript consisted of the entire Psalter as translated by
St Jerome in the Latin Vulgate. It was venerated as a relic and
custody of it became disputed between various families. Eventually
and sadly – so tradition or legend tells us – the manuscript and its
shrine became the centre of a battle, the battle of Cul Debene, which

was won 'through the prayers of Colm Cille'. In repentance for his part in this blood-letting – so the tradition continues – Colm Cille left his native land and went as a pilgrim monk to Iona. The *'tituli'* or 'titles' given to the psalm in the *Cathac* show traces of Alexandrian and Greek influence, suggesting a relationship between the sixth-century Church in Ireland and the Greek and Coptic churches.[55] The manuscript also indicates the love of the psalms which was present already in the sixth-century Irish Church, as well as the close links between that Church and the Christian Churches across the whole of mainland Europe.

It is a recurring theme in the psalms that sacrifice of animals is not what God wants, but rather delight in keeping God's law. We find this in Psalm 39(40):

> You do not ask for sacrifice and offerings
> but an open ear.
> You do not ask for holocaust and victim
> instead here am I.
>
> In the scroll of the book it stands written
> that I should do your will.
> My God, I delight in your law
> in the depth of my heart. (Ps 39(40):6-8)

I have already argued that scriptural passages like this do not necessarily mean rejection of the tradition of offering animal sacrifices. However, in the case of Psalm 39(40), the Letter to the Hebrews interprets these verses as meaning that the sacrifices formerly required by the Law have been abolished and are now 'quite incapable of taking sins away'. They have been replaced by Christ's 'one single sacrifice for sins', whereby he 'achieved the eternal perfection of all whom he is sanctifying' (Heb 10:1-18).

Many of the psalms are contemplative in nature and aspire to that silence and quiet and peace which are characteristic of contemplation. Romano Guardini, one of the great forerunners of the Second Vatican Council, stressed the importance of contemplation and contemplative prayer for authentic celebration of the liturgy as does Pope Benedict. The Vatican Council itself frequently recalls the necessity for contemplative prayer in the mission of the Church. Some such psalms are the prayer of Jewish exiles, living among unbelievers and longing to see Jerusalem, God's Holy City, and the Temple, God's House, the special place of his Presence. Psalms 41(42) and 42(43) express this longing:

> Like the deer that yearns for running streams,
> so my soul is yearning for you my God.
>
> My soul is thirsting for God,
> the God of my life.
> When can I enter and see
> the face of God. (Ps 41(42):1-2)
>
> O send forth your light and your truth
> let these be my guide.
> Let them bring me to your holy mountain,
> to the place where you dwell. (Ps 42(43):3)

Other psalms find rest only in God:

> In God alone is my soul at rest,
> my help comes from him.
> He alone is my rock, my stronghold,
> my fortress: I stand firm. (Ps 61(62):1-2)
>
> Oh God, you are my God,
> for you I long.
> For you my soul is thirsting.
> My body pines for you
> like a dry, weary land without water.
> So I gaze on you in the sanctuary
> to see your strength and your glory. (Ps 62(63):1-2)

The waters of a river give joy to God's city,
the holy place where the most High dwells.
God is within, it cannot be shaken.

Be still and know that I am God,
supreme among the nations,
supreme upon the earth. (Ps 45(46):4-5, 10-11)

O that I had wings like a dove
to fly away and be at rest.
So I would escape far away and take refuge in the desert.
(Ps 54(55):6-7)

When I fear, I will trust in you.
In God whose word I praise,
in God I trust, I shall not fear,
what can mortal man do to me? (Ps 55(56): 3-4)

Have mercy on me God, have mercy,
for in you my soul has taken refuge.
In the shadow of your wings I take refuge,
till the storms of destruction pass by. (Ps 56(57):1)

A group of psalms called 'Pilgrimage Songs', sung and prayed by Jews living far from Jerusalem or living in exile but now on pilgrimage to Jerusalem, express this passionate desire to be near to God in his holy 'house'. These are Psalms 119(120) to 133(134). Psalm 125(126), sung by returned exiles, speaks of their return to Jerusalem as 'like a dream', when those who 'sowed in tears sang when they reaped'. Israel's age-old longing is expressed: 'May you see your children's children in a happy Jerusalem.' (Ps 127(128))

Another of these psalms longs for silence and peace in the embrace of God, like the peace of a weaned child on its mother's breast:

> Truly I have set my soul
> in silence and peace.
> A weaned child on its mother's breast,
> even so is my soul. (Ps 130(131):2)

Elsewhere in the Psalter the psalmist expresses his envy of the sparrow or the swallow, which are allowed to build the nest for their young close to God's altar in the Temple – a closeness which the Jew in pilgrimage hopes soon to share:

> My soul is longing and yearning, is yearning for the courts of the Lord. (Ps 83(84):2)

The growing secularism in our society can make Christians feel at some moments as if they were exiles of faith in their own land! These psalms can well express our feelings at such moments, indeed our feelings at any time in the midst of the stresses and the pressures of modern life.

The psalmist expresses a certain envy of the priests who live in the Temple and whose lives are spent in the service of God in his holy Temple. He encourages them to 'bless the Lord through the night'. In turn, the priest calls down the Lord's blessing on the psalmist: 'May the Lord bless you from Sion.' (Ps 133(134))

The psalmist's great desire would be to spend his life in God's presence in the Temple:

> One day within your courts
> is better than a thousand elsewhere.
> The threshold of the House of God
> I prefer to the dwellings of the wicked. (Ps 83(84):10)

The Psalter has psalms for all times and seasons, all sorts and conditions of men and women, all varieties of human experience. The joys of old age are expressed, as well as the energies and enthusiasms of youth. Psalms 70(71) and 91(92) are prayers of old people or of people anxious to prepare well for a fruitful old age:

> It is you Lord who are my hope,
> my trust, Lord, since my youth.
> On you I have leaned from my birth,
> from my mother's womb, you have been my help.
> My hope has always been in you. (Ps 70(71):5-6)

> Do not reject me now that I am old,
> when my strength fails do not forsake me. (Ps 70(71):9)

> O God, you have taught me from my youth,
> and I proclaim your wonders still. (Ps 70(71):17)

St Thérèse of Lisieux loved this psalm, and particularly this last verse, which vibrated with her own life experience. She prayed with great fervour the line: 'When my strength fails do not forsake me.' (Ps 70(71):9) With her, we too can pray: 'You have taught me from my youth' – through your Word; 'I proclaim your wonders still' – through the Eucharist. The older among us can pray:

> Now that I am old and grey headed,
> do not forsake me, God.
> Let me tell of your power to all ages,
> praise your strength and goodness to the skies,
> tell of you who have worked such wonders,
> O God, who is like you? (Ps 70(71):1-9)

Psalm 91(92) opens on a note of joyful praise: indeed, music and song might better serve the psalmist's mood:

> It is good to give thanks to the Lord,
> to make music to your name, O Most High,
> to proclaim your love in the morning
> and your truth in the watches of the night,

on the ten-stringed lyre and the lute,
with the murmuring sound of the harp. (Ps 91(92):1-3)

Your deeds, O Lord, have made me glad,
for the work of your hands I shout with joy.

Thérèse of Lisieux again made these words her own. Her translation of this last couplet read: 'Lord, you fill me with joy by everything that you do.' For those of us who are old, it is consoling to recall the final strophe of Psalm 91(92):

Planted in the house of the Lord,
they will flourish in the courts of our God,
still bearing fruit when they are old,
still full of sap, still green,
to proclaim that the Lord is just,
in him, my rock, there is no wrong. (Ps 91(92):13-15)

It is good to think that, despite grey hairs and failing strength, people can still be 'full of sap, still green', still fruit-bearing, because they can 'proclaim [God's] wonders still', and can 'tell of God [in whom] there is no wrong'. Each stage of life has its special grace and joy; the joy of old age, and its grace, is that it enables one to call both on one's faith and on one's long life – experience to proclaim to the world: 'Who is like God?'

There are, of course, moments of spiritual darkness and distress, when God seems distant or even unreal; St Thérèse knew such moments, as did Mother Teresa of Calcutta. The psalmist too knew such moments:

I have become like a pelican in the wilderness,
like an owl in desolate places,
I lie awake and I moan
like some lonely bird on a roof. (Ps 101(102):6-7)

At such moments, one can only cry out repeatedly for God's mercy; one can only express in words what one can scarcely feel in one's heart, that God in his mercy will have pity for those who fall and cannot rise without help, but lie prostrate and helpless in the dust:

> You will arise and have mercy on Zion:
> for this is the time to have mercy,
> (yes, the time appointed has come)
> for your servants love her very stones,
> are moved with pity even for her dust. (Ps 101(102):13-14)

In such moments, Thérèse of Lisieux, helpless in her wheelchair, said that she 'kept repeating what she wanted to believe'. This psalm ends:

> Long ago you founded the earth
> and the heavens are the work of your hands.
> They will perish but you will remain.

The psalm has a special resonance for me. I distinctly recall reciting it in the Divine Office on the day of my ordination to the priesthood, on 22 June 1941. Looking back, and thinking of all the changes in the world and in Ireland which have occurred since then, I realise anew today the force of the concluding words of this psalm:

> They will perish but you will remain.
> They will all wear out like a garment.
> You will change them like clothes that are changed.
> But you neither change nor have an end. (Ps 101(102):26-27)

What greater proof could we have of God's mercy and love than the daily Eucharist, which never changes, and yet is ever new.

Yet the psalmist's desire to be with God, as expressed in the pilgrimage psalms and elsewhere, is only a pale reflection of God's desire to be with us. This is powerfully expressed in Psalm 138(139):

O where can I go from your spirit,
or where can I flee from your face?
If I climb the heavens, you are there,
If I lie in the grave, you are there.

If I take the wings of the dawn
and dwell at the sea's furthest end,
even there your hand would lead me,
your right hand would hold me fast. (Ps 138(139):7-10)

As for us humans, we find our reasons for living and our human dignity in giving praise to God. The first in a series of seven psalms of praise of God which conclude the Book of Psalms says:

I will give you glory,
Oh God, my King,
I will bless your name forever. (Ps 144(145):1)

Our greatest offering of praise and thanks is the Eucharist, and this is why we pray:

The eyes of all creatures look to you
and you give them their food in due time.
You open wide your hand.
You grant the desires of all who live.

We exist in order to praise God; we find our glory in praising God. God is, in a beautiful phrase from the psalms, 'enthroned on the praises of Israel'.

Gather us from the nations
that we may thank your holy name
and make it our glory to praise you.
Blessed be the Lord, God of Israel,
forever, from age to age.
Let all the people cry out:
Amen! Amen! Alleluia! (Ps 105(106):47-48)

Psalms 104(105) and 105(106) are classical examples of Berakah – psalms of praise and thanks to God for his mighty interventions on behalf of his people throughout Israel's history.

Psalm 144(145) ends with the words:

> Let me speak the praise of the Lord,
> let all mankind bless his holy name
> forever, for ages unending. (Ps 144(145):21)

In Christian tradition, the last stanza of Psalm 144 has eucharistic overtones; recited in Latin, it used to form part of the 'Grace before meals' in seminary.

> The eyes of all creatures look to you
> and you give them their food in due time.
> You open wide your hand
> and grant the desires of all who live. (Ps 144(145):15-16)

Similar eucharistic allusions are found in Psalm 145(146):

> It is [God] who gives bread to the hungry
> the Lord who sets prisoners free. (Ps 145(146):7)

Psalm 147[56] is commonly sung as a eucharistic hymn and is associated with eucharistic processions, as at Lourdes:

> He established peace on your borders
> he feeds you with finest wheat ...
> He sends out his word to the earth ...
> He makes his word know to Jacob,
> to Israel his laws and decrees.
> He has not dealt thus with other nations;
> he has not taught them his decrees.
> Alleluia. (Ps 146(147):14, 19-20)

Psalm 149(150) has the wonderful line: 'The Lord takes delight in his people.' (Psalm 149(150):4) In Psalm 150, the last in the Psalter, the praise of God seems to mount in a great crescendo of praise leaving one breathless, until in the last line all is calm again and one quietly and peacefully prays:

> Let everything that lives and that breathes
> give praise to the Lord. (Ps 150(151):6)

The praise and thanks to God which fill the psalms are continued and infinitely surpassed in the Eucharist. I quote Eucharistic Prayer IV to illustrate this point. In this Prayer the eucharistic community prays that it may wholly become 'a living sacrifice of praise'. The Prayer began with the Preface, where the priest, in the name of the congregation, speaks of a united cosmic community of angels and human beings who join together in praising God's glory in the words of the Isaian Theophany: 'Holy, holy, holy Lord, God of power and might …' The Prayer, in the Berakah style, enumerates reasons, taken from both Old and New Testaments, for praising and thanking God. Later, the Holy Spirit is invoked, first, to change the elements of bread and wine into the Body and Blood of Christ, and, second, to change the whole community 'into the one body of Christ, a living sacrifice of praise'. Towards the end of the Prayer, the priest prays that all present may 'enter into [their] heavenly inheritance' and that then, 'in your Kingdom, freed from the corruption of sin and death, [they may] sing your glory with every creature through Christ, our Lord, through whom you give us everything that is good'.

In the Eucharist, we do not depend on our own merits to give God perfect praise; we are offering Christ's 'holy and perfect sacrifice, the bread of life and the cup of eternal salvation' (Eucharistic Prayer I). This is why, in spite of our own sinfulness, we can confidently end each Eucharistic Prayer with the words:

> Through [Christ], with him, in him, in the unity of the Holy Spirit, all glory and honour is yours, Almighty Father, for ever and ever, Amen.

PART II

NEW TESTAMENT: EUCHARIST UNVEILED

New Testament

The Eucharist has been at the heart of the Christian community ever since the death and resurrection of Jesus Christ. One of the earliest groups of Christian martyrs, the martyrs of Abilène, were put to death in the second Christian century for their faith in Christ. Abilène is near Carthage in North Africa, and this Province of the then Roman Empire was, in the early centuries of Christian history, one of the most thriving regions of the Catholic Church. The martyrs, fifty in number, were arrested after the celebration of the Eucharist. They were interrogated as to whether they had shared in eucharistic worship and why they had done so. Their leader and spokesperson declared on behalf of all: 'Without the Eucharist we cannot live.' Another speaker added: 'How could a Christian live without the Eucharist, how could the Eucharist be celebrated without Christians?' Addressing the judge, he continued: 'Do you not know that Christians make the Eucharist and the Eucharist makes Christians and neither of these can exist without the other?'[57]

One is reminded of the words of Augustine Birrell, a former British Chief Secretary in Ireland who said: 'Between Dublin [and the capital cities of neighbouring countries] it is the Mass that matters.' His words may be less justified now than they were a century ago; but they are still true of a very large number of Irish people, at home and abroad.

Just as the Old Testament cannot be understood in its fullness of meaning without the New Testament, so the New Testament itself often reveals its full meaning only by the light of the Old Testament. This is true of the doctrine of the Eucharist. For example, the Sapiential themes of the Wedding Feast and the Messianic Feast in the Old Testament form the background to the many references in the gospels to a feast in celebration of a wedding or some other joyful event. The wedding feast at Cana is a case in point. The Sapiental and Messianic feasts or banquets are recalled in the meals eaten publicly by Jesus with notorious sinners, to the great scandal of the Pharisees and of many bystanders. The Messianic Banquet, celebrating the great return of God's people and the final accomplishment of the covenant, included the forgiveness of sins; and this was the symbolism also of Jesus' eating with sinners.[58] Jesus speaks of those who will come from east and west to take their places with Abraham and Isaac and Jacob at the feast in the kingdom of heaven (Mt 8:11-12). St Paul tells us that in the Eucharist we are 'proclaiming the death [of Christ] until he comes' (1 Cor 11:27); and this death was freely accepted by Christ 'for the forgiveness of sins' (Mt 26:28).

One of the parables of the Kingdom of God compares it to a king's feast for his son's wedding. Those on the invitation list make excuses and do not come. Finally, all are invited to come to the wedding. One, however, fails to wear the wedding garment and he is excluded; for 'many are called but few are chosen' (Mt 22:2-14). This image recurs in the Book of Revelation, where we read: 'Happy are those who are called to the wedding feast of the lamb.' (Rev 19:9) The image is recalled in our eucharistic liturgy, when the priest says at the communion: 'Happy are those who are called to his supper' – although the present banal translation almost obliterates the original biblical meaning.[59]

There are allusions to the Messianic Banquet also in the parable of the servants served at table by their master and in the parable of the ten virgins (Mt 25:1-13). Jesus certainly intended the Eucharist to be a foretaste of the great universal feast to which he would invite all his people, in celebration of the final coming of God's kingdom. Thus the Eucharist would be a sign of redemption, of reconciliation and of forgiveness, of resurrection and of a consummation of the covenant, a pledge of unity with God in Christ and an anticipation of eternal joy.

The Words of Institution

It seems appropriate to begin these reflections on the Eucharist in the New Testament by studying the words Jesus used at the institution of the Eucharist, which have been repeated in its celebration across two millennia from the death of Jesus until the present day. Correct understanding of these words is obviously vital for our understanding of the Eucharist. Among the most exhaustive and authoritative studies of the words is that of Joachim Jeremias, the German Lutheran, in his book, *The Eucharistic Words of Jesus*.[60] The words are quoted with minor variations in each of the three Synoptic Gospels, Matthew, Mark and Luke, and also by St Paul in his first Letter to the Corinthians. A table setting the phrases of the different accounts in parallel lines is provided by Jeremias, and I have adapted his table, using the Jerusalem Bible translation. The adapted version is printed on the next page. The juxtaposition helps us to identify the similarities between the four accounts of the institution of the Eucharist, as well as to note the differences. The agreement between the four narratives is striking and this has importance for both the accuracy of the words as reported and for the historicity of the events described.

I begin with the historicity.[61] The earliest in date of the four reports is that of St Paul in his first letter to the Corinthians. The context is that of abuses in the celebration of the Eucharist which had crept in among the Church community in Corinth and which St Paul feels obliged to correct. Some were using the occasion to divide the community into separate factions and some to eat and drink to excess while others went hungry. Such behaviour, St Paul insists, is a failure in respect for the community; it is also 'behaving unworthily towards the body and blood of the Lord'.

The first letter to the Corinthians is reliably dated to the spring of the year AD 54. Paul speaks of his teaching about the Eucharist as being the same teaching that he had earlier proclaimed to them by word of mouth. This would have been at the time of his missionary work in Corinth, in the autumn of AD 49, some twenty years after the crucifixion of Jesus. Paul claims that his teaching is what he himself had received directly 'through a revelation of Jesus Christ' (Gal 1:12). This is most probably a reference to Paul's encounter with the Risen Lord near the gates of Damascus;

The Words of Institution of the Eucharist

1 Corinthians 11:23-25	Luke 22:19-20	Mark 14:22-24	Matthew 26:26-28
The Lord Jesus took some bread,	Then he took some bread	and as they were eating he took some bread,	as they were eating Jesus took some bread,
and thanked God for it,	and when he had given thanks,	and when he had said the blessing	and when he had said the blessing
and broke it, and he said;	broke it and gave it to them, saying	he broke it and gave it to them.	he broke it and gave it to the disciples.
'This is my body which is for you.	'This is my body which will be given for you;	'Take it,' he said 'this is my body.'	'Take it and eat,' he said; this is my body.'
do this as a memorial of me.'	do this as a memorial of me.'		
In the same way he took the cup after supper and said:	He did the same with the cup after supper and said:	Then he took a cup, and when he had returned thanks he gave it to them and all drank from it and he said to them:	Then he took a cup and when he had returned thanks he gave it to them.
'This cup is the new covenant in my blood. Whenever you drink it, do this as a memorial of me.	'This cup is the new covenant in my blood, which will be poured out for you.'	'This is my blood, the blood of the covenant, which is to be poured out for many.'	'Drink, all of you, from this,' he said, 'for this is my blood, the blood of the covenant, which is to be poured out for many for the forgiveness of sins.'
Until the Lord comes, therefore, every time you eat this bread and drink this cup, you are proclaiming his death.'			

and this has been reliably dated to the year AD 33, three years after the crucifixion of Jesus, which is usually dated to the year AD 30. Three years after his conversion, that is to say, some six years after the crucifixion, Paul visited Jerusalem and met Cephas and spent two weeks in his company. Fourteen years later, Paul went to Jerusalem again. This time, he met the 'leading men' of the Church[62] and laid before them the Good News as he (Paul) proclaimed it. These leaders fully approved of Paul's mission and endorsed his preaching of the Good News as Paul had received it directly from the Risen Lord.[63]

After minute study of the Words of Institution, Jeremias notes that, in the relevant passages, there occur 'peculiarities which present the most distinctive characteristics of Jesus' manner of speaking'; for example: 'Amen, Amen, I say to you', which, Jeremias says, is 'without parallel in entire Jewish literature and in the New Testament outside the gospels'. He declares that he finds this fact 'astonishing'.[64] He points out that St Paul's wording is close to that of St Luke. At the same time, on the basis of traces of Semitic language which he finds in Mark and Luke and also in St John's account of the washing of the feet, Jeremias concludes that 'the chain of tradition goes back unbroken to Jesus himself'.[65]

The significance of all this for the unending debate on the historical reliability of the gospels, and of the Christian faith in general, is profound. The eucharistic words of Jesus contain in concentrated form the central doctrines of the Christian faith: namely belief in the Godhead of Jesus Christ, the atoning and saving character of the death of Jesus, the forgiveness of sins. Only God can make a covenant with mankind. God made the original covenant with the Jewish people on Mount Sinai, amid great and awesome signs and wonders of divine majesty and power. Only God could change this into a new covenant with the whole of mankind, and Jesus did this at the Last Supper, saying: 'This cup is the new covenant in my blood.' Jesus was thereby implicitly claiming to be God, and the claim historically goes right back to Jesus himself.

Only God can forgive sins. Jesus brings about the forgiveness of all the sins of all mankind by his death on the Cross, saying at the Last Supper: 'This is my blood which is to be poured out for all.'[66] These words go right back to Jesus himself. Jesus died for our sins. He said at the Last Supper:

> This is my body, given up for you.

The words go right back to Jesus himself. Jesus said at the Last Supper:

> Do this in memory of me.

The words are an indication that his followers are to continue as a communion of saints or Church, perpetually remembering and celebrating the death and resurrection of Jesus and the forgiveness of sins. All of this is repeated substantially in our Apostles' Creed. The words of our Creed, therefore, have their authority from the historical Jesus Christ himself.

The gospels tell us that Jesus once, 'filled with joy by the Holy Spirit', said:

> I bless you, Father, Lord of Heaven and of earth, for hiding these things from the learned and the clever and revealing them to mere children. Yes, Father, for that is what it pleased you to do. Everything has been entrusted to me by my Father; and no-one knows who the Son is except the Father, and who the Father is except the Son, and those to whom the Son chooses to reveal him. (Lk 10:21-22)

When we say our Creed, we are not simply repeating what our parents and our teachers and our priests taught us. We are repeating what Jesus himself has revealed to us. We have the privilege of being able to apply to ourselves the words that Jesus spoke to the disciples as he sat in a boat near the lakeside in Galilee:

> Happy are your eyes because they see, your ears because they hear! I tell you solemnly, many prophets and holy men longed to see what you see, and never saw it; to hear what you hear, and never heard it.

Karl Barth once said that preachers should no longer tell people: 'You are bound to believe …', but rather: 'You are allowed to believe … You are privileged to believe.' Since there is convincing evidence that the words of the institution of the Eucharist go back in essence to Jesus himself, then we must surely conclude that, contrary to some modern theories, the essential message of the gospels goes back to Jesus himself.

All of the four accounts of the words of the institution of the Eucharist agree in having Jesus refer to the new covenant. Paul and Luke are in complete agreement about the words spoken by Jesus over the cup: 'This cup is the new covenant in my blood.'

Mark and Matthew also share a common formula for the words over the cup, though in a slightly different form: 'This is my blood, the blood of the covenant.' Mark and Matthew add the words: 'which will be poured out for many', Matthew further adding: 'for the forgiveness of sins.' The Hebrew word 'many', as we have noted, is regularly used as a synonym for 'all'. Luke uses the words, 'for you'. St Paul alone adds the words: 'Whenever you drink [this cup] do this a memorial of me.'

Peculiar to St Paul also are the words: 'Until the Lord comes, therefore, every time you eat this bread and drink this cup you are proclaiming his death.'

The Words of Institution, which Jeremias calls 'the eucharistic words', and which we now call the 'words of consecration', appear in the Roman Missal in the form:

> Take this, all of you, and eat it:
> this is my body which will be given up for you.
> Take this all of you and drink from it:

> this is the cup of my blood,
> the blood of the new and everlasting covenant.
> It will be shed for you and for all
> so that sins may be forgiven:
> Do this in memory of me.

The term 'covenant' is central to the meaning of the Eucharist. Following the covenant God established with Noah, a 'covenant between [God] and the earth' (Gen 9), God entered into another and still more solemn and specific covenant with Abraham and his descendants, the people of Israel, 'a covenant in perpetuity' (Gen 17). This covenant was solemnised amid great signs and wonders on Mount Sinai, where Moses spoke with God and God with him. Sacrifice was offered to God to ratify this covenant. Moses took up in two basins half of the blood of the sacrificed animals; he cast half of the blood on the altar and the other he cast towards the people, saying: 'This is the blood of the covenant that the Lord has made with you.' (Ex 24:8)

These words are substantially the same as those spoken by Jesus at the institution of the Eucharist, the sacrifice of the new covenant. As we have seen earlier, blood in the Old Testament is a synonym for life and the rite of sprinkling of blood is a sign of the sharing of life between God and his people, Israel. Much of the Old Testament is taken up with the history of the covenant, marked on Israel's side with repeated infidelities and betrayals of the covenant, and on God's side with fidelity, mercy and forgiveness and repeated renewal of the covenant.

Another element enters this history with God's promise, through the prophets, of a new covenant, a covenant 'written on the hearts' of God's people (Jer 31:33), a covenant of peace, whereby God will be a 'true shepherd' to his people (Ezk 34:11). Hosea used the language of marriage, promising reconciliation of God with his unfaithful wife, Israel, in a renewed union. This new covenant is a covenant between God, whose essence is mercy and forgiveness, and his people:

Ephraim, how can I part with you,
Israel, how could I give you up? ...
My heart recoils from it,
my whole being trembles at the thought. ...
for I am God, not man,
I am the Holy One in your midst,
and have no wish to destroy. (Hos 11:8-9)

We must note also that the three synoptic gospels place the institution of the Eucharist on the Jewish feast of Passover, and specifically they place it within the context of the Passover Meal which was special to this feast. Christians know the occasion as the 'Last Supper' of Our Lord, Jesus Christ. Jeremias presents a series of powerful arguments to back up the 'definite conclusion' that the Last Supper was in fact a Passover meal.[67] St John, in his gospel, while dating the Last Supper to the day before the Passover, nevertheless sets the meal in a Passover context: he identifies Jesus as the True Paschal Lamb, of whom it had been prophesised, 'not one bone of his will be broken' (Ps 33(34):20; Ex 12:46). St John gives a timing for the Crucifixion of Jesus which coincides with the time laid down for the ritual slaughter of the lambs which were to supply the main meal for the Passover feast.

It is important to note, however, that the liturgical tradition of the Eucharist was never seen as a perpetuation of the Passover ritual. The synoptic linkage of the eucharistic meal with the Passover is, therefore, the recording of an historical fact rather than being deduced from subsequent Christian liturgical practice.[68] The accounts of the institution of the Eucharist given both in the Synoptic Gospels and in St Paul agree in reporting the Lord's commandment, 'Do this in memory of me'. Taking this along with the injunction quoted by St Paul to 'proclaim the death of the Lord', we know that, in the breaking of the bread and in the cup, we are remembering particularly Christ's death. This is symbolised by the broken bread and by the separation of the bread and the cup. But what we are really proclaiming is not Christ's death alone but his death and his resurrection and ascension into heaven. This remembering and recalling and proclaiming are to mark a new period of history, the history of Christ's glory, his 'sitting at the right hand of the Father'. This period begins with Christ's resurrection and will be made fully manifest at the End-time, when Christ comes again in glory.

This eschatological longing and expectation are included in every celebration of the Eucharist. It was a feature of every Passover Meal that the head of the 'Seder' or Passover gathering would be asked by the youngest participant to explain the meaning of the various elements of the meal which were peculiar to this particular feast: the guests reclining, rather than sitting; the bitter herbs; the unleavened bread. These questions required an answer, and the answer was a prescribed part of the Passover ritual. The so-called 'words of interpretation', which answered these questions, were spoken before and after the main course of the Passover meal. They are not reported as such in the gospels or in St Paul's writings. We can, however, see the eucharistic discourse of John 6 as being perhaps an expanded interpretation of the eucharistic meal by Christ himself. The language of John 6 is certainly remarkably close to that of the words of institution of the Eucharist. As Jeremias points out, 'all the witnesses [Paul, Luke, Mark, Matthew and John], transmit the sentence: "this is my body/my flesh"'. Common to all of them also, except John, are the words: 'this [wine] is my blood of the covenant' – which Jeremias translates as: 'my blood [shed for the concluding] of the covenant.'[69]

Jeremias, in his very thorough study of the Eucharistic Words of Jesus, gives convincing evidence for two other conclusions which are relevant to the present study. First of all, he shows that Jesus himself did not partake of the Passover meal proper (i.e. the paschal lamb) but fasted. His words are usually translated as: 'I have longed to eat this Passover with you before my death'; but Jeremias demonstrates that Luke's use of the relevant infinitive denotes an 'unfulfilled wish' and the proper translation would be: 'I would very gladly have eaten this Passover with you before my death.' The implication is that he is not going to eat it. Jesus explains his abstinence as follows: 'I shall not eat it until it is fulfilled in the Kingdom of God.' When passing round the Cup, Jesus says the following words, unusual for a Passover meal: 'Take this and divide it among yourselves.' This seems to indicate that Jesus himself did not partake of the Cup. Furthermore, as the Cup was being passed around, Jesus said: 'From now on I shall not drink of the fruit of the vine until the Kingdom of God comes.'

The abstinence of Jesus would seem to have two motives: first, it is an act of mourning and sorrow and atonement for sin; second, it is an intensification of Jesus' prayer that God hasten the day of his inauguration of the Kingdom of Salvation. This abstinence later took the form of fasting before the Eucharist, a practice still required of communicants, though of shorter duration now than formerly. This two-fold longing is expressed in Eucharistic Prayer IV:

> Father, in your mercy,
> grant also to us, your children,
> to enter into our heavenly inheritance
> in the company of the Virgin Mary
> … and your apostles and saints.
> Then, in your Kingdom,
> freed from the corruption of sin and death,
> we shall sing your glory
> with every creature through Christ our Lord,
> through whom you give us
> everything that is good.

The abstinence of Jesus introduces into the Passover of Christians, and into the Eucharist, a two-fold element of reparation of sin and of eschatological longing for the eventual overcoming of sin and the final achievement of God's gift of eternal life.[70]

Finally, Jeremias sheds an important new light on the words of Jesus, 'Do this in memory of me'. These words are usually understood as an injunction given by Jesus to his disciples; and this is certainly part of Jesus' meaning. The faithful celebration of the

Eucharist over 2,000 years in memory of the saving death of Jesus is the Church's response to this mandate. But there is an added meaning: 'In memory of me' means also 'that God may remember me'. Jesus offers himself in death to God the Father and we offer his self-offering to the Father so that God, in view of his Son's self-offering, may hasten the coming of God's kingdom, when, as we pray in Eucharistic Prayer II:

> [Christ] will raise our mortal bodies and make them like his own in glory ... There we hope to share in [God's] glory when every tear will be wiped away. On that day we shall see you, our God, as you are, we shall become like you and praise you for ever through Jesus Christ our Lord, from whom all good things come.

The Feast for the Prodigal Son

The parables of Jesus frequently include a reference to a wedding feast or to a feast celebrating some other joyful occurrence. Notable among these is the parable of the Prodigal Son (Lk 15:11-32). The younger son in this parable has all the marks of a rebellious and spoiled and self-centred young person, who insists on going his own independent way, no matter whom it hurts. He demands his 'share of the estate' (one third of the value of the father's property) and goes off to 'get a life' for himself. But his money is soon squandered on the usual excesses, ('He and his women,' growls the elder son!). The young man's lifestyle had gradually alienated him from home and family and from his religion and his immediate faith community.

This alienation is eloquently expressed in the description of how this well-bred young man is reduced to feeding pigs – animals which were 'unclean' in Jewish eyes. The job of feeding them, the reference to his being willing to eat even the husks left behind by the pigs, were indications of the low level to which this young Jew had sunk. The young man begins to reflect on his condition and to realise the disgrace and the degradation of his present life. He begins to feel sorry for himself and decides to return to his father and seek reconciliation. He is now prepared to work, no longer as a son but as a slave, on his father's farm. But the father had missed his young son sorely and longed for his homecoming. The old man of the parable had repeatedly scanned the horizon in hope of seeing his boy trudging home. A day comes at last when he does see his son in the distance. The father runs to meet him – an undignified thing for a respectable senior citizen to do in that culture.[71] He 'clasped him in his arms and kissed him tenderly'. He called for the best ceremonial robe to be brought and put it on the young man, put a ring on his finger and sandals on his feet – all these being signs of special honour and dignity, reserved for distinguished guests, but now conferred on this wayward and worthless son. The father called for the fatted calf that they had been preparing for a special family occasion: 'We are going to have a feast, a celebration,' he said, 'because this son of mine was dead and has come back to life, he was lost and he is found.'

The whole parable has undeniable eucharistic allusions. It illustrates God's merciful love, even, perhaps especially, for the most undeserving. It hints at the connection between penitence and reconciliation and the Eucharist. It encourages sinners – which we all are – to seek reconciliation with God before sharing 'the feast, the celebration' of the Eucharist with him. The parable reminds us that God always takes the initiative in reconciliation; he always loves us first. The parable illustrates perfectly one of the most beautiful of the Collects of the Roman Missal, which addresses God as the One 'who manifests his almighty power most of all by sparing and by showing mercy'.[72]

The Multiplication of Loaves

The first formal teaching given by Jesus about the Eucharist, which he was later to institute, was given in signs and in words by his miracle of the multiplication of loaves. This miracle has an important place in the life and teaching of Jesus, and it is reported, with minor variations, in each of the four gospels.[73] Indeed, Mark and Matthew report two such miracles, distinguished by minor differences of detail.[74]

The relation of the miracle to the Eucharist is hinted at in various ways in all of these accounts. In Luke's version, we read of how Jesus:

> ... took the five loaves and the two fish,[75] raised his eyes to heaven and said the blessing over them, then he handed them to the disciples to distribute among the crowd.

The similarity of these actions and words of Jesus to his words and actions at the Last Supper cannot be accidental.

There are similarities also with the eucharistic discourse in St John's gospel, to which I return on pp. 150–60 In both the Johannine discourse and in all the accounts of the miracle of the loaves we find reminiscences of the manna given by God to his people in the desert and hints that Jesus is repeating that miracle still more powerfully and is not just equal to Moses but is incomparably greater; he is indeed the very Son of God.

The parallel with Moses is implied in all the accounts of the miracle of the loaves. The place where the miracle of the loaves is performed is a 'lonely place', a desert place, recalling the desert through which the people of God wandered for forty years. The crowd are arranged there in 'squares of hundreds and fifties' like the people of God whom Moses led.[76] The crowd whom Jesus miraculously fed 'all ate as much as they wanted', just as, in the case of the manna, each one could gather 'only as much as was needed' for one day.[77] The scraps of bread and pieces of fish left over filled twelve baskets, recalling the twelve tribes who formed the people fed by the manna from heaven in the desert.

Another important feature of the loaves narrative is often overlooked, namely the context in which the miracle is inserted by the gospel writers. The account in Matthew situates the miracle in a context 'framed' on one side by the beheading of John the Baptist and on the other by the Transfiguration of Jesus. This pattern corresponds broadly with the narratives of Mark and Luke. This segment of Matthew's gospel is sometimes called 'the Section on the Loaves'. It is marked all through by the emphasis Jesus places upon his mission of teaching: notably the need for faith in his teaching and in his person, the affirmation of this faith by Peter, who is spokesperson for all the believers, and the attestation by God at the Transfiguration of the divine identity of Jesus and of his teaching. We need to look at each of these features of the loaves narrative.

Mark tells us that, after Jesus arrived at the place of the miracle and saw the large crowd which had followed them, he 'took pity on them because they were like sheep without a shepherd', and he 'set himself to teach them at some length'. We recall that, in the Old Testament, the shepherd is seen as one who feeds his sheep in rich pastures and protects them from false shepherds who allow them to stray. Mark continues with the account of how Jesus made the disciples get into the boat in which they had crossed and go over to Bethsaida where he dismissed the disciples. Then Jesus went into the hills alone to pray. A strong contrary wind blew up and the disciples became increasingly aware of how distant from Jesus they were in this time of danger; for they were now far out on the lake and he was alone on the land. About the fourth watch in the night – a time when in a stormy sea panic can set in even for hardened seafarers – Jesus came towards them walking on the lake. They were terrified. Jesus said: 'Courage. It is I. Do not be afraid.' The words, 'It is I', could be understood in a banal sense as saying merely, 'I am here; don't be afraid'. But the disciples could scarcely have failed to recognise the words[78] as the same words spoken by God to Moses when Moses asked for his name: 'I am who I am. This is what you must say to the sons of Israel: "I am" has sent me to you ...' (Ex 3:14) Jesus is saying on his own behalf what God said to Moses: 'I am.' This can stand as an implicit statement by Jesus himself of his divine nature.

The words 'Do not be afraid' run like a refrain throughout the Old Testament, coming from the lips of God as his characteristic words of reassurance to his people. Even the disciples, however, were slow to understand and slow to believe. They still could not see the real significance of the miracle of the loaves, namely that the bread which is Jesus himself and his teaching is more important than material food. In another boat at a later time the disciples had forgotten to take food with them and had only one loaf on board. Naturally, they were upset and anxious. But Jesus rebuked them for having no perception. He said to them: 'Are your minds closed? Have you eyes that do not see, ears that do not hear. Or do you not remember?'(Mk 8:18)[79]

Jesus then reminded them of the two miracles of the loaves and asked them: 'are you still without perception?' (Mk 8:29) He is reminding them that faith in his person, faith in who he is and in his teaching, is essential if one is to understand the meaning of the loaves – and, as he will make clear later, essential if one is to understand the meaning of the Eucharist which the loaves foretell. The cure of a blind man at Bethsaida, which follows in the gospel of Mark, is a further indication to the disciples that lack of faith is a form of blindness and that only Jesus can bring the light of faith to the spiritually blind (Mk 8:22-26). The same is true of the cure of a deaf man, which is reported in the section on the loaves in Mark (Mk 7:31-37). Lack of faith is a form of spiritual deafness and only Jesus can bring the gift of faith which enables the spiritually deaf to hear his words.

Just after this, in the gospels of Mark and Luke, Jesus returns to the question of faith more directly when he asks the disciples: 'Who do people say that I am?' The disciples reply in terms of what various contemporary schools of thought were saying about him – more or less as some people might answer the same question today in terms of various modern theories of Christology. But this is not what Jesus wants to hear. He wants our personal faith and not just academic debate. He insists: 'But you, who do *you* say that I am?' There follows Peter's great confession of faith on behalf of all the disciples:

'You are the Christ.' (Mk 8:30) This is the heart of Mark's gospel, as it is the heart of Christian faith. Peter, however, has much to learn yet about true faith in Christ; he still has to learn what St Paul calls the language of the Cross.

The Transfiguration

Jesus prepares Peter for his lessons in the language of the Cross by the Transfiguration. Peter and James and John are invited by Jesus to accompany him in climbing a high mountain, where they would be alone. Luke, evangelist par excellence of prayer, characteristically tells us that they went there in order to pray (Lk 9:28-30).[80] As Jesus prayed,

> the aspect of his face was changed and his garments became brilliant as lightning, dazzlingly white, brighter than any earthly bleacher could make them.

Suddenly, two figures appeared, talking with Jesus. They were Moses and Elijah, and they were 'speaking of his passing[81] which he was to accomplish in Jerusalem'. Thus two of the greatest authorities in the whole history of Israel come to authenticate the person and the teaching of Jesus. They represent respectively the Law and the Prophets, the two great expressions of the covenant and of the way of life of a covenant people. Above all, they come to give their sanction to a new Exodus, and to a new covenant which Jesus is to accomplish. Finally, the Lord, God the Father, speaks: 'This is my Son, the Beloved, the chosen One, listen to him.'

As at the baptism of Jesus in the Jordan, God himself attests that Jesus is his Son and that faith in the person and the teaching of Jesus is inseparable from faith in God himself. Three times in close proximity to the account of the Transfiguration we read of Jesus' prophecies of his coming passion; in Mark, the first of these follows immediately after Peter's confession of faith in Jesus as the Christ. Peter needed the experience of the Transfiguration and of the divine attestation of Jesus' messiahship and divine sonship to enable him to reconcile the marks of suffering on the dying face of a scourged and crucified Jesus with 'the glory of God shining on the face of Christ'. Whether or not he be the author of the 'Letters of Peter' in the New Testament, it remains true that Peter never forgot in the darkness of Calvary what he had seen and heard in the light of the Transfiguration, 'when we were with him on the holy mountain', and when 'the Sublime glory itself spoke to [Jesus]' and said, 'This is my Son, the Beloved; he enjoys my favour' (2 Pet 1:17-18).

The miracle of the loaves, seen in the context in which it is situated in the gospel accounts of Matthew, Mark and Luke, points back to the manna in the desert, and points forward to the Eucharist. From our reading of the gospel accounts of the miracle of the loaves it is also clear that the miracle, with the future Eucharist to which it points, is set in the context of teaching by Christ, leading to faith in Christ. This, as we shall see on pages pp. 150–60 is made still more clear in St John's account of the same miracle of the loaves, where the miracle is followed by the great eucharistic discourse of John's sixth chapter. We recall also the Synoptic accounts of the temptation of Jesus, where Jesus quotes his heavenly Father in Deuteronomy as saying of the manna that it teaches us to understand that man does not live on bread alone but on every word that comes from the mouth of God.[82] Always, throughout the whole Bible, the Eucharist is preceded by teaching which evokes and deepens faith. The Church's liturgy is faithful to that biblical prescription, placing the liturgy of the Word before the liturgy of the Eucharist, thereby to arouse and deepen the faith of the assembly before the celebration and reception of the Eucharist.

Emmaus and the Eucharist

A remarkable lesson on the Eucharist is reported as given by Jesus Christ himself in St Luke's gospel (24:13-35). It comes after the Passion and Death of Jesus and before the news of his resurrection has spread widely among the disciples. Many of these were still suffering from the shock of his death. The reaction of the two disciples of whom we read in St Luke's gospel can be taken as typical of the feelings of the disciples at large after the cruel and humiliating death of the Lord. These two were on the road to Emmaus, seven miles from Jerusalem – perhaps on their way back to their villages and homes which they had left to follow Jesus. There was nothing in front of them now but to resume their ordinary work and lives. Jesus had been the meaning of their lives. Now that he was dead, they were broken men, disillusioned, with nothing left to live for. A stranger joined them on their way. It was Jesus, but 'something prevented them from recognising him'. Luke gives us a sample of their conversation with the Stranger. 'What were you talking about?' the Stranger asked. 'All about Jesus of Nazareth,' they replied, 'who proved he was a great prophet.' But, they continued, the chief priests and leaders of the Jews had him crucified. 'Our own hopes had been,' they went on, 'that he would be the one to set Israel free.' Their talk about Jesus now was all in the past tense: 'we had hoped ... that he would have been' ... but now ... now it is all over. He is dead and buried. The hopes of the coming Kingdom of God, hopes for a New Israel, a new covenant, a New Creation, all are dead and buried with him in his grave. There had been a story that he was alive; but some of their friends went to the tomb to see if the story could be true; 'but of him they saw nothing'.

The Stranger then spoke. He said:

> 'You foolish men. So slow to believe the full message of the prophets. Was it not ordained that the Christ should suffer and so enter into his glory?' Then, starting with Moses and going through all the prophets, he explained to them all the passages throughout the scriptures that were about himself.

Later, in further instructions to his disciples, we read that Jesus said to them: 'Everything written about me in the Law of Moses, in the Prophets and in the Psalms, has to be fulfilled.' (Lk 24:44)

As was the case with the manna and with the multiplication of the loaves, the teaching of Jesus here on the road to Emmaus is a prelude to the recognition by the disciples of who Jesus is, and to the revival of their faith in him. Their recognition of Jesus is completed and their faith in Jesus as the Christ is confirmed in the meal which follows – a meal which clearly refers to the Eucharist. They had reached Emmaus, where the two disciples intended to stay; but Jesus 'made as if to go on.' They begged him to stay with them: 'Stay with us Lord: it is nearly evening and the day is almost over': '*Mane nobiscum Domine.*' He consented; and, as he sat with them at table,

> he took the bread and said the blessing, then he broke it and handed it to them. And their eyes were opened and they recognised him. But he had vanished from their sight.

They hurried back to Jerusalem – to resume their lives with Jesus; for now they knew he was alive: 'they had recognised him at the breaking of bread.' 'The breaking of bread', *fractio panis*, was one of the terms used for the Eucharist in the earliest Church, as we find in the Acts of the Apostles.[83] This is the reason for my choice of title for this book.

The reference to the Eucharist in the words and actions of Jesus at this table in the inn at Emmaus is unmistakable. It should be noted that, as in the eucharistic discourse in St John, the meal is preceded by a teaching given by Jesus about his person, his message and his mission. In both St Luke and St John, the teaching is primarily based on the claim of Jesus that he is 'the One who was to come', as predicted in the Old Testament, and that the message of the Old Testament, veiled in the past, is now unveiled in the person of Jesus. The Eucharist is thus a two-fold eating: first, an 'eating' of God's word, revealed fully in Jesus Christ; and then an eating of that word made flesh, crucified, raised from the dead, and now become 'life-giving Spirit'. The two-part structure of the eucharistic celebration, which we now know as the liturgy of the word and the liturgy of the Eucharist, is, therefore, already adumbrated in the eucharistic teaching of Jesus himself in the New Testament and anticipated in a veiled manner in the Old Testament.

An artist friend of mine, the late Ray Carroll, did a painting of the Emmaus scene which is now incorporated as the altar-piece in the Blessed Sacrament Chapel in St Mel's Cathedral in Longford. Jesus is shown at table with the disciples. The artist depicts one of the disciples as a woman. The male disciple is following Jesus' explanation of the scriptures, turning over the pages of his Bible as he listens and questions. The woman is looking lovingly at Jesus, listening, absorbing. A girl is serving the food: she wears the Star of David. She represents the first Israel, our elder sister in the faith of Abraham. She has prepared the Bread, foreshadowed by the manna in the desert. Jesus' hand is raised and his finger points to the scene outside the window behind him. The hand casts a shadow across his face. As God does in the Old Testament, Jesus at times hides his face; something prevents us from recognising him.

But faith in Christ transforms our earthly views. The hand of Jesus is pointing, pointing towards a road which winds up a hill. It is the hill of Calvary. But the Cross is empty now. Good Friday's darkness is gone now. The sky is bright with azure blue; it is a picture of calm and quiet, peace and silent prayerfulness. The room where Jesus and the disciples sit itself radiates a sense of peace. To enter it we pass beyond parted curtains, we go down steps. It represents the quiet place of prayer in our own hearts. Jesus is there. There is no need for words; heart speaks to heart. As Gerard Manley Hopkins put it, in 'The Half-Way House':

> See, Love, I creep and Thou on wings dost ride;
> 　love, it is evening now and Thou away.
> Love, it grows darker here and Thou art above,
> 　Love come down to me if Thy name be love.
> Here yet my paradox: Love, when all is given,

To see Thee I must see Thee, to love, love;
I must o'ertake Thee at once and under heaven
   If I shall overtake Thee at last above.
You have your wish; enter these walls, one said:
   'He is with you in the breaking of the bread'.

In Ray Carroll's painting, the finger of Jesus is pointing to the way that he walked – to Calvary. He tells us: 'I walked that way for you. I am the Way, follow me. Do not be afraid, I am with you.' The finger points also to Heaven, to God, whose 'glory shines on earth' (Ps 107(108)). Jesus has gone there to prepare a place for us, and he has promised that he will come again to take us to himself, so that, where he is, we may be too, in the eternal Communion where Sacrament becomes face to face vision. Meanwhile, we wait and watch for that Day when all waiting will end in our presence to the Divine Presence. With Hopkins we can say:

Oh! Till Thou givest that sense beyond,
   to show Thee that Thou art, and near,
let patience without chastening wand
   Dispel the doubt and dry the tear;
And lead me child-like by the hand,
   If still in darkness, not in fear.

Speak! whisper to my watching heart
One word – as when a mother speaks
   Soft, when she sees her infant start,
Till dimpled joy steals o'er its cheeks.
   Then, to behold Thee as Thou art,
I'll wait till morn eternal breaks.[84]

Eucharistic Discourse in the Gospel of John

The sixth chapter of the fourth gospel begins with the account of the multiplication of the loaves. The linkage of this miracle with the

Eucharist is, as we have noted, a feature of the synoptic gospels also. It is significant that St John places this event 'shortly before the Jewish feast of Passover', thereby situating it in the context of the Passover and hinting at the new Passover of the new covenant which Jesus had come to inaugurate. The miracle was performed in the 'desert place' along the shore of the lake where Jesus often went with the disciples. The disciples are struck by the abundance of the bread miraculously provided – twelve hampers of scraps are left over after everyone had eaten their fill, although there were only five loaves and two fish to start with and the crowd which was so amply fed numbered as many as 5,000 men. The crowd began speculating about who Jesus might be and began wondering whether he might be the Messiah. Jesus left the scene quickly, fearing that the excited crowd might try to make him king. The disciples, once the Master was gone, returned to the boat to cross back to Capernaum.

They encountered rough seas and then they saw Jesus walking on the waters and coming towards their boat. They were frightened; but Jesus said to them: 'It is I. Do not be afraid.' The disciples would have recognised the opening words as identical with those spoken by God himself when he revealed his Name to Moses, and repeated often in the Old Testament. The use of these words by Jesus on this occasion increased their awe and their wonder. St John, in particular, reports Jesus as frequently using these words, particularly in the great 'I am', passages of his gospel. Indeed these words are characteristic of the Johannine Jesus.[85] Although it is characteristic of the fourth gospel, the phrase 'I am' is found also on the lips of Jesus in the synoptic gospels.[86]

The multiplication of the loaves and the mysterious acts and words of Jesus on the lake form the background to the discourse which takes place on the following day. Some of the crowd had followed Jesus across the lake to Capernaum and found him in the synagogue. Jesus rebukes them for looking only for material bread, the food that cannot last, and neglecting spiritual food, bread 'that endures to eternal life'. It is this spiritual food that Jesus has come to give them. This food is received through faith in Christ, for he is the One that God has sent. This is the true bread, the bread of life, the bread which God the Father gives, of which the manna of old was only a sign (Jn 6:27). This is the true bread that comes down from Heaven; and Jesus Christ himself is that bread: 'I am the Bread of Life,' he says. Jesus is hereby proclaiming that he is in person the true manna, of which the manna of Moses was the image:

> It was not Moses who gave you bread from heaven, it is my Father who gives you the bread from heaven the true bread, for the bread of God is that which comes down from heaven and gives life to the world. (Jn 6:32-3)

Further reflection on the words of Christ in this passage shows that Jesus himself becomes the 'Bread of Life' for us through the 'teaching of the Father', which becomes life-giving for us through faith in Christ; and the life which this bread gives is everlasting life. Only Christ, the One who 'comes from God', the One who 'has seen the Father', can be this 'bread from heaven', and only the one who believes in Christ can truly receive it. In receiving the 'bread of heaven', the believer receives eternal life. Those who ate the manna of old suffered death; but the one who eats the true bread of life, which God gives us in Christ Jesus, 'will live forever'. For the believer in Christ, death as others know it is abolished; it is transformed into life, everlasting life. To be taught by the Father is to learn about Jesus Christ; this teaching is given to us in Holy Scripture, and those who believe in Jesus Christ as revealed in Holy Scripture have eternal life. This is not a promise that they will have eternal life after they die; it is a guarantee that they have eternal life already now, because of their faith.

The bread which is Jesus Christ is received by faith in God's word; doing God's work means 'believing in the one that God has sent' (Jn 6:29). In this discourse, Jesus contrasts two kinds of seeing: one could see Jesus with one's bodily eyes and yet see only a young itinerant rabbi; because one has not the faith, one sees without *really* seeing. When one sees Jesus with eyes enlightened by faith one sees the Son of God and believes in him and thereby has eternal life.[87] The distinction between the two kinds of seeing is characteristic of John's gospel. In most instances, two different words are used for 'seeing'; often it is the Greek word *theorein* which is used for seeing with faith and the word *idein* for seeing with bodily eyes only and without faith. The former suggests a contemplative, prayerful way of seeing, which is characteristic of a person of faith.

Since the gospel of St John, and specifically the eucharistic discourse, are sometimes dismissed as being personal meditations of St John or his circle rather than being historically reliable writings, it is important to note the close parallels which exist between the Johannine account and the synoptic gospels. The accounts in Mark, Matthew and Luke of the multiplication of the loaves and of Christ's walking on the water correspond closely with one another and with St John's account of the same events. In all four narratives, the multiplication of the loaves is preceded by reference to the teaching of Jesus. There are allusions in all these accounts to the manna in the desert; and, as in the manna narrative in Exodus and in Deuteronomy, the crowd is arranged in groups of 'hundreds and fifties' and each individual receives as much bread as each one wants – features which are found also in St John.[88]

The accounts in the synoptic gospels of the temptations of Jesus in the desert refer to the manna and are in agreement with John's eucharistic discourse in interpreting the manna as a sign of God's teaching about Jesus Christ, Son of God. When Jesus is hungry after forty days' fast in the desert,[89] the devil taunts Jesus: 'If you are the son of God turn these stones into loaves.' The devil interprets Jesus' hunger as being only for earthly food. Jesus insists, in St John's version, that the important hunger is hunger for God; so Jesus replies to the devil in the words of Deuteronomy: 'Man does not live on bread alone but on every word that comes from the mouth of God.' (Mt 4:4)[90] We have seen earlier that the words 'eating' and 'drinking' are frequently applied in the Old Testament, as in the New, to listening to God's words in Holy Scripture and putting them into practice in one's life.

Two modes of presence of Christ as Bread are found in the eucharistic discourse in St John's gospel. The transition from one mode of Christ's presence to the other is almost imperceptible; but from Verse 51 of Chapter 6 onwards it becomes clear that 'the bread which has come down from heaven' which is now being spoken of, is Christ in his bodily presence; it is Christ's 'flesh' in a real, one might say, physical, sense. This is indicated by the use of a new word for 'eat' in the second section of the eucharistic discourse: from verse 51 on, Jesus uses the word translated in Greek by *trogein* instead of the word *phagein*; *trogein*[91] carries a greater sense of literalness, or what one might even call 'physicality', than *phagein*. That another form of 'eating' and another sense of 'body' are now in question is indicated also by the use of the Greek word *sarx* for 'body'; it is the word used for the incarnation in John's Prologue: 'The Word was made flesh', *ho logos sarx egenoto*. The 'flesh' is the body of Mary's child, the body of Jesus of Nazareth. To make the meaning still clearer, Jesus specifies that the flesh in question is 'my flesh for the life of the world' (Jn 6:51). It is the flesh that was to be scourged, nailed to the Cross, the flesh which was to bleed to death and then to be raised from the dead in the power of the Divine Spirit – it is this same flesh that is to be eaten, this very blood which is to be drunk, if one is to have eternal life and be raised up on the last day (Jn 6:54). The words: 'The bread which I shall give is my flesh for the life of the world' bear a close resemblance to the words of institution of the Eucharist. 'This is my body which will be given for you ... This is my blood ... which will be poured out for you'. (Lk 22:19-20) The word used here for 'body' is the Greek word *soma*; in the present context it is a 'neutral' word, but the 'physical' reality of this *soma* is clear in the Greek syntax, which, literally translated, would read: 'This is my body, [namely] the [body] given for you'. ... 'This is my blood ... [namely] the [blood)] poured out for you.'

The 'literalness' of the words of Jesus is shown also by the reaction of the listeners to the words of Jesus. The disciples would have had no difficulty whatever with 'eating' the body of Christ, in the sense of absorbing Christ's teaching; as we have seen, this was an idiom abundantly familiar to them from the scriptures. The other listeners too would at least have understood the language of 'eating' Christ's body, understood as Christ's teaching; the notion was familiar from the scriptures to them also. Yet many in both camps were revolted by the idea of eating Christ in the flesh, as proposed in the second part of John's eucharistic discourse. They begin arguing with one another: 'How can this man give us his flesh to eat?'

Jesus could have dispelled their doubts at once by quoting scriptural texts and saying that he intended his words to be understood only in the Old Testament sense which we have described; or by saying that he meant his words to be understood only figuratively or metaphorically, but not literally. Instead he declared that, unless they did eat his flesh and drink his blood, they would not have life; for, he insisted, 'my flesh is real food, my blood is real drink'. He declared that eating his flesh and drinking his blood were essential if one was to have life, life drawn from Christ as Christ himself draws life from the Father. His flesh, Christ insists, 'is the bread come down from heaven; ... anyone who eats this bread will live forever'.

Christ's audience in the synagogue, including his own followers, were not impressed. They had not protested when Jesus spoke to them about his being the Christ spoken of in the scriptures; it made sense to speak of Jesus as 'the living bread come down from heaven'. This was 'bread' that they could 'eat'. But 'flesh chewed': that was different; to Hebrew ears it was even disgusting. This, they muttered, is 'intolerable language'; nobody could accept it.

But Jesus does not withdraw his words. Instead, he tries to help his hearers to see how the words can be literally true. He asked them to reflect on how they would feel about these same words if they were to 'see the Son of Man ascend to where he was before'. If this flesh were to be raised up in glory by the Holy Spirit through the Resurrection and then throned at God's right hand in the Ascension, would it not then be possible to eat it and thus draw life, everlasting life, divine life, from it? 'It is the Spirit that gives life,' he went on; 'mere flesh has nothing to offer.'

The language of Jesus here has to be compared with his language in the garden after the resurrection when he speaks to Mary of Magdala (Jn 20:11-18). Mary was inconsolable after the death and burial of Jesus. She could not stay away from his tomb and came to it to watch and weep and pray. When she arrived at the tomb, however, she noticed that the stone covering the tomb had been moved away, and she ran to give this news to Peter and John. The two disciples rushed to the tomb; they saw the linen cloths which had wrapped the dead body of Jesus lying on the ground, but saw no trace of the body. John remembered the teaching of scripture about Christ's resurrection, and he believed that Jesus had risen from the dead.

The two disciples went home, but Mary stayed on in the garden where the tomb was, weeping over the death of her Lord. She saw two angels, one at the head and one at the foot of the empty tomb. They asked her why she was weeping. She replied: 'They have taken away my Lord and I don't know where they have put him.' Then she saw a figure which she thought to be that of the gardener; it was in fact Jesus, but she didn't recognise him. He put the same question as the angels: 'Why are you weeping?' adding: 'Who are you looking for?' When Jesus called her name, 'Mary', she immediately recognised him and rushed to him and clasped his feet – obviously as a sign that she would never let him be taken away again. Jesus gently rebuked her: 'Do not cling to me,' he said; 'I have not yet ascended to the Father.' He asked her to go 'and find the brothers and tell them' that he is soon to ascend to his Father and theirs, his God and theirs. Mary, one of the first to see the risen Lord, brought the joyful news to the disciples.

The words spoken by Jesus to Mary in the garden of the resurrection are undoubtedly linked to the words he spoke to the disciples in the synagogue at Capernaum, where he said: 'What if you should see the Son of Man ascend to where he was before?' (Jn 6:62-3)

Jesus is teaching Mary, and through her is teaching us that in his risen and ascended state there is no need to cling to him with bodily hands. Risen from the dead and ascended to his Father's side in the power of the Spirit, his body can be with each of the brothers and sisters in faith more closely than he is now with Mary, each one clasping him more tightly with the clasp of faith than Mary holds him with her clasp of hands. There is a grip of faith that is more firm and unbreakable than the grip of hands, just as there is a 'seeing' of faith that is more reliable and more sure than the seeing of eyes, and just as there is a 'hearing' of faith that apprehends truth more surely than the hearing of bodily ears. The risen and ascended body of Jesus is freed of the limitations of matter and the senses. The words of St Thomas Aquinas in his great eucharistic hymn, *Adoro Te Devote*, translated by Gerard Manley Hopkins, apply to that risen and ascended body:

> Seeing, touching, tasting, are in Thee deceived,
> How says trusty hearing? That shall be believed.
> What God's Son has told me, take for truth I do;
> Truth himself speaks truly, or there's nothing true.

The resurrection and ascension make the Eucharist possible. The Eucharist makes the resurrection and the ascension present.

Christ's teaching here is the same as that given by St Paul. Speaking of the Resurrection, Paul writes:

> The first man, Adam, as scripture says, became a living soul; but the last Adam has become a life-giving spirit … The first man being from the earth, is earthly by nature; the second man is from heaven. As this earthly man was, so are we, on earth; and as the heavenly man was, so are we in heaven. And we who have been modelled on the earthly man will be modelled on the heavenly man. (1 Cor 15:45-49)

This is the same Paul who is the earliest witness to the words of institution of the eucharist. His eucharistic doctrine is strikingly similar to that of St John. Christ is the 'heavenly man'. His flesh, given up for the life of the world, has been raised up by the Resurrection and the Ascension, and is our food in the Eucharist; and, by eating his flesh, we live in him and he lives in us. The Eucharist is, therefore, given to us as our supreme way of sharing in Christ's own life in God. The Eucharist, as St Paul puts it, 'models' us on 'the heavenly man' who is Christ.

Christ's elaboration of his teaching is not accepted by the majority in the synagogue at Capernaum. They 'left him and stopped going with him'. The text suggests that only the Twelve believed and remained with Jesus. Any doubts which might have remained with them are finally dissipated by the resurrection and the ascension of Christ; for thereby Christ's body is liberated from the limitations of space and time, and freed from the conditions of matter and 'flesh'. The resurrected Christ becomes 'life-giving spirit' (St Paul); and it is 'the spirit that gives life' (St John). The Eucharist, therefore, is a true 'convivium', a sharing of life, a true communion. Through the Eucharist, by the bodily presence within us of the risen Christ, we share in the very life of God and God shares his life with us. As the heavenly man, Christ, is within us here on earth, so are we with him, in heaven. Thereby also, as we shall see, the Eucharist is a true sacrifice, for sacrifice, as we found in Part I, is a sharing by us in the life of God. This is a core meaning of sacrifice already in the Old Testament; but it reaches its true and full meaning in the Eucharist. Thereby also, the Eucharist is an ecclesial sacrifice: for it is a sharing of life, divine life, between Christ and the members of the body of Christ, which is the Church. I return on pages 189–203 to the question of the essentially ecclesial nature of the Eucharist.

In Capernaum, however, the sacrificial death and resurrection of Jesus Christ are still in the future. The faith of some disciples is as yet unformed and weak. Despite Christ's words, they still cannot accept any suggestion of eating Christ's flesh. 'Many of his disciples left him and stopped going with him.' The community of believers is reduced to its core elements, the Twelve whom he had named Apostles; but these twelve are still in germ the new Israel, the Israel of God, the Church. Christ is the One who gathers into unity the scattered children of Israel; and the greatest force for effecting and expressing that unity is the Eucharist itself.

Yet even these twelve are challenged by Christ: 'Will you go away too?' Peter, as always, speaks for the rest:

> Lord, whom shall we go to? You have the message of eternal life and we believe, we know, that you are the Holy One of God. (Jn 6:67-8)

Faith in Christ as the only Son and unique revealer of God, and faith in the real presence of Christ in the Eucharist, belong to the foundational faith of the Church. Faith in the Eucharist is an expression of the Church's faith in Christ, and Peter is its authoritative spokesperson.

It seems strange that St John, who has a rich theology of the Eucharist, reports the Last Supper of Jesus, his Passover Meal, without mentioning the words of institution of the Eucharist, while the other three gospels report these words in substantially identical terms. Instead, John highlights the washing by Jesus of the feet of the disciples. This action is presented to the disciples as an example for them to follow; it is an example of the kind of self-sacrificing love which is to characterise those who share in his paschal meal, the Eucharist. This is given by Christ as an example of the kind of leadership which the Twelve are to exercise in his community. It is an illustration of the kind of love which is to characterise those to whom Christ gives 'a new commandment': 'By this love you have for one another, everyone will know that you are my disciples.' (Jn 13:35)

The washing of the feet of guests was a duty normally performed by servants, who frequently were slaves. The towel and basin used by Jesus are significant; Jesus is taking on the attire and the work of a slave to do this most menial of tasks, washing the feet of his guests.

This is a vivid illustration of the kind of self-humbling service which is expected of those who share in the eucharistic meal. This is the kind of love that Jesus spoke of when he said: 'Love one another as I have loved you.'

But there is a still more important significance in Jesus' washing of the feet of his disciples at the Last Supper: it is his chosen way of demonstrating to the disciples that he is indeed the Servant of the Lord foretold by Isaiah in the 'Songs of the Servant': in that garb, at that menial task, Jesus is indeed 'without beauty, without majesty ... despised and we took no account of him' (Isa 53:3). It was a fitting figure of his death. Crucifixion was the most degrading as well as the most terrifying of deaths: Cicero called it *crudelissimum et teterrimum*, the most cruel and most hideous way of putting someone to death. Washing feet clean from grime is a symbol of washing souls clean from sin. As Jesus washed those dirty feet, he was anticipating the giving up of his own body on the Cross for the sins of the world and was already pledging the pouring of his blood for all for the forgiveness of sins (Mt 26:28). In the words of Isaiah, 'he was praying all the time for sinners' (Is 53:12).

The Eucharistic Vine

St John's chapter on the Vine and the Branches (Jn 15) repeats the teaching of the eucharistic discourse in John 6. Christ is the vine, the disciples are the branches; it is the presence of Christ in the disciples and their presence in Christ which is the source of their life and their action. The allegory of the vine recalls the Old Testament passages on the vine and the vineyard, to which I referred on pp. 78 – 80. An obvious connection with the Eucharist is already suggested by the wine, fruit of the vine, which in the Eucharist becomes the blood of Christ. Our offertory prayer at Mass says:

> Blessed are you, Lord, God of all creation.
> Through your goodness we have this wine to offer,
> fruit of the vine and work of human hands.
> It will become our spiritual drink.

Comparison of the chapter on the vine with the eucharistic discourse in the sixth chapter of St John shows the eucharistic import of Christ's words about the vine. The chapter opens with the words: 'I am the true vine', where the words 'I am' have, as usual, a two-fold reference, one to the statement in which Jesus compares himself to the vine, which is the immediate context; the other to the name of God as revealed to Moses, an allusion which could not but have had its impact on Hebrew listeners. Jesus is speaking with the full strength of his divine authority when he stresses the profound oneness between himself and his disciples, a oneness which has been called 'mutual immanence'.[92] The words used to express this are 'Remain in me', or 'Make your home in me'. Thus Jesus says:

> Make your home in me as I make mine in you. …
> Whoever remains in me with me in him
> bears fruit in plenty. (Jn 15:4, 5)

The words 'remain in me'[93] are repeated seven times in as many verses. They are accompanied by the words 'as I remain in you'. The in-dwelling, the inter-penetration, are reciprocal. The mutual in-dwelling is the work of love. It includes sharing of home, sharing of life, sharing of love, between Jesus and his disciples. It is the fruit of faith: the words of Jesus 'remain' in his disciples. His teaching challenges the disciples, testing the sincerity of their faith and life. His teaching 'prunes' believers to make them bear even more fruit. The disciples' oneness with Jesus in faith and love is the condition of their bearing fruit in holiness and in apostolic zeal. The love the disciples have for their Master finds its source and its model in the self-sacrificing love of Jesus for mankind: 'A man can have no greater love than to lay down his life for his friends.' (Jn 15:13) This is a direct reference to Jesus' death for us on the Cross; and at the same time there is an indirect reference to the Eucharist, in which that death is remembered and sacramentally re-presented to the Father. The words 'no greater love' apply also to the words of the eucharistic discourse in John 6: 'The bread that I shall give is my flesh for the life of the world.' (Jn 6:51)

The oneness between Jesus and his disciples goes to the point of Jesus' admitting the disciples into sharing in the intimate and unique relationship that Jesus himself has with his Father. Jesus makes known to his disciples 'everything [he has] learned from his Father' (Jn 15:15). His 'learning' from the Father becomes our faith as disciples. The faith of Christians, the Creeds, those great confessions of faith which the Church professes, are nothing less than Jesus Christ sharing with us all that he himself has learned from his Father. When we profess our faith as a eucharistic community in saying the Creed, or when we recite the Creed as personal prayer or when we make an 'act of faith', we are being privileged to give voice to what Jesus Christ has himself revealed to us. It is on his word that we believe, it is by his authority that we speak, when we proclaim our Creed. When we say, 'I believe in God ...', we are not just repeating what our parents or our teachers or our priests taught us to say; we are repeating what Jesus taught us. Jesus Christ, we read in St. Luke's gospel, was 'filled with joy by the Holy Spirit' when he said:

> I bless you Father, Lord of heaven and earth, for hiding these things from the learned and the clever and revealing them to mere children. Yes, Father, for that is what it pleased you to do. Everything has been entrusted to me by my Father; and no-one knows who the Son is except the Father, and who the Father is except the Son and those to whom the Son chooses to reveal him. (Lk 10:21-3)

The similarity here between the gospel of St Luke and that of St John is very striking.

We have the privilege of being among those to whom Jesus Christ chooses to reveal God, his Father, and our saying of the Creed is our repetition of the lessons Jesus has taught us. The Holy Spirit is the channel used by Jesus to make those lessons penetrate our minds, our hearts and our lives. André Feuillet has said that the Holy Spirit is like a mother, teaching her children to say 'Father' (or 'Abba') to God.[94] When we repeat the Creed meaningfully, sincerely and from the heart, we are being faithful pupils of Jesus, the Divine Teacher sent to us by God, and we are becoming more like Jesus through the working of the Holy Spirit in our hearts and minds.

Our faith admits us into the eternal secrets of God's being and God's love. We become, through faith, sons and daughters in the Son, members of the family of God, part of the 'family circle' of God. By faith we are given the special privilege of calling God by the intimate and affectionate name, 'Abba, Father', the name which only Jesus can properly use, but which he gives Christians permission to use.

This intimate relationship with God, which we share with Jesus through our 'remaining in' him and his 'remaining in' us, gives us the privilege of praying the special 'family prayer' of Christians, 'Our Father'. With this comes the amazing promise that when we 'make our home' in Christ: 'The Father will give you anything you ask him in my name.' (Jn 15:16)

Deification

The Eastern or Greek Catholic tradition speaks of 'deification' or 'theosis', as the process whereby the Christian becomes progressively more united with God the Father, through the Son, by the working of the Holy Spirit, a unification which is effected primarily by the sacraments and especially by the Eucharist. In this tradition, 'deification' is the consummation to which every Christian soul is called by virtue of baptism. The union with God which results is the other name for holiness; for God alone is the Holy One, and all human holiness is a sharing in the holiness of God, which is to say, a sharing by us in the life and in the very being of God.

It might seem that the Western or Latin Church may not have felt completely at ease with the term 'deification'. At least, the term occurs much less frequently in Latin texts. However, it must be kept in mind that the Greek Fathers who use the term were writing before the East–West schism and were writing in and for the undivided Church. Their writings are part of the patrimony of the Latin Church as well as of the Greek Church. I wish now to show how the term 'deification', though less common in the Latin Catholic tradition, is nevertheless fully at home there. It could not be but so, since the truth which the term expresses is a biblically revealed truth, as found particularly in the teaching of St Paul and of St John. I first give some examples from Catholic liturgical texts. I select them mainly from the Office of Readings of the 'Divine Office', because this forms the prayerful context in which the Eucharist is celebrated, particularly in monasteries, but also ideally – and, nowadays, increasingly – in parishes.

St Irenaeus (about AD 130–200) writes:

> As the earthly bread, once it has received the invocation of God upon it, is no longer ordinary bread but the Eucharist, and is made up of two elements, heavenly and earthly, so too our bodies, once they have received the Eucharist, are no longer corruptible but contain within themselves the hope of resurrection ...[95]

The 'hope of resurrection', or of bodily incorruptibility, is the result of a sharing in the life of God and this sharing is communicated to us by the resurrected Christ through the sacraments, and above all through the sacrament of the Eucharist.

St Hilary of Poitiers (AD 310–367) writes:

> If the Word was truly made flesh, and if we truly receive the Word made flesh in the Lord's food, why should we not hold that he remains within us naturally? For when he was born as a man he assumed the nature of our flesh in such a way that it became inseparable from himself, and he joined the nature of his flesh to the nature of his eternity in the sacrament of his flesh which he allows us to share. Accordingly, we are all one, because the Father is in Christ and Christ is in us. He is in us through the flesh and we are in him; and being united with him, what we are is in God.[96]

St Basil, called the Great, Bishop of Caesarea (AD 329–379) writes:

> Souls that carry the Spirit ... become spiritual themselves and send forth grace upon others. ... So do they acquire likeness to God; so – most sublime of all – do they themselves become divine.[97]

In his longer Rule, the same Basil writes:

> Christ was not content merely to quicken us when we were dead, but he bestowed the dignity of divinity ...[98]

Basil's great friend, St Gregory Nazianzen (AD 330–390) writes:

> I must be buried with Christ and rise with him again, be co-heir with Christ, become a son or daughter of God and indeed God himself. This is what the great mystery means for us; this is why God for our sake became man ... so that he might raise up fallen human nature and bring salvation to man who is made in his image.[99]

Elsewhere St Gregory writes:

> Acknowledge that you have been made a Son of God, a co-heir with Christ, acknowledge, and now I speak with daring, that you have been made divine.[100]

St Cyril of Jerusalem (AD 315–386) writes:

> Let us partake with the fullest confidence that it is the body and blood of Christ. For his body has been bestowed on you under the figure of bread, and his blood under the figure of wine, so that by partaking of Christ's body and blood you may become one body and blood with him. This is how we become bearers of Christ, since his body and blood spread throughout our limbs; this is how, in the blessed Peter's words 'we become partakers of the divine nature'.[101]

Elsewhere the same St Cyril writes:

> [Before the Ascension of the Lord] everything had been accomplished which remained to be done on earth; but it still remained necessary that we should share and participate in the divine nature of the Word.[102]

St Cyril of Alexandria (AD 376–444) writes:

> We have all received one and the same spirit, the Holy Spirit, and so in a certain sense are mingled with one another and with God. For although, taken individually, we are many, and in each of us there dwells the Spirit of the Father who is also the Spirit of Christ, nevertheless this Spirit is one and indivisible. ...

> If we put aside the natural way of life, and surrender once and for all to the laws of the Spirit, it is incontrovertible that, by denying, in a sense, our own life and assuming the heavenly form of the Holy Spirit so that he becomes woven into our being, we are transformed, so to speak, into another nature. We are no longer just men or women, but sons and daughters of God; we receive the name of heavenly persons because we are made partakers of the divine nature.

> Therefore, we are all one in the Father and in the Son and the Holy Spirit – one in identity of relationship, one in the likeness revealed in devotion, one in receiving the holy flesh of Christ and in sharing the one Holy Spirit.[103]

The same Cyril of Alexandria writes elsewhere about our being 'deified by grace', whereas Jesus Christ is 'true God made manifest in human form for us'.[104]

St Peter Chryologos, Bishop of Ravenna, (about AD 380–450) writes:

> And so Christ is born, that being born he may renew our corrupt nature ... Man, whom he had made an earthly creature, he now has made a heavenly creature; one who was animated by a human spirit, he quickens into a divine spirit. Thus he assumes him wholly into God, so that he leaves nothing in him of sin, of death, of toil, of sorrow, of earth, through our Lord Jesus Christ.[105]

I note once more that the early Church fathers whom I have quoted belong to the Eastern or Greek-speaking Church, but this was then part of the undivided Catholic Church. Their language is not different from that of St Thomas Aquinas, who, writing about the Eucharist, speaks of our deification, while not using the term:

> The only-begotten Son of God, wishing to enable us to share in his divinity, assumed our nature, so that, by becoming man, he might make men gods ... Now, in order that we might always keep the memory of this great act of love he left his body as food and his blood as drink, to be received by the faithful under the appearance of bread and wine. ... No sacrament contributes more to our salvation than this.[106]

Indeed, the term 'deification' or equivalent terms are used in current Catholic eucharistic texts. In our eucharistic liturgy, as part of the offertory prayers, the following formula is said as a drop of water is poured into the cup of wine before it is offered to God in the preparation of the elements for the Eucharist:

> Through the mystery of this water and wine,
> may we share in the divinity of Christ
> who humbled himself to share in our humanity.

I now quote several collects from the Roman Missal:

> Grant, Lord, that the Word that took flesh
> in the womb of the ever Virgin Mary
> may share with us his godhead.[107]
> God and Father ...
> grant that we who profess
> our firm and humble faith
> in the incarnation of Our Redeemer
> may have some share in his divine life.[108]

In the Evening Prayer of Christmas Day we pray:

> God, our Father ...
> our human nature is the wonderful work of your hands,
> made still more wonderful by your work of redemption.
> Your Son took to himself our manhood,
> grant us a share in the Godhead of Jesus Christ.

Indeed, in the first chapter of its Constitution on the Church *Lumen Gentium*, the Second Vatican Council stated: '[God's] plan was to dignify men and women with a participation in his own divine life.'[109]

If the Western or Latin Church may seem less than completely at ease with the term 'deification', this might perhaps be because of fear that it might be thought to imply some form of pantheism or pantheistic monism. However, the terms 'godly' and 'godliness', once commonly used of persons regarded as particularly saintly, reflect the concept of deification. The term 'Christ-like', more common in use, conveys the same truth: it is Christ's life in us, God's life in us, which is the source of all human holiness. Our struggle to be holy is our acceptance of God's will to 'deify us'. If the term is not commonly used in modern western Catholic theology, the substantial underlying doctrine is identical in the west and in the east.

None appreciated the identity of the reality named by these different 'languages' so much as the Christian mystics. For them, this was a fact of their experience of prayer, as being, at one and the same time, their own oneness with God in love and their sharing in the life of God, indwelling in us. St John of the Cross, for example, in his *Spiritual Canticle*, writes:

> The soul that is united and transformed in God breathes God in God with the same divine breathing with which God, while in her, breathes her in himself. ...
> There is no need to wonder that the soul should be capable of aught so high; for since God grants her the favour of attaining to being deiform and united in the Most Holy Trinity, wherein she becomes God by participation, how is it a thing incredible that she should perform her work of understanding, knowledge and love in the Trinity, together with it, like the Trinity itself, by a mode of participation, which God effects in the soul herself? ...
>
> The Father loves [souls] by communicating to them the same love as to the Son, though not by communication of the Divine Nature as to the Son, but, as we have said, by unity and transformation of love. ... Souls possess these same blessings by participation as He possesses by nature; for this reason they are truly gods by participation, equals of God and his companions.[110]

To 'be truly gods by participation', to 'share in the Godhead of Jesus Christ'; these are surely astonishing claims. Their presumptuousness is breathtaking. No human being would dare to speak thus if God himself did not take the initiative and authorise it. Yet, is it not the correlative of the '*admirabile commercium*', the 'marvellous exchange', whereby the Son of God took human flesh in Mary's womb at the incarnation? The author of the Second Letter of St Peter had no hesitation in speaking of how, through faith in Jesus Christ, we become 'sharers in the divine nature'. The offertory prayer (which I quoted on p. 160) uses the exact words of the Letter of St Peter.[111] Indeed, as I have suggested already and hope to show more fully later, the teaching of Jesus in his eucharistic discourse and in his allegory of the vine in St John's gospel is substantially the same as the teaching that St Paul received from the same Lord; and both stress our communal oneness with Christ in the community of faith and love which is Christ's body, the Church, and also our individual oneness with Christ in the communion of the Eucharist. Our oneness with Christ as individuals and our oneness through Christ in the Christian community are inseparably linked and both are hinted at in St John's first Letter:

> If we walk in the light as he himself is in the light, then we share together a common life and are being cleansed from every sin by the blood of Jesus, His Son. (1 Jn 1:5b-7)

I believe, however, that the concepts of union with God, divine indwelling, oneness in and with Christ, are interchangeable with the concept of deification. Indeed, the gospel of St John makes this clear, as I now hope to show.

The High Priestly Prayer

In what has been called the High Priestly Prayer in St John's gospel (Jn 17) Jesus develops his teaching on the mutual indwelling of his disciples in him and of him in his disciples. In this prayer, Jesus speaks of his indwelling, with the Father and the Holy Spirit, in the disciple and the reciprocal indwelling of the disciple in the inner life and mutual love of God, Father, Son and Holy Spirit. The unity of love of his disciples with one another and their unity in love with himself is, Jesus says, as close and intimate as is the love of the Father for the Son and the Son for the Father; indeed, it is a sharing in that indescribable trinitarian love which Jesus shares eternally with the Father and the Holy Spirit. The life of the disciples is henceforth inseparable from the life of Jesus himself. As Jesus does not belong to the world, neither do his disciples belong to the world. Jesus prays that they may be faithful – that faith may fill their lives and define their identities and become their reason for living:

> Father, consecrate them in the truth. ...
> May they be one in us
> as you are in me and I am in you
> so that the world may believe it was you who sent me. (Jn 17:21)

The prayer is offered not only for the Apostles, but 'for those also who through their words will believe in me' (Jn 17:20). Jesus prays for them all:

> May they all be one. Father, may they be one in us, as you are in me and I am in you, so that the world may believe it was you who sent me. ...With me in them and you in me, may they be so completely one that the world will realise that it was you who sent me and that I have loved them as much as you loved me. (Jn 17:20-23)

Jesus' ardent desire and passionate prayer is not just that his disciples may share with one another a oneness as close as is his own oneness with the Father; it is that his disciples may share in his very own oneness with God the Father in that divine love which is the Holy Spirit. He prays that his disciples may have a oneness that comes from his own indwelling in the Eternal Father in the unity of the Holy Spirit of love, and a oneness which comes also from his own indwelling in the disciples: 'as you [Father] are in me and I am in you.' He is praying that his disciples may share in the very life of the Most Holy Trinity. The words are one in meaning with the words of the eucharistic discourse in St John's gospel (Jn 6): namely, that all who believe in Christ have eternal life; for eternal life is a sharing in the life of God, 'who alone is immortal, whose home is in inaccessible light' (St Paul, 1 Tim 6:16).

The words are very rightly applied to the desire of Christ for unity between divided Christian Churches – a desire which all his disciples are called to make their own. This unity must indeed be expressed in structures and institutions; but this unity presupposes the deep personal and indeed mystical unity between each Christian disciple and Jesus Christ who dwells in him or her. The mystical and contemplative aspects of Christian unity should never be neglected and must never be separated from the search for institutional unity. The Eucharist is the most powerful agent of that personal and mystical unity of the individual Christian with Jesus, and also of the unity of the whole community of Christians. To share together the great eschatological Wedding Feast of the Lamb is the goal of all who work and pray for church unity. Meanwhile, the Eucharist is a manifestation of unity already achieved among those who celebrate it; and it is also an impetus to work for wider unity in all Christian Churches. The pain of present separation becomes a powerful incentive to work for future communion in the Church finally made one in the unity of Father, Son and Holy Spirit.

André Feuillet calls attention to the four-fold repetition of the term 'Your Name' in the High Priestly Prayer of Jesus (Jn:17) – a term which is rare in the rest of the four gospels. He finds in this unusual repetition a link with the liturgy of atonement of Yom Kippur. The Name of the Lord or the sacred tetragrammaton, Yahweh, was held in such awe by the Jews that it could not be pronounced. The same practice is observed among the Jews to the present day. Yom Kippur, however, was an exception: on that day, and on that day alone, the chief priest, and he alone, pronounced the sacred Name aloud several times. In his High-Priestly Prayer, which, in St John's gospel, is associated with the Last Supper, Jesus pronounces the equivalent, 'Your Name', repeatedly. He does so, Feuillet explains, in order to teach his disciples and 'those who through their words will believe [in him]', that, for them, God's Name is to be 'Father'. This name is not to be just another way of invoking God – vastly important though this title is in terms of people's prayer to God. It is to be much more than this. It is to denote a complete change in their relationship with God, indeed a complete change in their own very being. They are to become one with Christ through the Holy Spirit of Sonship; and thereby to become 'sons in the Son', daughters in the Son: Christ is to be in them and God is in Christ, so that God's people become completely one in the unity-in-Trinity of Father, Son and Holy Spirit; with the result that the world will realise that it was indeed God the Father who sent Jesus into the world and that God loves his people with the self-same love as that with which he eternally loves his Son, Jesus Christ (Jn 17:23).

This is Christ's founding charter for his Church: it is to be a community made one in the unity of Father, Son and Holy Spirit and living a life which makes present in the world the holiness of the Triune God. The Eucharist is the most powerful medium for the infusion of that holiness into the Church across the whole world: hence the Church's longing for holiness is its most eloquent witness to its truth. In the third Eucharistic Prayer, which captures the essence of Christ's High-Priestly Prayer, the Church prays:

> Father, you are holy indeed,
> and all creation rightly gives you praise.
> All life, all holiness, comes from you,
> through your Son, Jesus Christ, our Lord
> by the working of the Holy Spirit.
> From age to age you gather a people to yourself,
> so that, from east to west,
> a perfect offering may be made
> to the glory of your name.

This holiness is the Church's strength in all adversity. It is her certain hope of renewal, her sure means of recovery from sin and scandal among her members. Renewal and reform of institutions and structures and agencies within the Church are a continuing duty. Because its pastors and its members are human and imperfect, these institutions can come to obscure the Church's holiness and they require unceasing vigilance and repeated reform and renewal. But unless the Church is being constantly renewed in holiness all other reforms will fail. The Church's holiness, however, is not a holiness of sinlessness, but a holiness of forgivenness. We are a Church of forgiven sinners. The Father's love for us is that of the understanding father for his prodigal son. The name, Father, by which we are instructed by Christ to address God, is a name of love, of trust, of confidence; it is a guarantee that God loves us with the same eternal love with which he loves Jesus Christ himself. How could we be afraid? What can mortal man do to us?[112]

The 'Our Father' and the Eucharist

Hence our most familiar and most distinctive prayer as Christians is the prayer that Jesus taught us, the Lord's Prayer, the 'Our Father'. We have become so familiar with addressing God as Father that we forget how strange and even disturbing the appellation sounded in the ears of the hearers of Jesus. Jesus, as we find from the gospel record, never prayed without calling God 'Father'. Indeed, he used the still more intimate name, 'Abba'; this was, for Aramaic speakers, the 'in-family' term for Father: 'dearest Father'. Joachim Jeremias calculated that Jesus in the gospels used the term 'Abba-Father' one hundred and seventy times in speaking to God or about God.[113] The same writer points out that Jesus is unique in his use of this term, whether it be recorded as 'Father' or as 'Abba'. There is no record in Hebrew scripture or in the entire Hebrew corpus of prayer of 'Abba-Father' being used to invoke God. Jeremias writes: 'We can say quite definitely that there is no analogy at all in the whole literature of Jewish prayer for God being addressed as Abba.'[114]

In the sacred writings of Hebrew tradition, God is sometimes, though rarely, called Father; but never is he addressed as Father. Jeremias concluded that we hear in the words 'Abba-Father' the very voice (*ipsissima vox*) of Jesus himself. Indeed, Jeremias holds that Jesus' way of praying 'Abba' is at the same time his clearest statement of his own identity as the unique Son of God, the One who alone 'has seen the Father', and who alone is the definitive revelation of God to mankind.[115]

Jeremias notes that Jesus restricts the use of the term 'Abba' to the disciples: they are to 'call no-one on earth their Father' (Mt 23:9).

Indeed, the disciples, formed in the Jewish tradition of prayer, used the term, 'Abba-Father' with hesitation and even a certain trepidation. To quote Jeremias again: 'To the Jewish mind it would have been disrespectful and therefore inconceivable to address God with this familiar word.'[116] His conclusion is that Jesus' use of this term is 'new and unheard of'; it 'reveals the heart of Jesus' relationship with God' – a relationship which is that of a child to his father, 'simple, inward, confident'. What is still more astonishing is that Jesus, in authorising and teaching his disciples to call God 'Abba-Father', is thereby giving them a share in his own relationship with God: we become sons and daughters of God as he is Son of God.[117]

The disciples never got quite used to praying 'Our Father'. They certainly never took it for granted. They never said the prayer mechanically or by rote, as we often do. They needed reassurance that this way of addressing God was allowed, and indeed commanded, by Jesus. Consequently, before saying the prayer that Jesus taught them, the 'Our Father', they always felt the need to remind themselves that Jesus had prayed in this way and had instructed them to pray likewise. Every time they prayed the 'Our Father', they prefaced it with a short introduction. This survives in our liturgy in the formula which introduces the 'Our Father', prayed by priests and people before the Communion in the eucharistic celebration: 'Because we are so advised by salutary instructions and have been so authorised by divine teaching, we make bold to say ...' The Latin words are *Audemus dicere*, which, literally translated, means 'We dare to say: Our Father ...'. The present banal translation (which is more like a substitution) for this introduction[118] misses the point completely. It would be well for us to try to recover something of the thrill and the excitement and the sense of privilege and gratitude for being allowed to call God 'Our dearest Father'.

St Paul implicitly reminds his converts that this prayer is truly the Lord's prayer by retaining the Aramaic word used by Jesus, even in the Hellenistic and Roman cultures where he evangelised.

Paul also emphasises the special power of this prayer in insisting that it is by the inspiration of the Holy Spirit that we pray 'Abba-Father':

> The proof that you are sons and daughters is that God has sent the Spirit of his Son into your hearts; the Spirit that cries 'Abba-Father', and it is this that makes you a son. (Gal 4:6)[119]

Jeremias concludes that, when we pray 'Abba, Father', our divine sonship and daughtership is actualised, even as we pray it: 'Whenever you cry "Abba", God assures you that you can be absolutely certain that you really are his children.'[120] Since the ultimate destiny of disciples of Jesus is to be at home finally with Jesus in our Heavenly Father's house, Joachim Jeremias can state that the 'Our Father' is 'eschatology fulfilling itself' even as we pray it.

All this shows how appropriate it is to pray the 'Our Father' in the celebration of the Eucharist. The Eucharist is not merely our prayer, it is the prayer of Christ on the Cross, 'aloud and in silent tears' (Heb 5:7), offered to the Father on our behalf. By the will of the Father and the power of the Holy Spirit, the prayer of Jesus fulfils itself, makes itself true, even as we pray it. Thus, as the Eucharist is celebrated, God's Name is being called holy, his Kingdom comes, God's will is being done on earth as in heaven, we receive as much of God's grace and life as we want and as much as we need for today, knowing that tomorrow brings another Mass and every grace that we need for tomorrow; we are reconciled with God and we receive the grace that we need to forgive others as God has forgiven us; and finally we are assured by our dear Father that he will not let us fail in the testing of our faith. Truly, as the Eucharist is celebrated and as the exposed Eucharist is adored, the Lord's Prayer is being answered and eschatology is being anticipated, even as we celebrate and adore.

St Paul's Eucharistic Teaching

I turn now to St Paul's teaching on the Eucharist. An important aspect of this teaching is that it comes from a source quite independent of the sources in the oral tradition on which the four evangelists drew, and yet is in complete agreement with them. Furthermore, St Paul's teaching is the earliest in date of all the New Testament passages dealing with the Eucharist. Paul claims to have been 'specially chosen to preach the Good News' and to have been 'appointed by God to be an Apostle' (1 Cor 1:1-5). He introduces himself to the Christians of Rome as one who had received his mission through Jesus Christ, the risen Lord, and had 'received grace and our apostolic mission to preach the obedience of faith to all pagan nations' (Rom 1:1-5). Obviously, the reference is to his dramatic experience at the gates of Damascus, where, as a young Jewish zealot called Saul, he had arrived with the intention of apprehending and killing any Christian converts he could find. The scene is described in Chapter 9 of the Acts of the Apostles. A bright light suddenly shone, so intense as to leave Saul blind. Around the same time, a disciple in Damascus called Ananias had a vision in which he saw the Lord, who said to him: 'This man is my chosen instrument to bring my name before pagans and pagan kings and before the people of Israel.' (Acts 9:15)

St Paul constantly claims that this encounter with the risen Christ is the source both of his knowledge of the gospel of Jesus Christ and of his apostolic mission to preach that gospel. He insists that the Good News that he preached was 'something [he] learned only through a revelation of Jesus Christ' (Gal 1:10-11). He tells us that after his conversion, he discussed his revelation with no-one, but went off to Arabia (presumably to pray in the desert), and then returned to Damascus. After three years, he tells us, he went up to Jerusalem to visit Cephas and spent two weeks with him. He saw none of the other Apostles except James, brother of the Lord. It was 'not till fourteen years had passed' that he had contact with any of the Twelve again; then, going up to Jerusalem, he met 'the leading men' and shared with them the Good News as he [Paul] preached it. He found that they 'had nothing to add to the Good News as I preach it'; indeed, James, Peter and John 'recognised that [Paul] had been commissioned to preach the Good News to the uncircumcised pagans, just as Peter had been commissioned to preach it to the circumcised' (Gal 2:1-10). In other words, the leaders of the Church recognised that, although Paul had not known Christ in the flesh or listened to his teaching, as the other Apostles had, nevertheless his [Paul's] account of that teaching equally came from Christ himself and was furthermore identical with the account of Christ's teaching preached by the Apostles: 'What matters,' writes St Paul, 'is that I preach what they preach, and that this is what you all [the Corinthian Christians] believed.' (1 Cor 15:11)

The sequence of events as described in the First Letter to the Corinthians and in the Acts of the Apostles and in the Letter to the Galatians enables us to determine the approximate date of Paul's Damascus conversion. The First Letter to the Corinthians is generally dated to AD 54 or 55, some twenty to twenty-five years after the crucifixion and the resurrection of Jesus, which can be reliably dated to AD 30. Paul's conversion and his 'learning the Good News through a revelation of Jesus Christ' probably occurred three years later, in AD 33. Paul's first visit to Jerusalem and his days spent with Peter, which must have included comparing their respective accounts of the gospel of Jesus Christ, would have occurred in AD 36. The earliest gospel, which is Mark's, was written about AD 64; the gospels of Matthew and Luke belong probably to the decade AD 70. The earliest testimony to the institution of the Eucharist is found in St Paul's First Letter to the Corinthians. This testimony of St Paul, based on his personal encounter with the risen Lord, is earliest in date, indeed probably dating only three years after the actual institution of the Eucharist. It is independent of the accounts in the four gospels. Yet, this Pauline testimony is in full agreement with the eucharistic teaching found in the Synoptic Gospels and with the more developed eucharistic doctrine found in St John. These facts are obviously of crucial importance in relation to both the early date and the historical authenticity of the eucharistic doctrine and practice of the Church. Indeed they are a strong confirmation of the historical authenticity of the whole Jesus narrative of the four gospels; for the Eucharist contains the whole gospel in concentrated form and it can be historically shown that the Eucharist has been celebrated in memory of Jesus by his followers without interruption ever since a date very close to the actual events of his passion and death, resurrection and ascension.

St Paul's most important teaching about the Eucharist is given to the Corinthian Christians, not in the course of a formal catechetical instruction, but on the occasion of a rebuke delivered to them by St Paul because of abuses occurring on the occasion of gatherings of the community. The gatherings had a two-fold character: they took the form of a social gathering in the house of a member of the community, which included a meal in which all partook; and this was followed by the celebration of the Eucharist. The meal, as reported to St Paul, sometimes led to factions and cliques, where some were left with nothing to eat and others over-indulged, especially in drink. This behaviour, St Paul warned, destroys the whole concept of community. Above all, it was quite incompatible with the meaning of the Eucharist which followed the meal. St Paul reminded the Corinthians of the account which he had given them earlier of the institution of the Eucharist – the account which he had 'received from the Lord and in turn passed on' to them (1 Cor 1:17-34). Consequently, remembering what Our Lord said and did at the Last Supper, and realising that 'when they eat this bread and drink this cup, they are proclaiming the death of the Lord', Christians must recollect themselves before receiving the Eucharist and must make sure that they are not 'behaving unworthily towards the body and blood of the Lord'. They must realise that, when they eat this bread and drink this cup, 'they are proclaiming the death of the Lord'.

Paul concludes that 'a person who eats and drinks without recognising the body is eating and drinking his own condemnation'. It is clear from the context, where 'respect for the community of God' and 'proclaiming the death [of the Lord]' are equally emphasised, that 'recognising the body' has a two-fold meaning: first of all, it means recognising the real presence of the crucified Lord in the appearances of bread and wine, and second, it means recognising the presence of the living Lord in the community which celebrates the Eucharist; for the community of believers form one body with the Lord.

The latter injunction is part of a conviction which for St Paul is a revealed truth of faith, and also a deep personal experience – both originating in his Damascus road conversion. Struck to the ground near the gates of Damascus, Paul hears a voice, saying: 'Saul, Saul, why are you persecuting me? ... I am Jesus and you are persecuting me.' (Acts 9:4) Saul, soon to become the great Christian Apostle, Paul, was being given a revelation about the nature of the Church of Christ, as well as about the Eucharist: Christ and his believers are one, one in the Church, and one in the eucharistic celebration. Jesus had indeed revealed this to his disciples on many occasions: as, for example, when he said to his disciples, 'He that hears you hears me', or when he said to his disciples: 'So long as you did [this kindness] to the least of these brothers or sisters of mine, you did it to me.' (Mt 25:40)

This oneness of Jesus with his followers is put in a eucharistic context in St John's gospel, when Jesus says, in the synagogue at Capernaum: 'He who eats my flesh and drinks my blood lives in me and I in him. ... Whoever eats me will draw life from me.' (Jn 6:56-7)

This teaching is directed to Paul personally at the gates of Damascus by the question: 'Why are you persecuting me?' This is the original source of Paul's rich doctrine of the Church as the Body of Christ. In the first part of the twentieth century, theologians spoke of the Church as the Mystical Body of Christ. Fr (later Cardinal) Henri de Lubac showed that, in the history of theology, the term 'mystical body' was used first of the Eucharist and only later of the Church. In either usage, the term 'body' used of the Church, and used also of the Eucharist, indicates close connection between the Church and the Eucharist. It is important to note that this connection goes back to St Paul himself and to the very beginnings of Christianity.

The sequence of topics treated by St Paul in Chapters 11–13 of First Corinthians is significant. St Paul's great discourse on the Eucharist (1 Cor 11:17-34) is followed by his paragraphs on spiritual gifts in the Church – all of them emanating from the work of 'one and the same spirit' (1 Cor 12:1-11). 'In the one spirit we were all baptised, Jews and Gentiles, slaves and citizens, and one Spirit was given to us all to drink.' (1 Cor 12:13) This is followed by his comparison of the Church with the human body, and finally by his wonderful paean in praise of love, the 'way that is better than any of them' (1 Cor 1-13).

Our eucharistic liturgy follows a similar pattern: the Holy Spirit, the one body of the Church, the love which flows from the Spirit and permeates the Church – all have their place. The Holy Spirit is invoked twice in each of our Eucharistic Prayers II, III and IV. The Spirit's role in the Eucharist is two-fold: as we have mentioned earlier, he is invoked first by both word and sign, to transform the elements of bread and wine into the body and blood of Christ; and he is invoked second to transform the gathered assembly into the one community of love, the one body of Christ, which is the Church.

As the words are spoken over the bread and wine before the consecration of the Eucharist, the priest's hands are extended over the elements; this is the same sign as that used to call down the Holy Spirit on the confirmands in the sacrament of confirmation and on the candidate for ordination as priest or as bishop in the sacrament of holy orders. In the Eucharist, we call the word and sign the *epiclesis*.

With hands extended over the bread and the chalice, the priest prays in Eucharistic Prayer II:

> Let your Spirit come upon these gifts
> to make them holy,
> so that they may become for us
> the body and blood of Our Lord, Jesus Christ.

The corresponding prayer in Eucharistic Prayer III is:

> And so, Father, we bring you these gifts.
> We ask you to make them holy
> by the power of your Spirit,
> that they may become the body and blood
> of your Son, our Lord Jesus Christ,
> at whose command we celebrate this Eucharist.

In Eucharistic Prayer IV, the words are:

> Father, may this Holy Spirit
> sanctify these offerings.
> Let them become the body and blood of Jesus Christ, our Lord
> as we celebrate the great mystery
> which he left us as an everlasting covenant.

The Holy Spirit is invoked a second time, after the consecration, and this time, it is to transform the people gathered for the Eucharist into the one body of Christ, a body made one in faith and love and peace. In Eucharistic Prayer II, we have:

> May all of us who share in the body and blood of Christ
> be brought together in unity by the Holy Spirit.

Eucharistic Prayer III has the words:

> Grant that we who are nourished
> by his body and blood
> may be filled with his Holy Spirit
> and become one body, one spirit, in Christ.

In Eucharistic Prayer IV the priest says:

> Lord, look upon this sacrifice
> which you have given to your Church,
> and by your Holy Spirit

gather all who share this one bread and one cup
into the one body of Christ,
a living sacrifice of praise.

In the text of the Eucharistic Prayer for 'The Church on the way to Unity' found in the 'Eucharistic Prayers for Various Needs and Occasions', is the following prayer:

Renew by the light of the Gospel
the Church of N. [diocese/place].
Strengthen the bonds of unity between the faithful and their pastors,
that together with Benedict our Pope, N. our Bishop
and the whole college of bishops
your people may stand forth
in a world torn by discord and strife
as a sign of oneness and peace.

The two invocations of the Holy Spirit in each eucharistic liturgy echo the teaching of St Paul in chapters eleven, twelve and thirteen of the First Letter to the Corinthians. The section on love in Chapter 13 might be thought to be unconnected with the preceding two chapters. It was St Thérèse of Lisieux, with the insight of the saint rather than the erudition of the scholar, who saw the connection between Paul's teaching on the Church and on the Eucharist, as being each the Body of Christ, and his teaching on love as the greatest gift of the Spirit. For her, the heart was the symbol of love, and the heart is the most vital organ for the whole life of the human body. So it must also be for love in the life of the body which is the Church. Hence her own vocation was to 'be love at the heart of the Church', and this is how she was going to be able to 'be everything at once', and thus exercise all vocations in the Church together.

It is when we are 'guided by the Spirit', as St Paul says, that love becomes, through us, the life of the whole community which is the Church. It is when we are 'led by the Spirit' that the fruits of the Spirit become manifest in the life and work and in the institutions of the Church: these fruits are 'love, joy, peace, patience, kindness, goodness, trustfulness, gentleness and self-control' (Gal 4:15-25). It is by showing these qualities, by 'being the truth in love', that the Church witnesses most effectively to the truth of Christ which she proclaims. The Eucharist, sacrament of the greatest love mankind has ever known, is the great conduit by which God transmits his love into the daily lives of individual Christians and into the life of the whole Church. This is why Pope John Paul was able to write, at the beginning of his Encyclical Letter, *Ecclesia de Eucharistia*, 'the Church draws her life from the Eucharist'. This is why he could write, in his Apostolic Letter, *Mane nobiscum Domine*:

> May [the Eucharist] encourage a more lively and fervent celebration of the Eucharist, leading to a Christian life transformed by love. (28)

The Christian life for St Paul is the life of Christ in us; indeed it is Christ himself living in us. Paul develops this theme particularly in his Letters to the Galatians and the Romans. His teaching is given to us in condensed form in a passage in the Letter to the Galatians:

> I have been crucified with Christ and I live now, not with my own life but with the life of Christ who lives in me. The life I now live in the body I live in faith: faith in the Son of God who loved me and who sacrificed himself for my sake. (Gal 2:19-20)

Our 'being crucified' with Christ begins with our baptism: we go down into the water with Christ as Christ went into the tomb for us, and, as Christ rose from the tomb, we rise up to a new life of faith which is 'the life of Christ who lives in me'. This new life is the beginning of eternal life in our mortal bodies.

This 'Christ-life' continues in parallel with our mortal life; and, if we are living as Christians should, this 'Christ-life' will gradually more and more pervade our being until our whole being is at one with Christ's being and we come to think like Christ, to love God and love others like Christ, to live like Christ, to forgive like Christ. To adapt Pope Benedict's words, 'we want the same things as God and reject the same things as God', and so we develop with God a 'communion of will', which 'increases in a communion of thought and sentiment', and thus 'our will and God's will increasingly coincide'. To put Pope Benedict's words slightly differently, God's will is no longer for me an alien will, imposed on me from outside by the commandments; but it is now my own will, because God is more deeply present to me than I am to myself.[121]

St Paul says, 'You must live your whole life according to the Christ you have received, Jesus, the Lord' (Col 2:6). It is not a question of knowing and observing a list of prohibitions, or of knowing and avoiding a set of 'things that are forbidden'. Living the Christian life thus becomes for me not a question of 'keeping the rules', not even of simply 'obeying the commandments'. It is rather the spontaneous expression of a communion of will and indeed person between myself and Jesus Christ to the point that his will becomes my will and I want only what he wants. As Pope Benedict points out, the Christian life is not an ethical code, it is a 'mysticism' centred on Jesus Christ. It cannot be properly understood or lived without some degree of contemplation – through scripture reading and the liturgy and prayer and above all through the Eucharist. The question is not: 'What are the rules?' but 'What does Jesus Christ want?' – for he is my true and real self. The question regarding the Church is not: 'Who makes the rules?' but 'What does Jesus Christ want?', for Christ is the one whose body is the Church.

The communion of will between myself and God is, to use the modern phrase, 'driven' above all by the communion between myself and Jesus Christ which is the holy Eucharist. This is ultimately the reason why Christ says so simply and so categorically:

> Anyone who does eat my flesh and drink my blood has eternal life. ... He who eats my flesh and drinks my blood lives in me and I live in him. (Jn 6:54, 56)

If one may be forgiven the play on words in this sacred context, one could say that the Christian life consists in letting Christ's Real Presence in Holy Communion become his permanent real presence in the whole of our life. But contrary forces are also at work within us and around us. St Paul speaks of a death to be endured by us so that Christ may live in us. We have to 'die' to sin and to everything within us that is in league with sin. For there still is within us a complicity with sin which resents and resists our communion of life with Jesus Christ. The resulting struggle is long and bitter, a struggle unto death, a struggle between life and death. St Paul used a variety of descriptions for this conflict: it is a struggle between the 'sin living in me', 'the law of sin which lives inside my body', and my spiritual self, or 'the law of the spirit of life in Christ Jesus' within me (Rom 7:28, 8:1); it is a struggle between my spirit and my body, my spiritual self and my unspiritual self; it is a 'war between the impulses of nature and the impulses of the spirit' (Gal 5:17); a struggle between 'the world around us' and our 'new mind' in Christ (Rom 12:2); it is a dying to 'the things that are on the earth' and living a life that is 'hidden with Christ in God' (Col 3:2-4). The outcome of the struggle for the Christian must be the progressive transformation of our whole behaviour until it fully corresponds to our 'new mind' as Christians (Rom 12:2):

> Our minds must be renewed by a spiritual revolution so that we can put on the new self that has been created in God's way in the goodness and holiness of the truth. (Eph 4:24)

The struggle St Paul is speaking about is not a dualism between an evil body and a good and holy soul. The body too is holy and good in virtue of being created by God and in the image of God, and in virtue of the incarnation, whereby God takes on a human body, like to our human bodies. What is even more extraordinary, our bodies, through baptism and the Eucharist, become members making up the body of Christ. To commit fornication is to 'join Christ to the body of a prostitute' (1 Cor 6:13-14), thereby sinning against one's own body. One's body is the 'temple of the Holy Spirit' who dwells in us through baptism; and therefore our bodies are to be used only for God's glory (1 Cor 6:15-20). Our bodies too are sacred and sin committed in our body has to be seen as a form of sacrilege. The sanctification of our body in Christ begins with our baptism and is increased by each Holy Communion.

St Paul does not hesitate to call the struggle against sin a way of sharing in the crucifixion of Christ. It is thus that we live out our baptism, for baptism, as we have noted, is a way of 'dying' to sin and 'rising again' to new life in Christ. A common term for baptism is 'christening'. If we pronounce the word differently as '**Christ**-ening', we obtain a new insight into the meaning of baptism: through baptism our whole being is 'Christified'; it becomes 'Christ-being'. Sad experience shows us that, on our side, this does not happen easily or overnight. There remain within us instincts, passions, desires, that resist our '**Christ**-ening'. It is literally the struggle of a lifetime to overcome all these elements within us and to 'crucify' them so that we can '**Christ**-ify' them. Baptism is not a past one-off event only; it is also a lifelong task, completed only at our death. An early Christian tombstone has the inscription: 'She has completed her baptism.'

Like baptism, the Eucharist, the second sacrament of Christian initiation, bears the sign of crucifixion: the separate consecration of bread and wine symbolises the separation of Christ's body and blood in death on Calvary, just as the dropping of a broken fragment of the sacred host into the cup of Christ's blood before the communion symbolises his resurrection. As the priest drops the fragment into the chalice, he prays: 'May this mingling of the body and blood of Our Lord Jesus Christ bring eternal life to us who receive it.'

The sacraments of baptism and of Eucharist are inseparably linked. The Eucharist is our most powerful resource for living out that radical transformation of our whole being into Christian being, or 'Christ-being', which begins at baptism. It is interesting in this connection to note that the Orthodox Churches administer Holy Communion to baptised infants. Just as baptism acts in us as an ongoing process while being itself a once-only event, something similar is true of the Eucharist. Christ 'grows' in us through our repeated eucharistic communions with him. St Paul frequently speaks of the gradual 'growth' of Christ in us. He likens it to the growth of a child in the womb. He even speaks of himself as a mother in faith to his Galatian converts, needing to go through the pains of giving birth 'until Christ is formed' in them (Gal 4:19-20). All this is the work of the Holy Spirit. The Holy Spirit, given to us in baptism, makes us 'sons and daughters in the Son', and gives us an entirely new relationship with God our Father. We have seen that this new relationship entitles us, indeed obliges us, to a new way of praying, in which we call God 'Abba', 'dearest Father'. It begins for us a whole new way of living which is a sharing in the life of Christ. The ancient prayer 'Anima Christi', which has been put to music in the hymn, 'Soul of my Saviour', has an opening line which has been translated as follows: 'May all that is you flow into me.' The words suggest the appropriateness of the symbolism of eating the body and drinking the blood of the Lord. When we eat ordinary bread, a process of biological metabolism transforms the bread into our bone and muscle. In our recieving of the Eucharist, by a kind of reverse spiritual metabolism, the Lord, whose flesh we eat, transforms us into his own likeness. As St Paul so often reminds us, this spiritual metabolism takes place through the power of the Holy Spirit. St Paul prays for his Ephesian converts: 'May [the Father] give you the power through his Spirit for your hidden self to grow strong.' (Eph 3:16)

The 'hidden self' is Christ's life in ourselves, becoming more and more indivisibly one with our own self, until 'there is only Christ' in us (Col 3:11) and our life becomes, as Christ's life was and is, a life of self-giving love for God and for others. St Paul's prayer continues:

> ... so that Christ may live in your hearts through faith, and thus, planted in love and built on love, you will with all the

saints have strength to grasp the breadth and the length, the height and the depth, until, knowing the love of Christ which is beyond all knowledge, you are filled with the utter fullness of God. (Eph 3:16-19)

In Eucharistic Prayer IV the priest prays:

> That we might live
> no longer for ourselves but for him
> [Christ] sent the Holy Spirit from you, Father,
> as his first gift to those who believe,
> to complete his work on earth
> and to bring us the fullness of grace.

As our life becomes more and more truly the life of Christ in us, then God becomes truly 'all in us all'. Thus, our life in Christ here on earth becomes continuous with our life with Christ in heaven. That consummation of an individual Christian life is already the beginning, here on earth, of that final and universal consummation which is the 'handing over of the Kingdom' by Christ to his eternal Father. St Paul describes it in these words:

> After that will come the end, when he hands over the kingdom to God the Father, having done away with every sovereignty, authority and power. For he must be king until he has put all his enemies under his feet, and the last of the enemies to be destroyed is death. … And when everything is subjected to him, then the Son himself will be subject in his turn to the One who subjected all things to him, so that God may be all in all. (1 Cor 15:24-28)

In this last quotation we have an early statement of a doctrine which St Paul develops systematically over a group of his writings – the doctrine of the Church as the Body of Christ. I have suggested earlier that this concept can be traced back to the time of his conversion, when he heard the voice of Christ on the Damascus Road saying: 'I am Jesus and you are persecuting me.'

St Paul seems to have reflected over and over again on these words and on the revelation he had received from Christ at that moment, and had later found to be identical with the tradition about Jesus that was proclaimed by Cephas or Peter and other leaders of the Church in Jerusalem. Through this renewed reflection and under the guidance of the Holy Spirit, St Paul came to a profound insight into what he called 'the depths that I see in the mystery of Christ' (Eph 3:4). This mystery, hidden in the past and revealed now 'through the Church', is that pagans 'are part of the same body' with Jewish believers in Christ, and this 'same body' is the very body of Christ (Eph 3:1-13).

The first letter in which Paul explicitly expounds this doctrine is in his Letter to the Galatians.[122] Hence Paul writes:

> All baptised in Christ you have all clothed yourselves in Christ and there are no more distinctions between Jew and Greek, slave and free, male and female, but all of you are one in Christ Jesus. (Gal 3:27-8)

It is to be noted that the Greek word for 'one', in the phrase 'all of you are one', is masculine in gender (*h'eis*) not neutral (*h'en*): the phrase means 'you are one person' in Christ, not 'you are one thing'. The 'one person' in this context is Jesus Christ: all members of the Church are *one person* in Christ Jesus.

It would seem to have been this passage which Gerard Manley Hopkins had in mind when he wrote:[123]

> The just man justices;
> keeps grace: that keeps all his goings graces;
> Acts in God's eye what in God's eye he is –
> Christ – for Christ plays in ten thousand places,
> lovely in limbs and lovely in eyes not his
> To the Father through the features of men's faces.

Christians form one body, the body of Christ. But this is a oneness in which each member retains her or his own identity and each one resembles Christ in his or her own particular way. All Christians together in unity reflect to the world the many-splendoured beauty of Christ, and at the same time give praise and glory to God through the endless variety of their Christ-like features.

This doctrine is developed further in First Corinthians. Here the oneness of all believers in Christ is presented as oneness in the same body; but, very importantly, the oneness is now linked explicitly to the one Eucharist which we all receive. St Paul writes:

> The blessing-cup that we bless is a communion with the blood of Christ and the bread that we break is a communion with the body of Christ. The fact that there is only one loaf means that, though there are many of us, we form a single body, because we all have a share in this one loaf. (1 Cor 10:16-17)

This truth becomes for St Paul the ontological basis for teaching about Christian moral living. For example, it is wrong for Christians to share in pagan idol worship by taking part in banquets where meats sacrificed to idols are eaten. Idols, St Paul teaches, are really only demons in disguise, and to share in rites of sacrifice to pagan idols would be to try at one and the same time to be in intimate communion with Christ, with whom we are one body and one blood through the Eucharist, and at the same time be in communion with demons (1 Cor 10:14-22).

We are one body in Christ through baptism and this oneness is intensified through eucharistic communion. Christian morality has, therefore, a eucharistic dimension: in holy communion, we receive what we are – Christ's body; and in receiving Christ we become what we are – Christ's body. We recall here a saying of Nietzsche, that the fundamental principle of morality is: 'Become what you are.' St Augustine put it: 'Become what you receive.'

Another problem which arose in the Corinthian Christian

community was the disciplinary problem of the ordering of special spiritual gifts or charisms. This was becoming a factor for division in a community called to be one in the one body of Christ. Such gifts, St Paul teaches, are all intended for the service of others and should be exercised in an orderly fashion for the good of the whole body of Christ which is the Church:

> Just as a human body, though made up of many parts, is a single unit, because all these parts, though many, make one body, so it is with Christ. ... If the foot were to say 'I am not a hand, so I do not belong to the body', would it stop being part of the body? ... The eye cannot say to the hand, 'I do not need you', nor can the head said to the foot, 'I do not need you'. ... As it is, the parts are many but the body is one ... If one part is hurt, all parts are hurt with it. If one part is given special honour, all parts enjoy it. Now you together are Christ's body. (1 Cor 12:12-30)

Each part of the body should seek, not to exaggerate its own importance, but to serve the common good of the whole body. Each 'gifted' person should use his or her gifts for the betterment of the whole body; and 'gifted' for Christians describes one to whom God has given gifts to be used for the service of the Church and of others – not a reason to feel self-important, but a call to self-giving.

St Paul teaches that all of this ordering of gifts for the good of the whole Church is the work of one and the same Holy Spirit, who is a Spirit of unity and of love and of peace, and who pervades the whole body of Christ which is the Church. Consequently, far more important than any particular gift or charism in the Church is love; and here St Paul leads us into his great hymn in praise of love (1 Cor 13). Without love, he insists, even faith is of no value and hope is of no worth; even the most eloquent preaching based on the most advanced erudition, but without love, is just a hollow drum that booms on the ear but has no solid content and leaves nothing with the hearer but noise. In the area of spiritual gifts, what matters is not that they be spectacular but that they are for 'the benefit of the community'.

St Paul, in his Letter to the Romans, restates once more the primacy of love; and here he links this again with the doctrine of the oneness of all members of the Church in the one body of Christ. He writes:

> Just as each of our bodies has several parts and each part has a separate function, so all of us in union with Christ form one body, and, as parts of it, we belong to each other. ... Do not let love be a pretence, but sincerely prefer good to evil. Love each other as much as brothers and sisters should and have a profound respect for one another. ... Work for the Lord with untiring effort, with great earnestness of spirit. If you have hope, this will make you cheerful. Do not give up if trials come and keep on praying. (Rom 12:4-13)

It is timely to point out here that these chapters in St Paul's first Letter to the Corinthians have a special relevance for the Church in our time; for love or mutual respect between different tendencies within the Church – 'progressives'/'conservatives', 'traditionalists'/'liberals', etcetera – are rarely evident, while anger against the Church and its leaders seems to become more vociferous. Anger can be justified – when it springs from love; but when there is no love, anger brings no healing and no reform; it benefits no-one. It damages unity, it excludes respect for others, it prevents dialogue. It hurts the whole body of the Church. We need to be reminded, again and again, of St Paul's words: 'You must want love more than anything else.' (1 Cor 14:1)

The Eucharist is our God-given means of overcoming divisions in the Church which threaten its essential internal unity. This is one of the great challenges facing the Church in our time. The Eucharist impels us to change our attitudes if they promote disunion or are lacking in charity and to seek strategies which foster unity within the Church. When we read books or articles by fellow-Catholics which we feel to be at variance with orthodox teaching, we should not rush to condemn, nor should we impute unworthy motives. We should presume the writer to be in good faith and ask ourselves why he or she writes (or speaks) like this. We should examine whether some of our own words or attitudes might be such as to foster misunderstanding or to evoke criticism.

In our comment or response, we should give positive statement of the truth priority over condemnation of error – necessary though this latter may be if the truth of faith is to be preserved. Above all, we must at all times preserve the primacy of love. We must speak the truth, but speak it always and only in love. 'Speaking the truth in love' (Eph 4:15) – St Paul's guiding principle – must dominate all dialogue between Catholics. Great progress has been made in developing a methodology for dialogue between divided Christians. We must now develop a similar methodology for dialogue between divided Catholics. Pope Paul VI, in his first encyclical in 1964, *Ecclesiam Suam*, gave us a superb outline of the kind of approach which the Church should adopt in dialogue with the modern world. The same approach should mark dialogue between Catholics. Here, more than anywhere, what St Paul says about love in the Church is relevant. We must preserve unity in the bond of peace (Eph 4:3). The golden rule of St Vincent of Lerins is as relevant today as in his own fifth century:

In necessariis unitas.
In dubiis libertas.
In omnibus caritas.

In necessary matters, unity.
In doubtful matters, liberty.
In all matters, charity.

The theme of love as the defining attribute of the Church is propounded repeatedly and with great intensity by St Paul in his first Letter to the Corinthians and in his Letters to the Romans, the Colossians and the Ephesians. Paul relates this theme to the Eucharist. I wish to look briefly at what Paul says on these matters in each of these Letters. Writing to the Romans, he reminds them that:

> All of us in union with Christ form one body and as parts of it we belong to each other. Our gifts differ according to the grace given to us.

Each person should accept his or her 'grace' and use it for the common good, respecting the 'grace' of others and realising that all are working together for the same Lord, and that the work of each one is necessary if the Church is to fulfil its mission (Rom 12:3-13).

Writing to the Colossians, Paul outlines the way of living which should characterise Christians – a 'life hidden with Christ in God', a life without distinctions of social class, race or ethnicity: there is no room for such distinctions. There is only Christ: he is everything and he is in everything (Col 3:11).

The 'clothing' over all virtues, 'to keep them together and complete them', is love. Fr Conleth Kearns likens this to a cincture or belt which clasps all these virtues together.[124] Inseparable from love is peace, for it is to this that Christians are 'called together as parts of one body'. This is only what is expected of those who 'let the message of Christ in all its richness find a home' in themselves (Col 3:14-17). One of the Easter hymns (in Latin) in the Liturgy of the Hours speaks of Christ as the 'bread of sincerity'. There is often great insincerity in our calling ourselves Christian when our lives and attitudes are decidedly not Christian.

The same message is repeated in the Letter to the Ephesians. Christian morality is simply a living out in behaviour and in relationships of what Christians *are* – the body of Christ. The way of living of Christians is the consequence of their belonging to 'one body, one Spirit … one Lord, one faith, one baptism and one God who is Father of all, over all, through all and within all' (Eph 4:4-6). Christians (whom Paul calls 'the saints') 'together make a unity in the work of service, building up the body of Christ'.

In this way we are all to come to unity in our faith and in our knowledge of the Son of God, until we become the perfect Man, fully mature with the fullness of Christ himself. (Eph 4:12-13).

This growth is compared to the development of an individual from childhood to adulthood. The completion of the process of development is none other than Christ himself – the 'completed Christ', what St Augustine called the 'total Christ', Head and members together in the same body. The degree of growth is measured by the degree of love:

If we live by the truth and in love we shall grow in all ways into Christ, who is the head by whom the whole body is fitted and joined together, every joint adding its own strength for each separate part to work according to its function. So the body grows until it has built itself up in love. (Eph 4:15-16)

Earlier in the same Letter, Paul had felt obliged to invent a new word of his own to express the realism of the oneness of Christians in the one body of Christ. The word is *sussomoi*, 'sharers of the same body'. There seems to be no other example of this word anywhere.[125] Paul is commenting on the mystery which brings it about that 'Jewish and pagan believers in Christ now are parts of the same body' – the body of Christ. Paul is so overwhelmed by this truth that he can only fall on his knees and pray:

Out of his infinite glory may God give you the power through his Spirit for your hidden self to grow strong so that Christ may live in your hearts through faith and then, planted in love and built on love, you will with all the saints have strength to grasp the breadth and the length, the height and the depth, until, knowing the love of Christ which is beyond all knowledge, you are filled with utter fullness of God. (Eph 3:16-19)

Then comes one of Paul's great doxologies:

> Glory be to him whose power, working in us, can do infinitely more than we can ask or even imagine, glory to him from generation to generation in the Church and in Christ Jesus, for ever and ever. Amen. (Eph 3:20-21)

This whole rich teaching of St Paul on the body of Christ which is the Church, the fullness of Christ (Eph 1:23), is embedded in his teaching about the Eucharist. The passage about the blessing cup and the bread, his first Letter to the Corinthians, which I have quoted on p. 191 , comes just before his instruction about the Lord's Last Supper, and about the need to 'recognise the Body' and preserve its unity in love.

Sharing 'at the table of the Lord' marks Christians as a distinct group in society, with a distinctive pattern of behaviour. We have noted St Paul's insistence that it is unthinkable for Christians to share in the idolatrous feasts of the pagan cultures surrounding them. Similarly, we, the Christians of today, who live surrounded by a secularised and increasingly God-less culture, must shun the various new 'idolatries' of today's world. We must instead draw life and strength from the Eucharist, allowing Christ to grow in us individually in order that he may grow in the Church as a whole, until Christ becomes everything in each and every member of the Church and we approximate more and more to the point where God is all in us all.

St Paul writes:

> You must live your whole life according to the Christ you have recieved – Jesus the Lord; you must be rooted in him and build on him and hold firm by the faith you have been taught, and full of thanksgiving. Make sure that no-one traps you and deprives you of your freedom by some second-hand empty, rational philosophy based on the principles of this world instead of on Christ. (Col 2:6)

This is why the road to reform and renewal in the Church passes through the Eucharist. This is why the faith-filled, reverent and fervent celebration of the Eucharist is itself a 're-formation' and a 're-newal' of the Church. When Mass is celebrated, the Church is brought back to its first beginnings, when the Apostles gathered around their Lord at the Last Supper and again when, united in prayer with Mary, the Mother of the Lord, they waited in the Upper Room at Pentecost to receive the Holy Spirit. Christ shares his Body with today's disciples at Mass in order that they may share his Body in the Church, each disciple drawing life and strength, energy and vitality, love and hope from Christ, so that the whole Church may be built up in faith and in love. The collective result of our Masses and Holy Communions should be that those who look at the members of the Church or who listen to members of the Church, may see and hear, not quarrelling factions speaking ill of one another, or ambitious individuals or groups competing with one another for precedence and power, but Jesus Christ himself, living and present in the Church, speaking to the Church in our world and speaking to our modern world through the Church, and saying: 'Seek first the Kingdom of God and his justice.' (Lk 12:32)

It is in the measure in which we become 'one body, one spirit in Christ' that we become 'a living sacrifice of praise' to God and living signs of Christ's peace to our world. Before the Holy Communion in every Mass we exchange the sign of peace, wishing peace to our neighbour, the peace which the Lamb of God, the Son of the Living God, 'by the will of the Father and the work of the Holy Spirit' brought into the world. Through that internal peace the Spirit is at work making us into a people made one in Christ 'so that the world may believe'.

We have perhaps tended to see our Mass and Holy Communion as acts of individual devotion, and to be less conscious of their ecclesial dimension. Yet St Thomas Aquinas, our greatest theologian, declared that the first effect of the Eucharist is the growth in numbers and in holiness of the Church. This is part of the meaning of St Paul's words about 'recognising the Body'.

To 'recognise the Body' of Christ at Mass is also to be aware that our sins hurt the whole Body of Christ which is the Church and that our faith in Christ and our love of him can help to heal that hurt. Nowadays, attendance at Sunday Masses is less than it was formerly, and, as a result, the body of the Church at large and of the Church in each particular parish suffers spiritual loss, and each diocese and each parish is weakened and diminished. The personal growth in faith and love and in prayer of each of us, particularly at Mass, can in some degree make up for that loss and can by God's grace help to attract back the missing. We must listen to St Paul's appeal:

> Do not make God's Holy Spirit sad, for his Holy Spirit is God's mark of ownership upon you, a guarantee that the day will come when God will set you free. ... Be friends with one another and kind, forgiving each other as readily as God forgave you in Christ. (Eph 4:30-32)

As for those of us who have the privilege of being regular members of the eucharistic community at Mass, we must resist the temptation to join those who fail to attend. We should see ourselves as personally and individually invited by Christ. He is saying to us as he said to the Apostles in the Synagogue at Capernaum: 'Will you go away too?' Let our response be firm and clear:

> Lord, who shall we go to? You have the message of eternal life, and we believe, we know that you are the Holy One of God. (Jn 6:67-8)

One test of the quality of liturgical celebration in a parish is the degree to which it helps to create a sense of community in faith and love within the parish and the diocese, and indeed within the neighbourhoods where the worshippers live. This sense of community must be open also to friendship and fellowship and mutual understanding and respect with people of different Christian denominations and indeed people of different faiths within the same neighbourhood. If we truly are the Body of Christ, and if we are open to the Spirit of God who fills that Body, then our relationships will be marked by 'love, joy, peace, patience, kindness, goodness, trustfulness, gentleness and self-control' (Gal 5:22); for these are the fruits of the Spirit and the signs of his presence. These are the marks of the eucharistic community which the parish is supposed to be. Let us never forget that a eucharistic community is one which 'builds itself up in love' (Eph 4:16).

Mutual support and sharing, whether in joy or in sorrow, between people with different gifts and different strengths is for St Paul a mark of a Church that recognises itself as the body of Christ. As in the human body, so also in the Church:

> Each part must be equally concerned for all the others. If one part is hurt, all parts are hurt with it. If one part is given special honour, all parts enjoy it. (1 Cor 12:25-26)

Each individual has his or her part to play. All together are Christ's body, but each one is a different part of it, each with its own indispensable role and importance for the well-being of the whole body. But, as St Paul so often reminds us, the most important of all is love (1 Cor 12:27; 13:13).

Suffering may seem to lessen a person's capacity to serve the Church. St Paul, however, sees suffering, on the contrary, as being in itself a very special way of serving the Church. He himself knew suffering in many forms: hardships at sea and on land in the course of his missionary journeys, violence and even assault at the hands of the enemies of the gospel, floggings, sometimes till near death, beatings, stonings, starvation, imprisonment, all these Paul suffered for the sake of the gospel. His pastoral care for his convert communities brought him daily worries, as part of his 'anxiety for all the churches' (2 Cor 11:23-33). There are references in his writings to some physical ailment, seemingly an eye problem, which caused him great embarrassment. It was of such a nature as could have caused revulsion or disgust to the Galatians were it not for their deep faith; but their faith made them ready instead to donate their own eyes to him if this were possible (Gal 4:13-16).[126]

Paul, however, saw all this suffering as his way of sharing in the sufferings of Christ on behalf of the whole body of Christ which is the Church. His own sufferings were seen by him as 'the overflow of the sufferings of Christ' into his own life (2 Cor 1:5). Through his sufferings, therefore, Paul felt that he was making up in his own body 'all that has still to be undergone by Christ for the sake of his body, the Church', of which he, Paul, was the servant (Col 1:24). It was not that Christ's personal sufferings were in any way incomplete; Paul's point was that the salvation won for the human race by Christ's sufferings needed still to be applied to the individual members who are being added, generation after generation, to the body of Christ.

This is why Paul can say that Christ has sufferings still to be undergone in his body which is the Church. By accepting his or her share in Christ's sufferings, the individual Christian strengthens the Church to endure whatever sufferings or scandals may assail it in the course of history, and to survive the storms which, from time to time, may afflict it, from within and from without. Paul himself derived great consolation from this truth; it was this that enabled him to 'struggle wearily on', through disappointment and weariness of spirit, 'helped only by [Christ's] power driving [him] irresistibly' (Col 1:29). This thought can inspire all of us in the present difficulties through which the Church is passing and from which we all suffer. It can act as a night-light 'for lighting a way through the dark until the dawn comes' (2 Pet 1:19).

Just as in a human body, when any member of the Church is in pain, the whole body of the Church suffers; conversely, each member of the Church should feel the pain when the Church body is hurt. Each member is used by God to transmit healing and health, courage and grace from Christ the Head to the other members of Christ's body which is the Church. It is *our* body which is affected when one member is unwell, corporally or spiritually. When one member is strong – particularly when the heart is strong – the whole body benefits. We recall again St Thérèse's saying: 'At the heart of the Church I shall be love – and so I shall be all things [for the Church].' We are all members of one another in the Church, all 'sharers of the same body' with Christ and with one another. The supreme moment of this sharing is the Eucharist; for it brings us into the deepest communion with Christ, and, through him, with the Church.

We should try like St Paul to accept suffering of body or of mind as the 'overflow' of Christ's sufferings into our lives. As Christ 'sacrificed himself for the Church to make her holy … and glorious, with no speck or wrinkle … but holy and spotless', so, in the 'communion with the blood of Christ' which is the Eucharist, we can offer our sufferings, united with Christ's, that the Church may be cleansed from the sins of its clergy and its lay members and made glorious 'without spot or wrinkle' (Eph 5:25-27). St Paul says:

> A man never hates his own body but feeds it and looks after it, and that is the way Christ treats the Church because it is his body, and we are its living parts. (Eph 5:29-30)

We should strive, particularly through the Eucharist, to be genuinely 'living parts' of the Church, so that Christ may use us to 'feed and look after' the needy members of the Church which is his body.

Suffering with Christ for the Church, however, is by no means a form of unhealthy 'spiritual masochism'. Christians do not seek suffering for its own sake. Their communion with Christ is – or should be – so close that they themselves, almost naturally, suffer as they contemplate the sufferings of Christ. They wish to share in some way in Christ's sufferings and they spontaneously accept their own sufferings as their way of sharing those of their Lord. It is significant that, when St Paul speaks of Christ suffering and sacrificing himself for his Church, he is speaking in the context of marriage. A husband or a wife shares and in some sense *feels* the pain of the other as if it were their own pain. This, as St Paul suggests, is what love means: a man becomes one body with his wife in marriage; husbands must love their wives as they love their own bodies (Eph 5:28-31). Paul applies this analogy to relations between Christ and his Church. The Church and Christ form one body as a husband and his wife form one body. Christ shares our pain as we share his (Eph 5:23).

It is above all by our prayer, offered through Christ our Lord, and by our sufferings freely and patiently accepted as a sharing in the sufferings of Christ, that we each help the whole Church to grow towards its full and final consummation in the glory of the risen Christ. To have Christ living in us is already a promise, and indeed a beginning, of that final glory; and the Eucharist is the most special way that Christ himself has chosen to live in us. St Paul writes to the Ephesians:

> The saints [i.e. all Christians] make a unity in the work of service, building up the body of Christ, until we attain in our totality to that state of being a perfect Man, to that measure of stature which belongs to the completion of Christ. Following the truth in love, we must in every way grow up towards him who is the Head, Christ himself. (Eph 4:13-16)[127]

Meanwhile, here in this world, through the Eucharist, we have Christ within us; but his presence in us is not visible externally except by such glimpses of it as are perceived by others through our way of Christian living. Each Christian is called to be a Christ-person, an 'icon' of Christ, a person in whom others can see something of what Jesus Christ is like. And St Paul tells us, when Christ comes again in glory the truth will shine out gloriously: 'When Christ is revealed – and he is your life – you too will be revealed in all your glory with him.' (Col 3:4)

Hence, St Paul says:

> Our homeland is in heaven and from heaven comes the Saviour we are waiting for, the Lord, Jesus Christ, and he will transfigure these wretched bodies of ours into copies of his own glorious body. (Phil 3:20-1)

Melchisedek, Priesthood and Sacrifice

As I promised earlier (see p. 23), I have reserved for this space my reflections on the third of the sacrifices enumerated in Eucharistic Prayer I, namely the sacrifice of Melchisedek. I do so because the figure of Melchisedek is an important part of the argumentation of the author of the Letter to the Hebrews, and therefore of the Church's teaching on the Eucharist as found in the New Testament – and this is my concern in this part of the book.

Let me recall that the present translation of the Melchisedek passage in Eucharistic Prayer I runs as follows:

> Look with favour on these offerings
> and accept them,
> as once you accepted …
> the bread and wine offered
> by your priest, Melchisedek.

The Latin original of this text puts this as follows:

> Accept them
> as once you accepted the offering made
> by your High Priest, Melchisedek,
> a holy sacrifice,
> an immaculate host.

What we have at present is a rather free translation, which scarcely conveys the sense of the importance given in the Church's tradition to Melchisedek and his sacrifice. Melchisedek was and remains a mysterious figure. In the fourteenth chapter of Genesis, we read about the great 'war of the Kings', when four great kings rebelled against a dominant coalition of kings, including Abraham. Their revolt was successful and they captured Abraham's nephew, Lot, and all his possessions. Abraham retaliated and defeated the 'rebels', releasing Lot and all the captured soldiers and possessions.

When Abraham returned home victorious from the wars, Melchisedek, King of Salem, who 'was a priest of God, Most High', came to greet him. Genesis tells us:

> Melchisedek, King of Salem, brought bread and wine; he was a priest of God, Most High. He pronounced this blessing: 'Blessed be Abraham by God, Most High, Creator of heaven and earth, and blessed be God, Most High, for handing over his enemies to you;' and Abram gave him a tithe of everything. (Gen 14:17-20)

Psalm 109(110) brings Melchisedek again into prominence, though shedding no more light upon his identity. The psalm may be a coronation hymn: it seems to hint at a Jewish coronation rite, part of which may have taken the form of the new King's 'drinking from the stream by the wayside and therefore he shall lift up his head'. There are other indications that the new king drank from the stream of Gihon in the course of his coronation. 'Drinking from the stream' was later interpreted by Christians as a sign of the passion of Christ; 'lifting up his head' after drinking was seen as a sign of the Resurrection. Our Lord himself quotes this psalm as a challenge to the disciples in their understanding of who Christ himself was. He quoted the first verse:

> The Lord's revelation to my master,
> Sit at my right hand
> I will put your foes beneath your feet.

Then Jesus said to the disciples,

> What is your opinion about the Christ? Whose son is he? If David [author of the psalm] can call him Lord, how can he be his son? (Mt 22:41-6)

Psalm 109(110) is regarded as a Messianic psalm. For this and other reasons it is seen as a revelatory psalm pointing to Jesus Christ as the Messiah and Universal King. This is what gives the psalm its particular importance in the eyes of the author of the Letter to the Hebrews.

This Letter follows closely what is said about Melchisedek in the Book of Genesis. Melchisedek is King of Salem, a word which is similar in meaning to 'Shalom' or 'Peace'. Coming to greet Abraham, Melchisedek brought bread and wine to offer in sacrifice. He was, Genesis tells us, 'a priest of God Most High'. He blessed Abraham, saying:

> Blessed be Abram by God Most High,
> creator of heaven and earth
> and blessed be God Most High
> for handing over your enemies to you.

Melchisedek tries to persuade Abraham to keep the possessions he had reclaimed in battle, but Abraham firmly refused. The Letter to the Hebrews interprets the name, Melchisedek, as King of righteousness as well as King of Salem or King of Peace:

> He has no father nor mother nor ancestry, and his life has no beginning or ending; he is like the Son of God. He remains a priest forever. (Heb 7:2-3)

The writer then recalls Psalm 109(110), and in particular verse 4:

> The Lord has sworn an oath
> he will not change.
> 'You are a priest forever,
> a priest like Melchisedek of old.'

This declaration, reinforced by divine oath, demonstrates that there has been a complete change in the priesthood as set up in the Jewish or Levitical tradition. The Levitical priests were entitled, and indeed obliged, to ask for tithes from the people. But here we have Levi, present already in his ancestor Abraham, paying tithes to Melchisedek. Levi is thereby recognising that the priesthood of Melchisedek is superior to his own and that the Levitical priesthood now has to yield place to a new priesthood, a 'priesthood of the same order as Melchisedek'. The author of this new priesthood is Jesus Christ, who is priest 'by the power of a indestructible life' (Heb 7:16-17). This new priesthood is inseparable from a new covenant. The Letter to the Hebrews calls it a 'better covenant … founded on better promises' (Heb 8:6-7). The Hebrews text quotes from Jeremiah to show the provisional and imperfect nature of the old covenant (8:6-12).

The priesthood of Christ, on the other hand, is an eternal priesthood:

> His power to save is utterly certain, since he is living forever to intercede for all who come to God through him. (Heb 7:25)

The sacrifice offered by Christ is the ideal and perfect sacrifice, offered by the ideal and perfect priest:

> The ideal high priest would have to be holy, innocent and uncontaminated, beyond the influence of sinners and raised up above the heavens; one who would not need to offer sacrifices every day, as the other high priests do for their own sins and then for those of the people, because he has done this once and for all by offering himself. The Law appoints high priests who are men subject to weakness; but the promise on oath, which came after the Law, appointed the Son who was made perfect forever. (see Heb 7:26-28)

The uniqueness of Christ's priesthood has many aspects. Christ is 'holy, innocent and uncontaminated, beyond the influence of sinners, raised up above the heavens' (Heb 7:26-28). He has offered himself once and for all; he is the perfect priest who:

> offered himself as the perfect sacrifice to God through the eternal Spirit [and who can] purify our inner self from dead actions so that we do our service to the living God. (Heb 9:14)

The Temple which he enters with the redeeming sacrifice of his own blood is not a material building, however sacred: it is heaven itself, so that he can 'appear in the actual presence of God on our behalf' (Heb 9:24).

Psalm 39(40) shows that the sacrifice acceptable to God is not animals' blood but the perfect submission to God of our human wills; and this is true uniquely of Jesus Christ, who is in perfect union with the Father's will, manifested 'by the offering of his body made once and for all by Jesus Christ' (Heb 10:10). It is thus that Jesus shows himself as the servant of the Lord, as foretold in Isaiah 53.[128] It is thus that Jesus shows himself as perfectly fulfilling the definition of sacrifice given in Psalm 39(40):

> You who wanted no sacrifice or oblation
> prepared a body for me.
> You took no pleasure in holocausts
> or sacrifices for sin;
> then I said,
> just as I was commanded
> in the scroll of the book,
> 'God, here am I!
> I am coming to obey your will'. (Ps 39(40):6-8)

The new Sacrifice inaugurated the new covenant and daily renews it. This is a covenant which gives us who were once excluded from the covenant the right to enter the sanctuary with our fellow believers in Christ. This should be our joy, a joy from which we should not exclude ourselves. The writer pleads: 'Do not stay away from the meetings of the community ... Encourage each other to go.' (Heb 10:25)

The Letter continues with a great paean of praise of faith and of the people who were our ancestors in the faith: Abel, Enoch, Noah, Abraham, Sarah, Jacob, Esau, Moses – all of them heroes of the faith. Yet it was not they who received what God had promised:

> Since God had made provision for us to have something better
> and they were not to reach perfection, except with us. (Heb
> 11:39-40)

It is Jesus Christ himself who is our Leader in faith. The writer
exhorts us: 'Let us not lose sight of Jesus.' (Heb 12:2) I feel a special
personal affinity with the Letter to the Hebrews, because it was from
this Letter that, forty years ago, I took my episcopal motto: '*Jesus
Christus heri et hodie*'; 'Jesus Christ is the same today as he was
yesterday and as he will be forever.' (Heb 13:8, 22, 25)

Through his word, particularly in the Liturgy of the Word,
Jesus is constantly at work transforming us into the likeness of
himself. His word can act like a surgeon's knife, slipping 'through
the place where the soul is divided from the spirit, or joints from
the marrow; it can judge the secret emotions and thoughts. No
created thing can hide from him; everything is uncovered and
open to the eyes of the one to whom we must give account of
ourselves' (Heb 4:12-13). Jesus is himself the caring and
compassionate surgeon. By his incarnation he has shared our
weaknesses with us:

> [So] it is not as if we had a high priest who was incapable of
> feeling our weaknesses with us; but we have one who has been
> tempted in every way that we are, though he is without sin. ...
> And so he can sympathise with those who are ignorant or
> uncertain because he too lives in the limitations of weakness. ...
> During his life on earth he offered up prayer and entreaty, loud
> and in silent tears, to the one who had the power to save him out
> of death, and he submitted so humbly that his prayer was heard.
> ... He learnt to obey through suffering. (Heb 4:15-16; 5:2, 7-10)

Reading and prayerfully pondering Holy Scripture, attentive
particularly to Holy Scripture read at the Liturgy of the Word at
Mass, we no longer remain at the stage of babies drinking milk; we
begin to be adults eating:

> solid food [which] for mature men and women with minds are trained by practice to distinguish between good and bad. (Heb 5:14)

This training comes from God himself and is corroborated by God's solemn covenant oath. This gives us:

> strong encouragement to take a firm grip on the hope which is held out to us and which reaches right through beyond the veil where Jesus has entered before us and on our behalf. (Heb 6:19-20)

Jesus carries with him into the holy presence of the Father his own blood, poured out for us in the greatest act of love the world has ever known. The writer of the Letter to the Hebrews calls his own message 'these words of advice', and asks its readers to 'take these words kindly'. He ends with the words: 'Grace be with you all.' (Heb 13:22-25) These concluding words show the loving concern which the writer has to share the truth about the Eucharist with this community whose Hebrew formation might isolate them from Greek-speaking Christians and might cause them to be deprived of some of the riches and joys of true and full eucharistic faith. For our Eucharist brings a new covenant for a new people, a covenant of Love which makes all things new and takes all sins away through God's mercy for the truly penitent. The old covenant inaugurated on Mount Sinai, with its awesome manifestations of God's almighty power, struck fear even into Moses himself. Our new covenant, renewed in each Eucharist, takes all fear away, leaving only love and joy and hope. For, as the writer of the Letter to the Hebrews reminds us, through the Eucharist, we have come to Mount Zion and to the city of the living God. We are admitted, with Jesus our priest, behind the veil into the very presence of God. We join with the millions of angels and with the saints in their celebration of the joyful festival of God's unending love. That is the grace and the joy of the Eucharist. Let us hold on to that grace, the Letter pleads, and use it to worship

God in the way that God finds acceptable, in reverence and in a new form of fear, a loving fear of ever letting ourselves be separated from God's incredible love.

'For our God is a consuming fire.' (Heb12:22-29)

The Cosmic Eucharist

The body of Christ is organically linked with the whole of creation. The Son of God, the Eternal Word, shares in the creative work of his Father. The Prologue of St John's gospel tells us that it was through the Word who 'was with God in the beginning', that all things came to be; 'not one thing had its being but through him'. When the Word was made flesh and 'was coming into the world', he was coming to his own domain and his own people did not accept him' (Jn 1:1-3, 10-11). This is true of the body of Christ in its mortal and in its resurrected state; it is true of the body of Christ which is the Church; it is true of the glorified body of Christ, who is to come again in glory. The incarnation and the Eucharist have cosmic significance.

The great christological hymns of St Paul convey the same teaching. These hymns may have been taken over by Paul from the liturgy of the Apostolic Church. They certainly were part of the faith and confession of the earliest Christian communities. The first of these is to be found in St Paul's Letter to the Philippians. It speaks of Christ 'emptying himself' in the incarnation and making himself still more humble in the Passion. But, for this very reason:

> [God] raised him high and gave him the name which is above all other names so that all beings in the heavens, on earth and in the underworld, should bend the knee at the name of Jesus and every tongue should acclaim Jesus Christ as Lord, to the glory of God the Father. (Phil 2:6-11)

Writing to the Ephesians, Paul, after greeting them as 'the saints who are faithful to Christ Jesus' at Ephesus, continues immediately with the words: 'Blessed be God, the Father of Our Lord, Jesus Christ.' These words are the beginning of an early Christian Berakah, a prayer form which, as we have seen, had its origins in Jewish liturgy and in turn influenced the structure of the Christian Eucharistic Prayer. Paul's hymn goes on to speak of the 'mystery of [God's] purpose', the 'hidden plan God had made from the beginning', namely: 'that he would bring everything together under Christ as head, everything in the heavens and everything on earth.'

In that vast universe, under Christ as its Head, we Christians have the special privilege of 'knowing the good news of salvation and believing it', and, consequently, we have the privilege and the responsibility of 'making Christ's glory praised' (Eph 1:3-14).

In particular, we are given the privilege of knowing God's power, at work in Christ, and of praising and worshipping

> [God who] has put all things under Christ's feet,[129]
> and made him, as the ruler of everything, the head
> of the Church, which is his body, the fullness of
> him who fills the whole creation. (Eph 1:17-23)

In the Letter to the Colossians, Paul hymns Christ as:

> The image of the unseen God and the first-born of all creation,
> for in him were created all things in heaven and on earth,
> everything visible and everything invisible. ... All things were
> created through him and for him. ... and he holds all things in
> unity. Now the Church is his body, he is its head. ... God wanted
> all perfection to be found in him and all things to be reconciled
> through him and for him, everything in heaven and everything on
> earth. (Col 1:15-20)

It is one and the same Christ, therefore, who shares one body with the Church as its Head and who, in his fullness as Christ-and-Church-together, 'fills the whole creation' (Eph 1:23). The Church is not alien to the cosmos or extraneous to it. Christ, who is head of the Church, is head also of creation. The Church, which shares one body with Christ, fills the whole creation and gives unity to all created things. The corollary is that the well-being of the Church contributes to the welfare of the cosmos and its inhabitants. The Church is, as many prayers in the Church's liturgy put it, a 'sacrament of unity and love', called to offer to all of humanity a model of loving and caring one another and for all living beings on the planet.

Christians, more than any other human group, are also called to care for the Planet, of which the Lord is head. In Eucharistic Prayer IV, we pray with the priest:

> Father, we acknowledge your greatness:
> all your actions show your wisdom and love.
> You formed man in your own likeness
> and set him over the whole world,
> to serve you his Creator
> and to rule over all creatures.

Humankind's 'rule' over creation is not despotic and absolute. It must serve God, the Creator, and his purposes. It must be marked by the qualities of God's kingdom – a kingdom of justice, love and peace. Men and women are shepherds of creation, caretakers of Planet Earth, answerable to God and to one another for their use or abuse of it.[130]

The cosmic dimension of the Eucharist is indicated particularly in the Offertory Rite in each eucharistic celebration. The gifts of bread and wine are brought to the altar processionally by representatives of the worshipping community.[131] The priest or deacon accepts the gifts and places them on the altar. The priest then offers them to God with a prayer of blessing. Offering the bread, he prays:

> Blessed are you Lord,
> God of all creation.
> Through your goodness we have this bread to offer,
> which earth has given
> and human hands have made.
> It will become for us the bread of life.

Offering the wine, the priest prays:

> Blessed are you Lord,
> God of all creation.
> Through your goodness we have this wine to offer,
> fruit of the vine
> and work of human hands.
> It will become our spiritual drink.

Earth and water, sun, air and rain, with human hands and brains and the tools and technology which work on these elements, are combined together to bring seed to crop in the soil and then bring wheat to harvest and then to mill and bakery and to bring vines to fruition and then bring grapes to vintage and on to wine cellar. The labour and the technology and science which produce bread from wheat and distribute it, or which produce wine from grapes and then store and later distribute it, are an exercise of the stewardship of earth entrusted by God to human beings. All this is consecrated to the praise and glory of God the Creator in the Eucharist. The bread and wine, product of earth and of human work and science and technology, are transformed in the Eucharist into the substance of the glorified body and blood of Christ. Thereby there is already a mysterious beginning of that 'hidden plan God made in the beginning ...' that he 'would bring everything together under Christ as Head, everything in the heavens and everything on earth' (Eph 1:10), so that, in the whole cosmos, as well as in redeemed humanity, 'God might be all in all'. Already, in the Eucharist, in principle and in anticipation of the eschatological End, 'everything is brought together under Christ as Head', and Christ, 'the Head of the Church which is his body' becomes 'the ruler of everything', and 'the fullness of him who fills the whole creation' (Eph 1:22-23). Christ 'holds all things in unity' and 'all things [are] reconciled through him and for him, everything in heaven and everything on earth' (Col 1:17-20).

God's creative power is at work in the Eucharist, as it is in the creation of the cosmos. Power to change the substance of things is the same power as that involved in creating them. St Ambrose, Bishop of Milan and one of the great theologians of all time, who died in AD 397, wrote a book entitled *De Mysteriis*, 'On the Mysteries'. He speaks of the many instances of 'change of elements' effected by divine intervention, as recounted in Holy Scripture. Most striking of all is the change from nothing into existence involved in the creation of the world. He quotes the Book of Genesis: 'God spoke and [the world was] made; He commanded and [the world was] created.'

Ambrose goes on to ask:

> Is he, then, not able to change existing things into what they were not before? Surely, creating is not less than changing the nature of things.[132]

The Heavenly Liturgy: the Book of Revelation

The Church's Liturgy is, therefore, earth-related, as befits the 'earthlings' which we, the worshippers, are. But it is also an echo of the liturgy of heaven. The Preface to the Eucharistic Prayer always ends with the singing or saying of the *Sanctus*, or the 'Holy, Holy, Holy'. This is always introduced by such words as:

> Through Christ, [our Lord]
> the angels of heaven offer their prayer of adoration
> as they rejoice in your presence forever.
> May our voices be one with theirs
> in their triumphant hymn of praise:
> Holy, Holy, Holy Lord,
> God of power and might,
> heaven and earth are full of your glory,
>   Hosanna in the highest.
> Blessed is he who comes in the name of the Lord,
>   Hosanna in the highest.

This, as we have seen, is a recall of the great passage in Isaiah which describes God's revelation of himself to the prophet and God's entrusting to the prophet of a message, to be proclaimed in God's name to the people of Israel:

> In the year of King Uzziah's death I saw the Lord God seated on a high throne; his train filled the sanctuary, above him stood Seraphs … and they cried out one to another:
> 'Holy, Holy, Holy, is the Lord of Hosts.
> His glory fills the whole earth.'
> The foundations of the threshold shook with the voice of the one who cried out and the temple shook. (Isa 6:1-5)

To cleanse the prophet's 'unclean lips' and make those lips worthy to pronounce the divine message, one of the Seraphs takes a live coal from the burning incense on the altar and touches Isaiah's lips, saying: 'See now, this has touched your lips, your sin is taken away, your inequity is purged.' (Isa 6:6-7) This is recalled in the prayers said by the priest or deacon as he prepares to proclaim the gospel reading. A deacon asks for a blessing from the priest celebrant, who prays over him:

> The Lord be in your heart and your lips that you may worthily proclaim his gospel. In the name of the Father and of the Son and of the Holy Spirit.

If the priest is himself proclaiming the gospel, he first bows before the altar and prays: 'Almighty God, cleanse my heart and my lips that I may worthily proclaim your gospel.'

There are further echoes of the Isaian passage in the sign of the Cross traced on forehead, lips and breast by priest and people before the reading of the gospel: this is a silent, mimed prayer that all present may be given the grace to understand with their minds the gospel reading, to use their lips to share its message with others, and to translate that message into their heart's choices.

The same Isaian scene is recalled in the last book of the New Testament, the Book of Revelation, when it describes the scene in heaven. A throne is seen there, resembling an emerald, and it is encircled by a rainbow. Around the throne twenty-four elders sit in a circle, wearing white robes with crowns on their heads. These represent the old Israel, with its twelve tribes, and the new Israel, represented by the Twelve Apostles. Closer to the throne are four animals, resembling a lion, a bull, a human being and an angel. These are often taken to be symbols of the four evangelists, Matthew, Mark, Luke and John. These never stop singing, by day and by night, the song of the Seraphs in Isaiah:

> Holy, Holy, Holy
> is the Lord God the Almighty,
> he was, he is and he is to come. (Rev 4:1-8)

God, the One sitting on the throne, is worshipped as the Eternal One, the Creator and Lord of heaven and earth. His eternity is expressed by the formula 'He was, he is and he is to come'. This formula is often used in the Book of Revelation, although the order of the three dimensions of time is constantly altering throughout the text. This is an attempt to express in chronological terms a mode of being which totally transcends the chronological order and is completely outside of time. It is an attempt to convey, in human-time terms, the reality of the *Nunc Stans*, the unchanging, eternal Now of the ONE WHO IS.

I have referred already to chapter five of the Book of Revelation, in reference to the breaking by Jesus of the seven seals that keep closed and hidden the full meaning of the scrolls of Holy Scripture. But this chapter also relates the heavenly worship of God to the earthly Eucharist; it incorporates into the heavenly liturgy 'a Lamb that seemed to have been sacrificed', while the twenty-four elders now sing: 'You are worthy to take the scroll and break the seals of it because you were sacrificed.' (Rev 5:9) It is to be noted that the Book of Revelation gives us the key to the meaning of worship, interpreting it as the service of which God is worthy, the expression by us of what God is 'worth'. This indeed is the etymology of the word 'worship', derived from 'worth-ship'; it is our attempt to render to God what God is 'worth'. Part of the message of the Book of Revelation is that we are utterly incapable of offering to God what God is worth – incapable, that is, until God gives his only Son to us as the Lamb, so that he may be our perfect sacrifice of praise and thanks.

After the song of the twenty-four elders, we are told that:

> Ten thousand times ten thousand and thousands upon thousands cry out: 'The Lamb that was sacrificed is worthy to be given power and riches, wisdom and strength, honour and glory and blessing.'

Then all creation joins in the celestial hymnology of praise:

> All beings in creation – everything that lives in the air and on the ground and under the ground and in the sea, cry out: 'To the One who is sitting on the throne and to the Lamb, be all praise and honour, glory and power, for ever and ever.'

And then, we read, the four animals said 'Amen'; and the elders prostrated themselves to worship (Rev 5:11-14). In the context of worship as 'worthiness' – what God 'deserves' in terms of praise and thanks – we may note in passing that one liturgist has interpreted in this sense the phrases introducing the *Sanctus* in our liturgy. The priest proposes to the people: 'Let us give thanks to the Lord our God.' The people respond: 'It is right to give him thanks and praise.' Fr Clifford Howell, SJ, argued that this very old formula comes originally from civic assemblies in the old Greek city-states. The person presiding might propose a vote of thanks or the conferring of an honour or some similar resolution. If the assembly were in favour, they would respond: 'It is right and proper [or fitting]'; the Greek words used were *'axion kai dikaion'*. The presiding person would then renew his own assent with the words: 'It is indeed right and proper ...' This language of the civic community was taken over into the language of the worshipping community and became the introductory formula for the Preface, the beginning of the great Eucharistic Prayer, which is the Christian's supreme 'resolution' of thanks and praise to God, 'proposed' by the priest and 'carried by acclamation' by the whole congregation in their response.

Fr Howell's argument seems well founded. Once more, however, our present translation into English falls far short of the original Latin or Greek. The priest's words, 'We do well', simply do not convey the sense and power of the words: '*Vere dignum et iustum est, aequm et salutare*': 'It is indeed right and proper, worthy and conducive to salvation.'[133]

It is impressive to reflect that these phrases introducing the Sanctus have been part of the eucharistic liturgy from the very early centuries. In the fourth century, St Cyril of Jerusalem describes the exchange between priest and people in the liturgy of the Eucharist. To the priest's invitation: 'Lift up your hearts', the people respond: 'We have lifted them up to the Lord.' To the exhortation: 'Let us give thanks to the Lord', the people reply: 'It is right and proper' (*axion kai dikaion*). Then follows a prayer similar to the Preface of our Eucharistic Prayer. The invocation of the Holy Spirit over the gifts follows; and, Cyril adds, 'Whatever the Holy Spirit touches is sanctified and transformed'. The Greek word 'transformed' (*metabebletai*, from the root word, *metabole*) is the near equivalent of the word 'transubstantiation'. The agreement of liturgical texts and of eucharistic doctrine over sixteen centuries is complete.[134]

In the Book of Revelation, all the martyrs who had been killed 'on account of the word of God for witnessing to it' join in the worship. When the seventh seal is broken by the Lamb and the meaning of the scroll is at last revealed, then an angel offers 'incense and the prayers of all the saints on the golden altar that stands in front of the throne'. Then the same angel takes burning embers from the thurible or censer and throws them down to earth. This is one example among many of the union between the heavenly and the earthly worship. Indeed, all through the Book of Revelation, the gaze of the narrator is moving back and forth between the unending liturgy which is heaven and the liturgy of the Church on earth. The latter culminates annually in the Easter Sunday liturgy, which is the climax of the liturgical year. This is when the newly baptised, wearing their white baptismal robes, assist for the first time at the liturgy of the Eucharist. This in turn is a sacramental anticipation here on earth of the eschatological 'Marriage of the Lamb' in the End time. The Book of Revelation refers to it thus:

> This is the time for the marriage of the Lamb. His bride is ready and she has been able to dress herself in dazzling white, because her linen is made of the good deeds of the saints. The Angel said: 'Write this: "Happy are those who are invited to the wedding feast of the Lamb."' (Rev 19:7-9)

Our eucharistic liturgy marks the connection with the Wedding Feast of the Lamb when, just before the Communion, the priest says: 'Happy are those who are called to his supper.' This, however, which is our present translation, fails sadly to convey the solemnity and the joy of the original invitation announced by the Angel with the words: 'Happy are those who are invited to the wedding feast of the Lamb.'

It is consoling to note that all those who have died in Christ join in the joyful celebration of the heavenly liturgy as depicted in the Book of Revelation. They are the 'saints' spoken of in the text; for 'saints' is the term commonly used in the New Testament for ordinary Christians. They are the ones dressed in their white baptismal robes. They are the ones invited to the Wedding Feast of the Lamb. Our own dear departed are, we may confidently hope, present with us at Mass, gazing at the same eucharistic Lord as we. We see him behind the veils of the sacrament, they see him face to face; but it is one and the same Lord. Our nearness at Mass to our dear departed is brought home to us in Ireland also by the fact that, in most rural churches, the cemetery is located around the Church. This practice dates back to early Celtic times, when the lay faithful were often admitted to bury their dead in the cemeteries of monasteries. There is a custom of visiting the family graves to pray for and with our dead before or after Mass. 'Cemetery Sunday' celebrations in many parishes bring large crowds annually to assist at Mass or a Service for the Dead, sometimes in the cemetery itself. All this points to the fact that the faithful departed also form part of the eucharistic community – a fact which is acknowledged in our liturgy by the memento of the dead which is made in every Mass.

Sacrifice and Eucharist

The earliest tradition of the Church, coming from the closest associates of Christ, the Twelve Apostles themselves, is that Jesus laid down his life in sacrifice for the sins of humanity. In all four gospel narratives, his death is seen as sacrificial. The words of the institution of the Eucharist, as reported by the gospels and by St Paul, define Christ's death as sacrificial. In all the gospels, the Passion and Death of Jesus are associated with the feast of the Passover, when the Paschal Lamb was sacrificed in memory of the Passover of Israel from enslavement in Egypt to liberation in the Promised Land. St Mark begins his account of the Passion with the words: 'It was two days before the Passover and the feast of Unleavened Bread.' (Mk 14:1) There follows the scene of the anointing of the feet of Christ by a woman at a meal in the house of Simon the Leper. Christ interprets this as 'anointing [his] body beforehand' for its burial.

The next day, 'the first day of Unleavened Bread', is the day 'when the Passover Lamb was sacrificed' (Mk 14:12). It is also the day when Jesus instituted the Eucharist in the course of the Passover meal which he celebrated with the disciples. At the end of the meal, the prescribed Hallel Psalm was chanted, and then Jesus with the disciples crossed the Kedron River for the Garden of Gethsemane, the agony and the betrayal.

The death of Jesus was seen by his immediate followers as the sacrifice of the true Paschal Lamb, of which the first Passover out of Egypt was a symbol. St John, in his account of the Passion, associates the timing of the Passion with the hour of the sacrifice of the lambs for the feast of the Passover. We have noted elsewhere the significance of John the Baptist's pointing to Christ as 'the lamb of God who takes away the sin of the world' and as the 'Chosen One of God'. In St John's gospel, the story of the wedding at Cana in Galilee is inserted immediately after John the Baptist's witness to Christ as the Lamb of God. John the Evangelist then brings Jesus to Jerusalem 'just before the Jewish Passover', and follows this with the story of his cleansing of the Temple. This sequence of events seems to be John's way, at the beginning of his gospel, of linking the death and resurrection of Jesus with the Passover feast. The words of Jesus at the cleansing of the Temple were: 'destroy this sanctuary and in three days I will raise it up.' This could have been heard as a prophesy about the material building of the Temple; but Jesus 'was speaking of the sanctuary that was his body' (Jn 2:13-25).

The description of the Christ as the Lamb of God comes originally from the fourth Servant Song of Isaiah, which says of the Servant of the Lord, that 'like a lamb that is dumb in front of its shearers, he never opens his mouth' (Isa 53:7). The first letter of St Peter asks his readers:

> Remember, the ransom that was paid to free you from the useless way of life your ancestors handed down was not paid in anything corruptible, neither in silver or in gold, but in the precious blood of a lamb without spot or stain, namely Christ. (1 Pet 1:18-19)

The Book of Revelation has repeated reference to 'The Lamb that was sacrificed', who is 'worthy to be given power, riches, wisdom, strength, honour, glory and blessing' (Rev 5:12). Innumerable ranks of angels and heavenly creatures cry out:

> To the One who is sitting on the Throne and to the Lamb be all praise and honour, glory and power, for ever and ever. (Rev 5:13)

The Lamb stands between the Throne and the circle of elders and before him stand 'innumerable ranks of angels and heavenly creatures' who cry out, giving praise to 'the One who is sitting on the Throne and to the Lamb'. Later on, in the same book of Revelation, the Lamb is seen standing on Mount Zion accompanied by one hundred and forty-four thousand people with the Father's name and the Lamb's name on their foreheads. The figure 144,000 is twelve times 12,000 – a reference to the twelve tribes of Israel as now made new in the Church of Christ. These are virgins, who have kept their faith intact and who 'follow the Lamb wherever he goes': they are 'first-fruits for God and for the Lamb' (Rev 14:1-5).

Moses and the Lamb are then introduced, singing 'the hymn of Moses, the servant of God, and of the Lamb'. This is a celebration of the new covenant, sealed in the blood of the Lamb, as the old covenant was sealed in the blood of the animals sacrificed to God at the inauguration of the Mosaic covenant on Mount Sinai. The old covenant entailed the defeat of Pharaoh's armies and the setting free from slavery of God's people. In a parallel fashion, according to the Book of Revelation, the new covenant brought about by Christ's sacrifice on the Cross entailed the fall of the imperial power of Rome and the freedom from persecution and from the ever-present danger of idolatry which Roman rule brought with it. At this victory, there are songs of triumph in Heaven, because 'the reign of the Lord our God almighty has begun ... the time for the marriage of the Lamb' (Rev 19:7).

Then the seer has a vision of 'a new heaven and a new earth'; he sees the holy city and the new Jerusalem coming down from God out of heaven, 'as beautiful as a bride dressed for her husband' (Rev 21:1-2). In this New Jerusalem, or End Time:

> The throne of God and of the Lamb will be in its place, his servants will worship him, they will see him face to face. ... It will never be night again and they will not need lamplight or

sunlight, because the Lord God will be shining on them. They will reign for ever and ever. (Rev 22:3-5)

The angel speaks: 'Very soon now I shall be with you again.' Then the Lord Jesus himself speaks: 'I am the Alpha and the Omega, the First and the Last, the Beginning and the End' … 'Then the Spirit and the Bride say, "Come". Let everyone who listens answer, "Come".' (Rev 22:7, 13, 17)

The congregation which gathers at Mass hears this invitation just after the Consecration; in the eucharistic acclamation it replies, 'Come', as it proclaims Christ's death 'until he comes in glory'. As in the Book of Revelation, so in the liturgy of the Eucharist, the people of God receive in faith an answering assurance from the Lord Jesus himself:

> The one who guarantees these revelations repeats his promise: I shall indeed be with you soon. Amen. Come, Lord Jesus. (Rev 22:20)

The Eucharist is, at one and the same time, a communion in the here and now with Christ, really and truly present under sacramental signs, and an eager anticipation of and a passionate longing for the face-to-face coming of Christ in the fullness of his risen glory. This, however, is no renunciation or condemnation of our life on earth, and is no abdication of our earthly responsibilities. The final Coming of Christ is also the final transformation of the earth and the coming of a 'new heaven and a new earth', and our work as Christians here on earth is already our contribution to that transformation, through the Eucharist. Our earthly tasks, permeated by the Eucharist, are our share in the 'redeeming of the times, for the days are evil' (Eph 5:16).

Christ certainly saw his own death as a loving sacrifice of himself, a sacrificial offering of his own life's blood, in loving atonement to God, his Father, for the sins of mankind, which he freely took upon himself. It is clear from the gospels that Christ saw his death in terms of the Deutero-Isaian Fourth Servant Song:

> Ours were the sufferings he bore,
> ours the sorrows he carried:
> on him lies a punishment that brings us peace
> and through his wounds we are healed. (Isa 53:4-5)

Some of the images evoked by the term 'sacrifice' and related terms – such as 'redemption', 'reparation', 'atonement' – have come to sound unattractive in our secularist age. So do terms like God's 'wrath', or 'punishment' for sin. The concept of hell is felt by some to be irreconcilable with the concept of a loving God. Redemption is seen by some as implying that God demands the death of his Son as a condition for forgiving human sins, or as restitution to God's outraged and offended Majesty. The thought of a 'price' paid by Jesus Christ to the Father for the forgiveness of human sins, is nowadays felt by some to be unworthy of a good and merciful and compassionate God. Such ways of thinking are misunderstandings of the truth about God revealed in Jesus Christ.

I wish to comment on some of these misunderstandings. Christ is our final judge; but he judges simply by being the Holy One, by being Love. When, in death, we come before God, our Judge, there is for us an overwhelming realisation of God's holiness and of one's own unholiness and sinfulness. But, if one is unrepentant of sin, then, by our own choice, we are rejecting God, refusing his love, and thereby rejecting that which alone can make us fulfilled and happy. Hell is the sense of self-inflicted rejection of love. It is the rejection of God, who himself is the eternal fulfilment and happiness which we call Heaven. God does not exclude us from heaven; we exclude ourselves. God does not 'punish' us; we punish ourselves. To reject God is to choose an eternity without God, and that is another name for Hell.

In death, we come face to face with Christ who is incarnate Love. We meet Christ who, even in glory, still bears on his hands and his feet the marks of the wounds he voluntarily suffered for us and the mark of the wound in his side which, more than any other, is the symbol of his heart's blood shed for us. In the presence of Christ, we either accept his love in faith and trust, and plead for and accept his forgiveness for our sins; or we reject Christ and reject his love and his forgiveness. The final rejection of Christ is the state which we call Hell. The final acceptance of Christ is the state which we call Heaven. Heaven is a perpetual communion in an eternal Eucharist. It is a state in which God has finally become All in all of us and the all of each of us. This hope of Heaven, this anticipation of Heaven, is implicit in our liturgy and often is given explicit utterance. One of the Easter Collects, for example, prays:

> Heavenly Father and God of mercy,
> we no longer look for Jesus among the dead,
> for he is alive and has become the Lord of life.
> From the waters of death you raise us with him
> and renew your gift of life within us.
> Increase in our minds and hearts
> the risen life we share with Christ
> and help us to grow as your people
> towards the fullness of eternal life with you.
> We ask this through Christ our Lord. Amen.

Heaven is a state of never-ending bliss through eternal communion with God. It is everlasting because never-ending, always beginning, always new. To borrow a phrase from C.S. Lewis, Heaven is a state in which one is perpetually 'surprised by joy'. God, and therefore Heaven, is an infinity of surprises. Hell is a state of lovelessness, where there is no point or meaning to existence, no hope, no better future, only unrelieved loneliness and the indelible remembrance of missed opportunities and failed possibilities, with perpetual guilt and self-blame.

All the vital elements of salvation are seen in a new perspective when we see them in the light of love. Love is the key to the understanding of Christ's incarnation; it was for love for us men and women and for our salvation that the Son of God became man, one of us. In St John's words, God is love; and Christ is God's love made flesh and living amongst us, living for us. It was his love for us, love seeking to take our sins away, that led Christ to offer to God the sacrifice of his life on our behalf. The sacrifice that he offered was precisely his love offered in atonement for our refusals of love – for this is what sin is, the refusal of love.

Salvation is the work of love: this is the teaching of Christ himself, as found particularly in the gospel of St John. Let us take as an example the parable of The Good Shepherd, where Christ says:

> I have come so that they may have life
> and have it to the full.
> I am the good shepherd; the good shepherd is one who lays down
> his life for his sheep ... (Jn 10:10-11)

> I am the good shepherd. I know my own and my own know me,
> just as the Father knows me and I know the Father; and I lay
> down my life for my sheep ... (Jn 10:14-15)

> The Father loves me because I lay down my life in order to take it
> up again. (Jn 10:17)

> No-one takes it from me. I lay it down of my own free will. ...
> And this is the command I have been given by my Father.
> (Jn 10:18)

In the parable of the Vine, Jesus says: 'A man can have no greater love than to lay down his life for his friends.' (Jn 15:13) St John, in his first letter, says that it is Christ's death of love for us that has taught us what love means:

> This has taught us love that he gave up his life for us and we too ought to give our lives for our brothers and sisters. (1 Jn 3:16)

The salvation of humanity was brought by a supreme act of love – Christ laying down his life for the human race; and this was the free and united decision of God the Father and of God the Son together. It is the free choice of the Son and, at the same time, the 'command of the Father'. The will of the Father and the will of the Son are one will, in the unity of the Holy Spirit, in the Three-in-One-ness of the Trinity.

There are obvious tensions between the Father's will and the will of Jesus, as shown in his struggle in the Garden of Gethsemane. But the tensions are between the human will and feelings of Jesus, crushed by the fore-knowledge of the humiliation and disgrace and the excruciating physical pain of the Passion which was to come and anxiety for the faith of the disciples and the future of his infant Church. But, throughout Christ's agony in the Garden, his 'settled will' remains firmly united, come what may, with the will of the Father to save humankind. The two wills were one, even though Christ's human feelings shrank back in dread and even in fear from what that will entailed.

It is significant that, when Christ speaks about the divine love which leads to human salvation, he uses words very similar to those of his great High Priestly Prayer. The saving love of God for mankind comes from the heart of the Trinity; it is the outpouring of the infinite love of Father and Son; it makes it possible for all humankind to become

> one in us [Father and Son], as you are in me and I am in you ... so completely one that the world will realise ... that I have loved them as much as you loved me. (Jn 17:21-23)

Christ's words about 'laying down his life for his sheep' and about 'laying down his life in order to take it up again' caused furious argument among the Jews who were listening. Many of them said that Jesus was possessed, a raving lunatic (Jn 10:19-20). St John is not specific about the precise element in the words of Jesus which provoked this outburst from his Jewish critics. But their reaction finds an echo in St Paul's words about the 'foolishness' of Christ's crucifixion. Paul wrote to the new Christians of pleasure-loving Corinth:

> While the Jews demand miracles and the Greeks look for wisdom, here are we preaching a crucified Christ; to the Jews a scandal, to the pagans madness ... [But] God's foolishness is wiser than human wisdom and God's weakness is stronger than human strength. (1 Cor 1:23-5)

God's 'foolishness' is surely the extravagant love he has shown towards the human beings whom he literally 'loves to death'. His 'madness' is the 'lunacy of love'. We find traces of the 'infatuation' of God's love for humankind in the language and behaviour of the 'Bridegroom' in God's love song for his 'Bride', the Song of Songs. It is not exaggeration to say that God is 'madly' in love with us humans. Every Eucharist is a fervent 'Thank you' to God for this love; it is part of the great universal love song of the Bride, the Church saying 'Yes' to God's love. Every Eucharist is a plea from Christ for our love – a repetition of Christ's question to Peter: 'Do you love me more than these others do?' The Eucharist is our response to Christ: 'Lord, you know everything, you know that I love you.' (Jn 21:15-17)

The centrality of love in the drama of salvation is clear also in the teaching of St Paul. 'What proves that God loves us is that Christ died for us while we were still sinners.' It was when 'we were helpless that Christ died for sinful men and women'; it was 'when we were still enemies' that we were 'reconciled to God by the death of His Son'. This is the source of our hope:

> ... because the love of God has been poured into our hearts by the Holy Spirit which has been given to us. (Rom 5:5-11)

The unbelievable nature of God's love for us – its 'foolishness' in worldly terms – is shown by the fact that we did not either deserve it or appreciate it; we were sinners, we were enemies, we were helpless and hopeless. Yet Christ loved us in spite of our sins; dare we say he loved us because of our sins? Only his unconditional love could make us lovable; only his 'keeping company' with us could make us 'fit company' for God – and this was precisely the 'hidden plan God so kindly made in Christ from the beginning' for the human race (Eph 1:9-10). From the beginning of his public ministry to its end, Jesus made a point of joining in company with known sinners, from his joining the queue of sinners at the Jordan riverbank waiting for baptism by John, to the dinner in Simon's house near the end of his ministry, when he allowed a woman who was a known sinner to anoint his feet. Jesus went further; in some mysterious way he took the sins of guilty men and women upon himself as if he were the guilty one. He, the Paschal Lamb, 'carried' their sins in order to 'carry them away'. The well-known words recall the words of the Fourth Servant Song of Isaiah:

> Ours were the sufferings he bore,
> ours the sorrows he carried.
> But we, we thought of him as someone punished,
> struck by God.
> Yet he was pierced through for our faults,
> crushed for our sins.
> The Lord burdened him
> with the sins of all of us.
> If he offers his life in atonement
> through him what the Lord wishes
> will be done. (Isa 53:4-6, 10)
>
> By his sufferings shall my servant
> justify many
> taking their faults on himself.
> He shall divide the spoil with the mighty

> For surrendering himself to death
> And letting himself be taken for a sinner. (Isa 53:11-12)

The author of the Letter to the Hebrews quotes Psalm 39(40) and applies it to the death of Jesus when he writes:

> Christ has made his appearance once and for all, now at the end of the age, to do away with sin by sacrificing himself ... Christ offers himself only once to take the faults of many on himself. (Heb 10:5-7 quoting Ps 39(40):6-8)

St Paul puts Christ's atoning sacrificial death still more starkly:

> For our sake God made the sinless one into sin so that in him we might become the goodness of God. (2 Cor 5:21)

'[Christ] who was sinless, [God] made sin for our sake': the words of St Paul are truly shocking. They add a whole new dimension to the words of Jesus: 'Greater love than this no-one has.' Jesus loved us so much that, in order to save us from our sins and make it possible for us to share the life of God, he takes the guilt of our sins – of all the sins of the whole of human history – upon himself. His holiness is outraged by the wickedness of all those sins; his purity is revolted by their filth; his goodness is insulted by their vileness; his love is affronted by the evil of their hate. Was this among the reasons for his cry from the Cross: 'My God, my God, why have you forsaken me?' If sin is the rejection of God, then Christ 'made sin' must feel rejected by God. If the Cross is the symbol of God's curse, then one who carries a cross and dies upon it must feel accursed by God. In this light, the Agony in the Garden takes on a new degree of anguish. This is expressed in Christ's distressful cry: 'Abba [Father], everything is possible for you: take this cup away from me.' (Mk 14:36) The 'cup' in question is undoubtedly the 'cup of God's wrath'[135] which Jesus freely chose to drink to its bitterest dregs on the Cross. I have already referred to Christ's cry on the Cross (taken from Psalm 21(22), where he addresses God not as 'Abba', but as 'My God' (see p. 101).

We arrive, therefore, at the conclusion to which Julian of Norwich arrived after fifteen years of contemplation of her 'Showings of Divine Love' and of her wonder at what was the Lord's meaning in all that he has done for us. The answer she found was 'Love was his meaning' and she is determined to 'wit it well'. At the end of her life of contemplation and at the ending of her book Julian wrote:

> Who showed it to thee? Love. What did he show thee? Love. Why did he show it? For Love. Hold thee therein and thou shalt witten and know more in the same. But thou shalt never know nor witten therein other thing without end. Thus was I learned that Love was our Lord's meaning.[136]

Mary Ever Virgin and the Eucharist

In our account of the heavenly liturgy as found in the Book of Revelation we did not mention the great figure of the Woman adorned with the sun. She is the Church, Mother of the disciples of Christ; she is also the Mother of Christ. She is placed at the point when 'the sanctuary of God in heaven opened and the Ark of the covenant could be seen inside it' (Rev 11:19), while 'flashes of lightning, peals of thunder and an earthquake' accompany her appearance (Rev 11:19). She is the one who stands constantly before the 'Holy of Holies', making intercession for us: the great *Orante*, as she is depicted in the iconography of the early Church, standing erect with arms outstretched in prayer. She is the devout Adorer, the great Pray-er, the powerful Intercessor. She is the Mother pregnant with Christ, her Son. She is the first communicant at the table of Communion; for, when the dragon who seeks to devour her new-born Son approaches, she is carried by God to a 'place of safety which has been made ready for her', where she will be 'looked after' by God (Rev 12:6, 14). The twice-repeated phrase 'to be looked after', (from the Greek *trephein*), could be translated as 'will have food provided for her' – and could be an allusion to the Eucharist, which Mary would have undoubtedly received at the eucharistic celebrations of the Apostolic Church.[137] Mary, Ever-Virgin, is our Protectress in the ongoing war waged by the Dragon against 'the rest of her children', that is, all who obey God's commandments and bear witness for Jesus (Rev 12:17).

The close connection of Mary with the Eucharist is borne out in the iconography of the early Church. An inscription found on the tombstone of Bishop Abercius of Hierapolis in Phrygia, in the time of the Emperor Marcus Aurelius in the second half of the second century, runs as follows:

> I am Abercius, disciple of the Immaculate Shepherd who feeds his flock through the mountains and valleys … He taught me the doctrine of life and sent me to Rome to contemplate a kingdom or a queen clad in gold and wearing golden shoes: here I saw a people adorned by a splendid sign … and everywhere I found brethren united together … And faith was always my guide and gave me as food the great fish which the Virgin took from the spring; and possessing most excellent wine, gave food to its friends, serving them with wine mixed with water along with bread.

The Virgin in this inscription could be identified with the Church; but that the Virgin was Mary is much more probable; it is in fact agreed by Joachim in his reference to this inscription.[138]

The fish was commonly used in the early church as a sign of Christ in the holy Eucharist: the Greek letters of the word 'fish' (*ichthus*) are the initials of the Greek words for 'Jesus Christ, Son of God, Saviour'. Another second-century inscription from the crypt of Lucina in the Cemetery of Callistus in Rome, dating from the same second century, depicts a fish, together with a basket of bread and a vessel of wine – such as were used to bring the Eucharist to faithful unable to come to the eucharistic celebration.

No Mass is ever celebrated without special reference to this Woman, Mary ever Virgin. In Eucharistic Prayer I we pray:

> In union with the whole Church
> we honour Mary
> the ever virgin Mother of Jesus Christ,
> our Lord and God.

In Eucharistic Prayer IV we pray:

> Father, in your mercy grant also to us your children to enter into our heavenly inheritance,
> in the company of the Virgin Mary, the Mother of God,
> and your apostles and saints.
> Then, in your Kingdom,
> freed from the corruption of sin and death,
> we shall sing your glory
> with every creature
> through Christ, our Lord.

In 2003, in preparation for the Year of the Eucharist[139] Pope John Paul II issued an Encyclical Letter on the Eucharist, with the title *Ecclesia de Eucharistia*. In 2004 he issued an Apostolic Letter, entitled *Mane nobiscum Domine*. In both of these Letters, the Pope spoke of the relationship of Mary, Mother of Jesus, with the Eucharist. He invited us to contemplate with Mary the face of Christ, and thereby to share in the Church's 'amazement' at this great mystery. The German poet, Rainer Maria Rilke, had already written of how Mary had followed her Son 'amazed'. We too cannot but be amazed at Jesus – amazed at his wisdom and grace, amazed like the Rabbis in the Temple at his knowledge and answers, amazed at his absorption in prayer to his Father, and amazed at his love for mankind, particularly for the poor and the suffering.

Mary's amazement at Jesus began with his conception in her womb. It grew during her pregnancy, when she was 'in some way the first tabernacle in history'.[140] This was Mary's Advent, her experience of Christ growing bodily within her as she grew in union of heart and mind and spirit with him. The way in which Jesus grew physically in Mary's womb is in some sense parallel to that in which, through the Eucharist, the presence of Jesus grows in us until, more and more, 'God is all in us all'. It is interesting to note that a Belfast writer, Mary Beckett, in her short story, *A Woman of Belfast*, speaks of an expectant mother who regularly prayed to Jesus for the welfare of her unborn child, and who at the same time also 'conversed' with her own unborn child, but sometimes confused the two conversations and spoke to her unborn child as if speaking to Jesus.[141] A pregnant woman, if she is also a woman of faith and prayer, is uniquely placed to live the season of Advent along with Mary; but we each can try to live spiritually, 'eucharistically', in union with Mary all year round, but especially during Advent and Christmas.

Mary, Pope John Paul II wrote, is the model of the 'eucharistic spirituality' which should characterise all Christians and which is needed more than ever in our time. This is a spirituality of union with Jesus Christ and of praise and thanks to God through Jesus, Mary's Son, who, as the same Pope said, is in person humanity's 'Yes' and 'Amen' and 'Thank you' to the holy will of God, our Father.[142] Mary's own 'Yes' to the Father's will was spoken when, at the Annunciation, she said her 'Fiat': 'May it be done to me according to your word.' Mary's close union with her Son in this 'Yes' is clear from her words on that same occasion: 'I am the handmaid of the Lord.' The word 'handmaid' is a milder word than that which is used in the Greek original: this is the word *doulé*, meaning 'slave-girl'. The word is the feminine form of *doulos*, meaning 'slave'. The word *doulos* is the very word used by Jesus of himself in the account of the washing of the feet at the Last Supper. This episode in turn, as we have seen, occupies, in the fourth gospel, the place of the words of Institution reported by the other three gospel writers. John is expressing one of the meanings of the eucharistic words instead of giving us the words themselves. The Eucharist, in which the death of Jesus on the Cross is re-presented, is Jesus' supreme act of self-abasement and of servant-hood to the

Father and to sinful humanity; it is the complete fulfilment by Jesus of the role of Servant of the Lord as this is delineated in the Songs of the Servant in Deutero-Isaiah. Mary's role as handmaid of the Lord is exactly parallel to Jesus' self-sacrificing role as Servant of the Lord.

Mary's life is fully conformed in this regard to the life of her Son. The union of Mary with Jesus was solemnly confirmed at the Presentation of Jesus in the Temple. She and Joseph, in obedience to the Law, brought the child Jesus to the Temple to present him to the Lord. As the Law required, Joseph, with Mary, spoke over the child and said: 'He is made over to the Lord.' Familiar as she would have been with the Servant Songs, Mary would have had some intuition here of her Son as 'suffering Servant', and of Simeon's 'sword of sorrow'; for Jesus was being 'made over' also to his Passion and Mary herself was being 'made over' to God as the closest associate of Jesus in his expiatory suffering on behalf of all humanity.[143]

Mary's whole spirituality, as Pope John Paul reminded us, is expressed in her Magnificat; and there is, the Pope said, 'nothing greater than this spirituality for helping us to experience the mystery of the Eucharist'. The Pope tells us that the relationship of Mary with the Eucharist 'can be understood more deeply by re-reading the Magnificat in a Eucharistic key'. The Pope concluded: 'The Eucharist has been given to us so that our life, like that of Mary, may become completely a *Magnificat*.'[144]

The author of the Letter to the Hebrews quotes two verses from Psalm 39 and applies them to Jesus Christ and to his sacrificial death on Calvary. The passage in question, as the Letter to the Hebrews translates it, reads:

> You who wanted no sacrifice or oblation,
> prepared a body for me.
> You took no pleasure in holocausts or sacrifices for sin;
> Then I said, just as I was commanded in the scroll of the book,
> 'God, here I am! I am coming to obey your will'. (Heb 10:6-7
> quoting Ps 39(40):7-9)

The Letter to the Hebrews interprets this as saying that God is abolishing 'the sacrifices, the oblations, the holocausts and the sacrifices for sin' of the Old Law and is replacing them with the single Sacrifice of the New Law; since God's will was 'for us to be made holy by the offering of [Christ's] body made once and for all by Jesus Christ' (Heb 10:5-10). The Hebrews text puts these words from the Psalm in the mouth of Jesus Christ at the moment when he was 'coming into the world'. There is a complete unity of mind and will between Jesus Christ and his mother, dating from the very moment of the conception of Jesus at the Annunciation. At the very instant when he is being 'made flesh' in Mary's womb, Jesus is saying to his heavenly Father: 'God, here I am! I am coming to obey your will'; and at that same instant Mary is saying to the angel Gabriel: 'I am the handmaid of the Lord, let what you have said be done to me.' 'Lord, here I am, I am coming to do your will' should be our response, each Sunday, or each morning, to that morning's or that Sunday's Eucharist; and Mary's example and her intercession are a powerful help to us in making that commitment real. The final 'dismissal' at the Eucharist: 'The Mass is ended, go in peace'; or, 'Go in peace to love and serve the Lord', is an invitation to all to live the Mass in the daily round of life and work and recreation. It is equivalently a call to us to say to the Lord, with Jesus and with Mary: 'God, here I am. I am coming today to do your will.'

The words can be applied also to the fulfilment in the Eucharist, through Jesus, with him and in him, of the eucharistic and eschatological longing of St Paul, that God may be all in each one of us and in us all, until we all together become 'a living sacrifice of praise' (Eucharistic Prayer IV).

This praising and thanking of God is, as I said earlier, our reason for existing. It is also our reason for rejoicing. Julian of Norwich wrote of 'enjoying' Our Lord, which she said 'is a full blissful thanking in our sight'.[145]

There will be struggle and setback in our efforts to live the Mass and to live the Christian life. There will be failure and apparent defeat. But we remember the words of Jesus: 'In the world you will have distress. But be brave; I have overcome the world.' (Jn 16:33)

Julian of Norwich, near the end of her *Showings of Divine Love*, wrote:

> This word, 'Thou shalt not be overcome', was said [by Jesus] full clearly and full mightily, for assuredness and comfort against all tribulations that may come. He did not say: 'Thou shalt not be tempested, thou shalt not be travailed', but he said: 'Thou shalt not be overcome.' God wills that we take heed to these words and that we be ever mighty in sure trust, in weal and in woe. For he loves us and likes us, and so wills that we love and like him and mightily trust in him; and all shall be well.[146]

Earlier she had written words she had heard from our Lord in her prayer:

> All shall be well, and all shall be well, and all manner of things shall be well.[147]

The Eucharist is God's everlasting guarantee to us, his solemn 'oath' to us, that 'all shall be well'. Jesus Christ is God's eternal 'Yes' and 'Amen' to this divine pledge. As St Paul put it: 'However many the promises God has made, the "Yes" to them all is in Christ.' (2 Cor 1:20)

I beg leave to be personal in my concluding remarks. Having witnessed in my pastoral life so many examples of God's saving work in people's lives, having gazed so often on the Sacred Host elevated for people's loving adoration, the Host which both reveals and conceals God's light and his glory, I like to end this book with the aged Simeon's words at the Presentation of Jesus in the Temple, his *Nunc Dimittis*. I quote these words as they are printed at the end of Book III of the *Divine Office*:

> Now Lord, you have kept your word;
> let your servant go in peace.
>
> With my own eyes I have seen the salvation
> which you have prepared in the sight of every people:
> a light to reveal you to the nations
> and the glory of your people Israel.

AMEN

NOTES

1. *In Psalmum*, 47.
2. The phrase 'hidden in the Old and the Old made manifest in the New' is taken from St Augustine.
3. Tertullian, *Adversus Marcionem*.
4. Genesis 4:1-16.
5. See Exodus 7:22, 8:15, 19.
6. Exodus 19.
7. This is the title of a study of the Noahic Covenant and related matters by Robert Murray, SJ, in a book with that title published by Sheed and Ward, London, 1992.
8. cf. Jeremiah 34:17-18.
9. See Exodus 16.
10. cf. *Bible Dictionary*, revised edition 1975, W.B. Eerdmans Publishing Co., Grand Rapids, Michigan, USA, 1987, p. 687.
11. cf. Mark 6:31-56; Luke 9:10-21: Matthew 14:13-36.
12. See The Constitution on the Sacred Liturgy, *Sacrosanctum Concilium*, 48, 51.
13. During the celebration of the Haj pilgrimage to Mecca – one of the 'five pillars of Islam' which every Muslim is expected to perform at least once in life – the pilgrim over three days hurls stones at three pillars representing Satan, at the very spot where, Muslims believe, the devil appeared to Abraham. This is an expression in mime of the rejection of Satan and the detestation of sin by Muslim believers.
14. Isaiah 42, 49, 50, 53.
15. See Isaiah 43:23, 56:6-7; Ezekiel 44:7-9; Jeremiah 17:24-7, 33:10-11; cf. Ecclesiastes 4:17.
16. Malachi 1:6-11; Isaiah 43:23, 56:6-7; Jeremiah 17:24-7, 33:10-11; Ezekiel 20:40-41, 46:24; Daniel 8:13-14.
17. Luke 12:50.
18. Matthew 4:1-11; Luke 4:1-13.
19. cf. Matthew 26:36-46; Mark 14:32-42; John 18:1-11.
20. cf. Matthew 16:21-3; 17:22-3; Mark 8:31-33, 9:30-32; Luke 9:22; 43-5.
21. See Feuillet, *La Sacerdoce du Christ et de ses Ministres*, pp. 116–8, 184–6.
22. As in the words of institution, the word translated as 'many' from the Hebrew is often used as the word for 'all'.
23. Luke 22:37, quoting Isaiah 53:12.

24. cf. 1 Corinthians 11:17-34.
25. For a description of the typical modern Passover, I refer to a book by Chaim Raphael, *A Feast of History*, Weidenfeld and Nicholson, Jerusalem, Tel Aviv, 1971.
26. When the dying of a crucified man was protracted, the soldiers would sometimes break his legs and thereby precipitate death by making it impossible for the dying man to push himself up on the cross to a position where he could draw a short breath, before slumping down again to a position where he could no longer breath; as a result of the breaking of his legs, the crucified man died rapidly and extremely painfully of asphyxiation.
27. *Eccelesia de Eucharistia*, 89
28. cf. Matthew 26:30; Mark 14:26.
29. The reference to the stone which 'has become the cornerstone' is applied to Jesus Christ himself by Matthew and Mark in their gospels: see Matthew (21:42) and Mark (12:10-11); and also by Peter in Acts (4:11) and by the author of the First Letter of St Peter (2:7-8).
30. The words 'Blessed in the name of the Lord is he who comes' is applied to Jesus Christ by Matthew, when he describes the triumphant entry of Jesus into Jerusalem before his Passion: see 21:9.
31. See John 1:29, 36; 1 Peter 1:19, Acts 8:32 and frequently in the Book of Revelation.
32. 1 Kings 17-21.
33. cf. Wisdom 2:10-16.
34. A. Feuillet, *Retraite Eucharistique*, pp. 59–68.
35. cf. Isaiah 45:15; Amos 8:12; Hosea 5:6; Jeremiah 29:13-14; Job 13:24; Psalm 43(44):25, 87(88):14.
36. See *La Bible avec Thérèse de Lisieux*, Conf, Paris, 1979, pp. 101, 106.
37. Even though there were six great stone water jars, each capable of holding twenty or thirty gallons.
38. For this last prayer, I have followed the translation of Eugene Geissler, in *The Bible Prayer Book*, published by the Ave Maria Press, Notre Dame, Indiana, 1981.
39. plural: *Berakoth*.
40. See Louis Bouyer, *Eucharistie*, Desclée, Belgium 1966, p. 47.
41. cf. ibid., p. 35; cf. p. 62.
42. We note again hints of the inseparable link between the Liturgy of the Word and the Liturgy of the Eucharist.
43. See *Adversus Haereses*, IV, 20. This is part of the reading for the Feast of St Irenaeus: see *The Divine Office* III, p. 77.
44. See Louis Bouyer, *Eucharistie*, Desclée, Belgium, 1966, pp. 45–7.
45. Matthew 27:43 and 27:35; see also John 11:23.
46. See Joachim Jeremias, *The Central Message of the New Testament*, SCM Press, London, 1965, p. 17.
47. *La Bible avec Thérèse de Lisieux*, Conf., Paris, 1979, pp. 73–4.
48. cf. Psalm 34(35):19 with John 15:25.

49. John 19:28-9 and Psalm 68(69):4 and 22; cf. Psalm 21(22):16
50. cf. 34(35):11.
51. Psalms 43(44), 73(74), 76(77), 78(79), 79(80), 84(85), 88(89), 101(102).
52. See *La Bible avec Thérèse de Lisieux*, Conf., Paris, 1979 pp. 79–80.
53. Psalm 6, 31(32), 37(38), 50(51), 101(102), 129(130), 142(143).
54. From the Greek word, *aletheuontes*.
55. See Michael Herity and Aidan Breen, *The Cathac of Colm Cille*, Royal Irish Academy, 2002.
56. In Latin, *Lauda Sion*.
57. See A. Hamman, *L'Eucharistie*, Desclée de Brouwer, 1981.
58. Feuillet, *Retraite Eucharistique*, pp. 52–5.
59. See Revelation 19:9 and cf. 3:20.
60. Joachim Jeremias, *The Eucharistic Words of Jesus*, English translation from the German, SCM Press, London, 1966.
61. cf. Gerald O'Collins, SJ, *The Easter Jesus*, DLT, London, 1973, pp 3–9.
62. Namely, James, Peter and John.
63. cf. Galatians 2:1 and 2.
64. Jeremias, op. cit., pp. 201–2.
65. Jeremias, pp. 188–9.
66. The gospel account says 'for many', but 'many' in Hebrew can serve as meaning 'all'; cf. Jeremias, op. cit., pp. 179–82, 229.
67. See Jeremias, op. cit., pp. 41–62. He outlines various objections to this view and argues against them: cf. pp. 62–88.
68. cf. Jeremias, op. cit., p. 62.
69. Jeremias, pp. 164–5, 169.
70. cf. Jeremias, op. cit., p. 218.
71. cf. Joachim Jeremias, *Rediscovering the Parables*, SCM Press, London, 1966, pp. 101–5.
72. See Roman Missal, 26 Sunday in Ordinary Time.
73. See Matthew 14:13-21; Mark 6:30-44; Luke 9:10-17; John 6:1-15.
74. Matthew 14:13-21 and 15:32-39; Mark 6:30-44 and 8:1-10
75. The fish were to be cut up and placed between the broken pieces of loaf so as to form something like what we call sandwiches.
76. Mark 6:40; cf. Exodus 18:21-2.
77. John says the disciples gave out 'as much as was wanted' – John 6:12.
78. In Greek, *ego eimi*.
79. There are recalls here by Our Lord of Jeremiah 5:21 and of Ezekiel 12:2.
80. See also Matthew 17:1-5; Mark 9:2-8.
81. The word used in the original text is the Greek word '*exodos*'.
82. Deuteronomy 8:3; Matthew 4:4.
83. See Acts 2:42, 46; 20:7.
84. Gerard Manley Hopkins, 'The Half-Way House' and 'Nondum', from *Gerard Manley Hopkins: A Selection of His Finest Poems*, Oxford University Press, 1995.
85. cf. John 8:58 ('I tell you most solemnly, before Abraham ever was, I am') John 6 ('I am. Do not be afraid'; 'I am the bread of life', 'I am the living

bread'); John 8 ('I am the light of the world', 'I am He'); John 9 ('I am the light of the world'); John 10 ('I am the gate of the sheepfold', 'I am the gate', 'I am the good shepherd', 'the Father and I are one'); John 11 ('I am the resurrection'); John 14 ('I am the Way and the Truth and the Life'; 'I am in the Father and the Father is in me'); John 15 ('I am the true vine'); John 17 ('Father, may they be one in us, as you are in me and I am in you'); John 18 ('I am he').

86. See, for example, Mark 6:51 and 8:27-30; Matthew 14:27-8 and 16:13-20; Luke 9:18-21.
87. cf. John 6:40.
88. cf. Mark 6:30-52; Matthew 14:13-33; Luke 9:10-17; John 6:1-15.
89. Which itself is a recall of the forty days in the desert of God's people, Israel.
90. cf. Luke 4:4.
91. Meaning to 'chew'.
92. André Feuillet, *Retraite Eucharistique*, p. 80.
93. Using the Greek word, *meno*.
94. Feuillet, *Retraite Eucharistique*, p. 24.
95. Irenaeus, *Adversus Haereses*, 4:18, 4-5. This is an extract from the Second Reading for Saturday, Week 2 of the Year. See *The Divine Office* I, pp. 433–4.
96. *De Trinitate* VIII, 13–16, being an extract from The Second Reading, on Wednesday of Eastertide, Week 4. See *The Divine Office* II, p. 563.
97. On the Holy Spirit, IX, 22-3. This is part of the Second Reading for Tuesday of Eastertide, Week 7. See *The Divine Office* II p. 671.
98. This is part of the Second Reading for Tuesday of the third Week of the Year. See *The Divine Office* I, pp. 446–8.
99. This is an extract from the Second Reading for Friday of Week 31 of the Year. See *The Divine Office* III, p. 729.
100. Orationes 14, 25. See *The Divine Office* II, pp. 97–8. This is part of the Reading for the first Monday in Lent.
101. From *Catechesis to the Newly Baptised at Jerusalem, Mystagogia* 4, 1.3-6.9. This is part of the Reading for Saturday of the Easter Octave; see *The Divine Office* II, pp. 565–6.
102. Commentary on John's gospel, Book X. This is part of the Reading for Eastertide, Thursday, Week 7. See *The Divine Office* II, p. 683.
103. Commentary on the gospel of St John, Book XI, XI. See *The Divine Office* II, pp. 610-1. This is an extract from the Reading for Eastertide, Week 6, Tuesday.
104. Extract from the Letters of St Cyril of Alexandria, being part of the Reading for the Feast of St Cyril. See *The Divine Office* III, p. 75.
105. Sermon 148; this is an extract from the Second Reading on the Feast of St Peter Chrysologos. See *The Divine Office* III, p. 140.
106. St Thomas Aquinas, Opusculum 57. See *The Divine Office* III, pp. 31–2. The passages quoted are extracts from the Second Reading for the Feast of Corpus Christi.

107. Collect of Mass of 17 December.
108. Collect of Mass of 22 December.
109. *Lumen Gentium* I, 2.
110. St John of the Cross, 'Spiritual Canticle', A, Str. 38. See *The Divine Office* III, pp. 397–8.
111. In the original Greek, the words are: '*Theias koinönoi physéos*', while the Latin translation reads: '*Divinae consortes naturae.*' (2 Pet 1:4)
112. cf. Psalm 55(56):11; 117(118)17(118):6.
113. Jeremias, *The Prayers of Jesus*, SCM Press, London, p. 29.
114. Jeremias, ibid., p. 57.
115. See Jeremias, *The Central Message of the New Testament*, SCM Press, London, pp. 9–30.
116. *The Prayers of Jesus*, p. 62.
117. *The Prayers of Jesus*, pp. 62–3.
118. 'Let us pray with confidence to the Father in the words our Saviour taught us.'
119. cf. Romans 8:15-16.
120. *The Prayers of Jesus*, p. 65.
121. Pope Benedict XVI, *Deus Caritas Est*, 17–18. The last phrase is quoted by Pope Benedict from St Augustine: *God is intimior intimo meo* – cf. Confessions III 6, 11.
122. 'The chronological order of the relevant Pauline writings is generally agreed to be as follows: Galatians, First Corinthians, Romans, Colossians, Ephesians. See Conleth Kearns, *The Church the Body of Christ*, Dominican Publications, Dublin, 1960, pp. 8–9.
123. 'As Kingfishers Catch Fire', published in a collection of poems by Gerard Manley Hopkins in the Oxford Poetry Library, The Oxford University Press, 1995.
124. Kearns, *The Church the Body of Christ*, Dominican Publications, Dublin, 1960, p. 39.
125. See Kearns, ibid., p. 33.
126. Galatians 4:13-16; cf. 2 Corinthians 1:3-7.
127. For part of this quotation I have followed the translation of Fr Conleth Kearns, *The Church the Body of Christ*.
128. Hebrews 9:28.
129. cf. Psalm 8:6.
130. I have written of this elsewhere: see *The Minding of Planet Earth*, Veritas, Dublin, 2004.
131. This rite is sometimes distorted by the bringing of other objects which, whatever their sentimental value (especially at a Funeral Mass, when they may include objects associated with the life and the interests of the deceased), have no relationship with the Liturgy and indeed distract from the true meaning of the Liturgy. The gifts properly carried up at the Offertory, by a tradition which goes back to the very beginning of the Church, consist of bread, wine and offerings for the poor.

132. St Ambrose, *De Mysteriis*, 50, quoted in Cardinal Caetano de Lai, *The Real Presence of Jesus Christ in the Eucharist*, Browne and Nolan, Dublin, 1925, pp. 89–90.
133. See Clifford Howell, SJ, *Mean what you say*, Geoffrey Chapman, London, pp. 55–7.
134. Cyril of Jerusalem, *Mystagogica* 5:5-7; see Conrad Kirch, *Enchiridion Fontium Historiae Ecclesiasticae Antiquae*, Herder, Barcelona, 1947, pp. 324–30.
135. To speak of 'God's wrath' is, as we have seen, a way of expressing our sense of the evil of sin, in utter contrast to the holiness of God.
136. See *Revelations of Divine Love*, by Julian of Norwich, edited and introduced by Dom Roger Huddleston, Burns Oates, (1927) 1952, p. 169.
137. A derivative of the verb *trephein* is used by St Paul in Ephesians 5:29 to describe the way a husband 'feeds and looks after his wife'.
138. See Jeremias, *The Eucharistic Words of Jesus*, p. 136.
139. October 2004–October 2005.
140. See *Ecclesia de Eucharistia*, 55.
141. See *A Belfast Woman*, Poolbeg, 1987, p. 80.
142. *Mane nobiscum Domine*, no. 26.
143. cf. Luke 2:22-28, with Exodus 13 and Leviticus 5.
144. cf. *Ecclesia de Eucharistia*, 58.
145. *Revelations of Divine Love*, edited by Roger Hudleston, Burns Oates, London, 1952, p. 74.
146. Ibid., p. 141.
147. Ibid., p. 49.

GENERAL INDEX

SCRIPTURAL INDEX